AF342023

NO TIME TO KILL

True Stories of an Arizona Bounty Hunter

VICTOR M. ALVAREZ

When you meet your antagonist, do everything in a mild and
agreeable manner.
Let your courage be as keen, but at the same time as polished as
your sword.

Richard Brinsley Sheridan

The Huntsman

Actual Stories of an Arizona Bounty Hunter

2nd Edition

Contents

Foreword

To say that Victor Alvarez has written just another bounty hunter book, is not doing justice to the chronicles of his authorization and empowerments by a bail bondsman — to seek a dangerous bail jumper, to lawfully arrest, detain and bring the jumper to jail in the precise time in order to avoid a bond forfeiture and of course to get his deserved bounty fee – has overlooked the fact that all of his captures were done without modern tracking devices.

To thoroughly immerse and enjoy his writings and adventures, one must be mentally transported back to the mid-and-late 80s of the 20th Century. His means of communication was limited to a beeper that required a public phone – and oh yes – to have coins readily available for such phone calls. There were no GPS, rather bulky and outdated maps which he used to navigate to his marked locations. He depended on his vivid and cunning recollection of an early scouted area for his nighttime apprehensions – without the use of night vision goggles.

Alvarez's captures were done employing his twenty years of disciplined military and police training, and his experiences as a youngster growing up in New York City, Spanish Harlem. But I have to say, Alvarez must had a sixth sense or skill of an animalistic magnitude to bring his bail jumpers to custody; a most remarkable achievement that earned him the respect and admiration of the bondsman of this tough Arizona and New Mexico region, and of the public media.

All of his arrest was made within the boundaries of the law — never risking a lethal situation that prevented him from going home or a costly and lengthily lawsuit. Much less, he did not antagonize the police force of the area he was working in. Instead, the police lent him a helping hand in some occasions, and bonded a rapport with several officers. Alvarez kept his bail bondsman harmless as well.

There were a host of proposition and temptations by the apprehended bail jumpers to corrupt him – by offer of money for their release, instead of jail. But he never relented and always returned them back into custody. There were plenty of threats of physical harm, but he was able to handle them successfully.

His stature as a writer of his adventures grows line by line, word by word, chapter by chapter. One can't bypass the fact that he projects, with a smile, or with a gesture and body language, either a friendly comforting support or the promise of the discharge of his lethal weapons, or a fist in the face. He held an outstanding *Macho Persona* in a world of bounty hunting, and in this, his continued adventures, permeates the adrenaline and the *Real Action*.

Victor's *NO TIME TO KILL*, it's simply addicting. It left me wanting for sequels of his adventuress life as an Arizona bounty hunter. Read his book, you won't be disappointed.

Lupita Shestko — Montiel, Bail Agent
Montiel Bail Bonds, Tucson, Arizona

Introduction

Mark Twain once wrote, "The two most important days in your life are the day you were born, and the day you find out why." I fully realized my purpose the day I became an Arizona bounty hunter. It was as if my experiences on both sides of the law suddenly made sense.

I have always lived on the edge of violence. Whether it was gang-banging in the slums of New York City's Spanish Harlem, to fighting in the Vietnam War, or chasing fugitives as an Arizona bounty hunter, I knew that at any given time, I stood to lose life and limb. It was a gamble I embraced, sometimes out of survival, sometimes out of patriotism and sometimes for the sheer adrenalin rush.

They say life is just a series of choices. Well I've made some good choices, and some not so good choices; some I'm still paying for and a few I've come to appreciate. Take for instance my gang days in New York City.

The gang life taught me two things; camaraderie and the ability to fight. Not just to fight, but to throw caution to the wind and not show fear in the face of danger. The US Army taught me more than just those qualities. They also taught me how to kill in various ways — techniques that were born of battle. I was taught to lose my inhibitions and fears. They motivated me to carry out mission orders no matter the cost — mission first and utmost! But the most important lesson I learned was to always look after your buddy, or the person next to you. In a 'fire-fight,' he could be the one that may save your life, or you his.

Survival was always important too. Staying alive and getting back to my family after a hunt was the tie that binds. I earned my past, and its one thing that can never be taken from me. Mind you, I was neither saint nor a fool, but there comes a time in everyone's life when you have to take life as it was given to you and run with it.

So this was me, running with it.

Victor Manuel Alvarez
San Antonio, Texas — September, 2016

Continuing the Adventures of *"The Huntsman, An Arizona Bounty Hunter. . ."*

"No Time to Kill," is the second book chronicling the adventures and life of Victor Alvarez, which began with "The *Huntsman – Actual Stories of an Arizona Bounty Hunter."*

We pick up where we left off, as the Huntsman is giving chase to a Mexican drug enforcer through the dark empty highway of Black Canyon City, Arizona.

And the hunt begins . . .

Prologue - The Chase

May 1987, Black Canyon City, Arizona

I was chasing a silver '72 Chevy Monte Carlo south on the Arizona Veterans Highway or I-17 as it was commonly known, and behind the wheel of my newly modified '82 Chrysler LeBaron, as I sped through the darkness and my jumper's taillights grew closer and closer. Kenny Loggins' *Highway to the Danger Zone* played from the car's radio as I kept my eyes on the road and my hands on the wheel.

I was tired, hungry and needed to catch this jumper. It was oven hot, and although it was after 3:00 a.m., heat still wafted from the roadway in front my headlights, thanks to the hot spell that still gripped Arizona.

I leaned slightly forward and adjusted the louvers on the car's air conditioner, so that I could get the cool air on my face. That position helped a lot and it brought a small smile to my lips.

The Bradshaw Mountains rose up to the right of the roadway in an area made famous when gold and silver was discovered there in the early 1800s. Those same mountains were later home to Apache Indians as they fought to protect their land and keep white settlers out. A few of the old settler homes and towns still stood and provided the backdrop for the car chase that roared along the mountainous periphery.

My newly suped-up 305cc engine and manual four-speed transmission easily pushed me closer to the fleeing Chevy. I didn't want to lose the jumper, but I didn't want to spook him either. I'd been in this situation before, and I knew things could take a turn for the worst in an instant. Dolores had told me to be careful and come home to her when she'd kissed me goodbye. For some reason, my wife had always told me I was handsome, though I didn't see it. Even with the scars on my face and hands, Dolores still saw me as a good looking guy, even after all our years together.

My years as a Spanish Harlem barrio gang member saw lots of fights, and sometimes a blade or two got in the way. Years later, it would be bullets that got in my way during two combat tours in Vietnam. While I was highly trained in hand-to-hand combat, I hoped I wouldn't have to bust a sweat – or bust a move – on the jumper in the Chevy that night. But I was ready nonetheless.

With 21 years of military service under my belt, I'd fought for my country and was a proponent of our criminal justice system. No bail jumper was going to avoid his day in court if I had anything to do with it. But the clock was ticking. I had to have the jumper back in Tucson in less than nine hours, by noon that same day, or else I'd forfeit my 10-percent fee, which in this case, was four thousand dollars. Triple 'A' Bail Bonds had hired me to find their jumper, who had disappeared without a trace, so they also stood to lose a lot of money and property too if the jumper wasn't brought in.

As I kept the Chevy in sight, I considered what I'd learned about him. I'd cut my teeth on finding some of the most elusive jumpers, and I'd always been successful because I took the time to learn all I could about them. Just like a hunter learns about his prey, their habits and their lifestyles. Fred Luna at Triple 'A' Bail Bonds had told me plenty about the man I pursued. His name was Jose Luis Aguilar, but best known as 'The Destroyer,' who worked for "The Locos," a crazy Mexican gang in South Tucson that boasted about 140 members. The membership fluctuated on any given day, depending on what The Locos had been up to, how many members were killed, and how many new members had been initiated into the crude gang known for its maniacal acts.

'The Destroyer' had been arrested on an attempted murder charge; but after posting bail, compliments of Triple 'A' Bonds, he went FTA (failed to appear) for his court date. My DEA contacts had also told me that the Mexican hood was suspected of having iced a couple of his gang's competitors who'd tried to muscle in on The Locos' operations. That's just how things were done with gangs, simply the cost of doing business. But it was this mindset that made my job even more dangerous since most of my jumpers had seen death many times and would stop at nothing to avoid jail time. Most of them had nothing to lose as they fled the law. They knew it; and I knew it too.

With a rap sheet as long as my arm, Jose Luis Aguilar had been in trouble since he was a kid, with arrests for aggravated assault, grand theft auto, sale and possession of crack cocaine, and now his newest pending indictments for attempted murder and attempted armed robbery. He was looking at twenty-to-life and possibly deportation; and he had no intention of seeing the inside of a prison cell.

Although I'd expected it might be fruitless, I had gone to see Aguilar's sister at the beginning of my manhunt.

"Where's your brother, Mary?" I asked through the cracked front door.

Without making eye contact she said, "No idea. I haven't seen him."

I knew Aguilar had once gone after a guy who'd attempted to rape his sister. This meant she 'owed him;' and besides that, in Mexican culture, you just don't mess with family. Everybody knows that can end dismally.

"Tell me the truth, Mary," I coaxed, using my best 'nice guy voice.'

"I am. I haven't seen Jose. Honest."

As she closed the door, I heard her lock it from the other side. My sixth sense told me, without doubt, that Mary had just lied to me. I knew Aguilar was inside that house, but I didn't want his sister to get hurt if I rushed the house and took him. Collateral damage would make my job messy and besides, it wasn't Mary's fault that her brother was a dangerous criminal. She shouldn't have to pay for his actions with her life.

I walked back toward my car to plan my next move.

Suddenly, a man's voice yelled out from the doorway where Mary had just stood.

"Hey! *Pinche Cabron!* You ain't takin' *ME* in!"

That's when the proverbial ball fell, and hell followed!

Not knowing if he had a gun on me, I still reacted as if he did. I figured with all the history of violence Aguilar was associated with, I wasn't about to take any chances. Besides, I knew he'd earned his nickname of 'The Destroyer' for a reason. Just like the old Chinese proverb says in *Sun Tzu* (The Art of War), "*If you know your enemies and know yourself, you will not be imperiled in a hundred battles . . .*" Those wise words rang true on this day, just as they had way back in the Sixth Century, BC.

With my back to the house, I flipped up the tail end of my coat and reached for my Colt holstered at the ready on my side. I drew and quickly spun around doing a 180-degree right pivot turn on my left foot as I tracked the figure at the door. With my Colt perfectly aligned on my target, as he stood in the doorway, a dark shadow silhouette against the interior light of the house, I was ready. Almost as if in slow motion, the figure raised his gun and tracked it until he stopped when it pointed straight at me.

'Plan for the worst, but hope for the best' had always sounded like such a sensible and cool-headed philosophy; that is until the scenario turns out for the worst! I hoped, in this moment, that the scenario would end well for me.

Aguilar got off a shot that sailed far to the right of me, as I heard the bullet whiz right past me, and almost instantly shatter in some glass somewhere behind me. I figured the bullet must have hit a windowpane in the distance. I also figured Aguilar must've been high on something because he had missed me by a mile.

With my ears still ringing from his errant gunshot, I tried to stay focused and to not let my anger get the best of me.

Instinctively my combat training kicked in, as I reflexively bent my knees and dropped down to the ground onto my left knee, affording the shooter as small a target as possible. I'd already had the hammer pulled back and I returned fire and let loose a shot of my own. It impacted with a loud *thump* on the door, just as Aguilar shut it again.

Although his shot was way off his mark, I still felt it was too damned close for comfort. *Am I getting too old for this shit?* I briefly wondered, but quickly let go of the thought. In the back of my mind, I knew that if I felt, for even an instant, that I was too old to be doing such work, that I would quit, and that my wife would be much happier for it.

'Christ, get up! Get up!' I silently yelled to myself. *'This ain't the time for a fucking breather!'*

I drew in a long, deep breath and smelled the strong odor of cordite as it wafted in the air. It was the same lingering telltale scent that I'd smelled many times before in my lifetime, it always arrives right after a bullet has been fired.

I slowly exhaled and decided to make my next move. I leapt up and ran toward the closed door and tried the knob as I stood to the side of it; but it was locked. Seconds later, I heard a car engine start up on the side of the house.

Oh Hell, NO! I thought, as I looked toward the direction of the sound.

I had a sinking feeling that things just weren't going to turn out well. This just wasn't my day.

The car sped off, away from the house and almost without braking, turned onto the main street. I caught sight of Aguilar's sister behind the wheel as her brother rode shotgun. I let them go, and decided not to fire into the car, since I didn't want a stray shot to hit or even kill Mary.

I sprinted back to my car, fired it up and shoved the LeBaron's gearshift into first. Almost in the same motion, I turned the steering wheel left, made a U-turn, and sped off after them.

Just moments later, I spotted the Monte Carlo's taillights in the distance.

My car was fast since I'd had the engine rebuilt and modified. Still though, I wasn't sure it was fast enough to catch up to the Chevy, but I was going to give it a try.

I knew Aguilar, with his sister beside him, had spotted me behind them as I steadily closed the gap between our cars. *Did he think just because his sister was driving, that I wouldn't fire at their car?* I asked myself. No, I wouldn't, unless she picked up a gun and fired it in my direction. If that happened, then all bets were off.

I realized now, as I trailed Aguilar's Chevy at 90 mph, that I should've just knocked down the door and taken him when I'd had the chance.

Right into the danger zone . . . Kenny Loggins sang from my radio as I shook my head and focused on Aguilar's taillights that kept getting closer.

The chase was on as I bore down on the taillights ahead of me. As I rounded a curve, about a car's length behind Aguilar and his sister, my right mirror suddenly exploded! Either he was a good shot, or just lucky; either way, I chucked it up to luck. No one was that good, shooting behind him and from a speeding car; anyway not someone the likes of Aguilar, a common street hood. *He might be just all juiced-up, I figured — running on adrenaline.*

The scene wasn't a Hollywood production though; it was for real as we raced through the empty desert landscape, leaving trails of dust in our wake. There were neither highway lights nor traffic on the lonely endless strip of highway; it was just the two of them and me.

The Chevy fast approached the Old Black Canyon Highway, a two-lane road. I figured they would shoot through it and stay on Highway-17. It surprised me when they didn't do that. Red brake lights lit up as the Chevy briefly slowed and then veered off onto the exit ramp, with me still about two car lengths behind.

Mary approached the intersection, but didn't slow down as she sped through a stop sign, clearly trying to put some distance between us. Seconds later, I also blew through the intersection, ignoring the stop sign too, careful not to lose even precious seconds. I put the pedal to the metal, as my car shot ahead, leaving a plume of white smoke behind me in the still night.

What happened next took just a few seconds, but there was no way I was going to let them get away from me. Neck and neck with the Chevy, I glanced at my speedometer as we raced along at over 90mph. The speed was just about right for what I had in mind.

In my peripheral, as I raced alongside their car, I saw Aguilar roll down his side window. I was sure he'd take a shot at me. And just as he stuck his arm out of the window, gun in hand, I jerked my steering wheel hard to the left and kept my foot hard on the gas pedal, forcing the Chevy off the roadway before he could get off a shot.

There was no shoulder of the road to speak of, just tall grassy areas as the Chevy tore through it. Mary somehow regained control of the car as it careened back onto the highway, jerking and rocking as she fought to steer it. By then, I was within spitting distance of the Chevy's rear end.

I thought about what I had to do next; hell, I'd done it once or twice before. *Well, practice makes perfect,* and what a better time to get my practice in, I thought, as I considered doing a *pit maneuver,* as it's referred to in law enforcement. The tactic is a precision immobilization technique — or my own personal abbreviation of it, anyway. In the military police, we called this technique a *takeout*, which is sort of self-explanatory.

With my hands tightly gripping the steering wheel, I rammed the Chevy hard against its left side bumper. This time, the technique's outcome was totally different. The car was completely out of control, as it swerved to the right, giving me a clear view of its side.

I saw my chance and too quick advantage. I accelerated hard on the gas pedal and rammed the Chevy's passenger side door, then reduced my speed, since I didn't want the Chevy to flip over on its side. I kept my speed to about 20mph as I pushed Aguilar's car clear across the road, and forced it into a clump of trees on the other side of the highway.

Suddenly, from the Chevy's driver's side, glass shattered; and then, with a loud thunderous clap and squelching boom of metal, the Chevy hit a tree hard and came to a hard stop. It was now sandwiched between the tree and the front of my car.

As the dust settled, all was quiet and still. I shifted my car into reverse and backed off a couple of feet. After I'd killed the engine, I climbed out of my LeBaron as my car's headlights illuminated the Chevy's side. In one motion, I pulled out my Colt, cocked back the hammer on a live round, and took a combat stance as I held my weapon in both hands, shoulders slightly turned and legs shoulder width apart. With my gun pointed at the Chevy's passenger door, I waited to see what Aguilar would do next.

There was no movement from inside their car, just moans and groans. With my knees slightly bent and my Colt still held in front of me, I slowly took three steps toward the Chevy and then cautiously stopped. I watched as Aguilar regained consciousness and started pushing with his shoulders against the passenger door, groaning with the effort, as he attempted to open the door that was twisted and wedged from the impact.

Wordless and dazed, Aguilar stared at me as I approached, and then I saw his eyes suddenly glaze over. Since I didn't see a weapon, I holstered my Colt and walked closer to the Chevy. After several tries, I forcefully opened the mangled door, then grabbed Aguilar and pulled him out of the car by his shoulders.

As I held his right arm, I shoved him to the ground and then bent his right arm up behind his back. I straddled him and then pushed him down at the back of his neck with my right knee, as I pulled out a set of cuffs. I got his left arm behind him and finished cuffing him.

With my right knee still on his neck, and Aguilar still dazed, confused and disoriented he wasn't about to give me any resistance. All the fight had been knocked out of him.

As blood dripped from a wound on the side of his head and still more blood ran from his mouth, reality started to sink in as he fought to focus. He seemed to be gathering his senses.

"Maria!" he cried.

His own health seemed only an afterthought to the hardened criminal, as Aguilar questioned his sister's condition. *You should've thought of that before you put her in the car with you!* I thought.

I went over and looked into the wrecked car that rested against the tree. Mary was motionless, slumped over the steering wheel, so I went back to finish with Aguilar.

I pulled him by his handcuffed arms up onto his feet and then shoved him toward my car. He must've twisted his ankle, because he limped along as blood continued to drip from his head and his mouth.

With one hand, I opened the right back passenger door, and with the other, I shoved him inside. Once he was safely seated, I reached in and cuffed him to the iron center post I'd installed for just such a purpose. He wasn't going anywhere, except back to jail, where he belonged.

Once again he cried out for his sister.

"Maria! Estas bien? Are you okay?"

I've always prided myself in trying to stay one step ahead of my opponents. It's something I've learned, not just in combat, or in my martial arts training, but even in playing chess. Still though, even I didn't see or sense what would happen next.

Just as I shut the car door on Aguilar, I heard shuffling sounds behind me. Before I could even turn around, I heard Mary crying, yelling and pleading.

"Mister, let my brother go!" she said.

Ever so slowly, I slid my right hand up to the comforting butt of my

Colt that waited faithfully at the ready. Not taking any chances, I turned around and faced Mary head-on. She stood beside the open passenger door of the Chevy holding a gun in both her hands. Mary barely pointed the gun in my direction though, as it canted more toward the ground than at me. Blood ran from her forehead and down into her eyes from a gash above her eye. I presumed she'd sustained the injury when she'd struck the steering wheel; and I could tell the blood in her eyes was obscuring her field of vision.

Madre De Dios! Just great! I thought. *Can this possibly get any worse?*

I was about to find out.

If it were anyone else beside Mary, I would have already been shot in the back without hesitation or even a second thought. No doubt about it, someone was definitely looking out for me in that moment.

I looked straight at her.

"I'm not going to do that, Mary. So, drop the gun or I'll pull this trigger and shoot you dead."

Aguilar yelled and shouted at his sister from the backseat of my car. He cried out in Spanish.

"Maria, he'll kill you. Do what he says!"

She said, "He . . . won't shoot me."

But something in her voice sounded as if she wasn't all that sure.

As I let her lock eyes with mine, I gave her a cold hard look.

I said, "Look at me very closely. Are you willing to bet your life on it?"

Her brother clearly was not important enough to die for, not this way and not tonight. He just wasn't worth it. Those thoughts kept going through my mind, as I stared into her blood-covered face as Mary tried to decide what to do next and how to end the standoff.

I grew impatient, actually bemused by her reluctance to drop her gun. She thought she was helping her brother though, just like family should do; and I couldn't take that away from her.

Mary stared back at me for a long moment, slowly shaking her head. Her sunken, defeated eyes, tinged with blood, seemed to have very little life left in them. I watched her torment as Mary let my words slowly penetrate her brain. I had never, and still today *have* never, drawn on a woman; but if she'd lifted her gun's muzzle toward me, even just an inch, I'd have had no choice but to reflex-ively draw and possibly kill her. It wasn't that I wanted to shoot her, not at all; but there would have been no other option. Her action would most certainly cause a *reaction* that none of us wanted to occur. The range between us was just a few feet, and I knew she'd be dead before she even hit the ground, no doubt about it. One simple motion could and would mean Mary would take her last breath; and all because of her brother, a man who'd spent a lifetime making his own bad decisions. I watched the frantic, defeated woman, as her eyes searched for an answer. I knew she was wrestling with potential scenarios, processing the situation and weighing her options, of which there were few.

Come on! Think about it. He's not worth it – not worth dying for, Mary! I thought, as I stared at her with my fingers lightly touching my Colt, poised to draw it in a split second.

As a cop, I'd taken my combat shooting skills to another level, and had trained in the art of quick draw and fire. I'd spent countless hours, using various targets and timing variables, to enhance my abilities to outdraw my opponents. In my world, I just never knew when that added *second* of reflex muscle memory could save a life, even *my own*. It was another example of 'practice makes perfect,' and something I took very seriously.

It was going to be either *Mary or me*; and I'd planned on going home to my wife and children, safe and sound, just like I'd promised.

The seconds ticked by as Mary agonized over what she should do. Deftly, my trigger finger slowly released the button on my holster that allowed my Colt to smoothly be drawn.

I realized I'd been holding my breath, careful not to move, not even to inhale or exhale, so I finally slowly exhaled and tried to keep as calm and still as I could. Everything depended on Mary in the do-or-die predicament. If I were fast enough, I'd live; and if I wasn't I'd die. It was that simple. My whole life came down to that moment; to Mary's response, to her decision and to how much she valued her own life.

Dark clouds had started forming on the eastern slopes of the moun-tains. The rainclouds behind Mary framed her and added to the dismal gloom that had fallen over the scene that played out beside her wrecked car. Raindrops suddenly started sprinkling down on us in the dark, sticky starless night.

Was one of us is feeling raindrops for the last time, I wondered.

With the LeBaron's headlights still shining on her, I watched Mary's eyes. She wore tight, khaki colored slacks, a blue shirt, now with fresh bloodstains, and sandals. Her long black hair fell below her shoulders. As the rain poured down harder, a cool breeze settled in from the east and flattened her dark hair against her face.

Even with her wet hair flung across her face, Mary's gun arm didn't waiver, though she still wasn't pointing the gun straight at me. I didn't start walking toward her, believing that if I did, she would reflexively bring the gun to bear; and I would then have to shoot her.

As I stood my ground, my thoughts briefly wandered to the killing I'd seen in 'Nam. Years ago, as I'd listened to the ominous sounds of death around me, even then I'd remembered the old quote that goes, *'This world is only the preparation for the next; and all I ask is that I live it having loved and being loved.'* In that moment, I was so grateful for the women I'd loved; but even more grateful for the woman I'd married.

I just hope I get back to her and in one piece, I thought.

As I snapped back to the here and now, I refocused my attention on the gun in front of me, and the person holding it. As a combat veteran and a police officer, I'd been taught and trained to never show panic in the heat of battle. For this reason, panic never entered my mind. It wasn't permissible; it wasn't what I'd learned and it wasn't a part of my conditioning.

Still though, it was totally unnatural not to know some small degree of fear when facing someone as he or she held a gun on you and held your life in their hands. To me though, the bit of fear I recognized wasn't for my own personal safety. It was the fear that I might have to shoot a *woman*, no matter the reality of the circumstance.

"God, Mister!" she cried her voice tight. "I'll shoot you!"

I didn't say a word as I watched her; but I gripped the handle of my Colt a little tighter, as I stared into her dark, uncertain eyes, illuminated by my car's headlights. Her eyes would betray her long before she lifted the gun barrel. I was sure I'd be able to read her eyes; and they didn't disappoint.

The scene played out that night was very fluid. Too many things could've happened that didn't.

Mary stared at me rather placidly, serenely almost, until a few seconds later, when her eyes slowly drifted away from me. Even still, the gun didn't waiver.

More seconds passed. It felt more like an eternity though, until Mary finally released a hand on her gun, then wiped the blood, rain and hair away from her defeated eyes. She inhaled deeply, and with a long loud sigh she wordlessly dropped the gun to the ground, and then slumped back onto the seat of the Chevy through the car's open door. With her hands covering her face, she slumped forward and sobbed heavy tears that seemed to come from somewhere deep inside her tortured soul. When she released hands from her face, she began to heave, almost convulsively sobbing, as the pain and torment flowed from her small frame.

Unmoving, I just stood there for a second or two, and allowed my own tension to slowly subside. Relief washed over me as I looked down on her; not relief for myself, but relief that I hadn't been forced to shoot her.

Wiping the rain from the upturned brim of my Stetson hat, I slowly walked toward her sobbing form. I stopped where she had dropped the gun and picked it up, released the magazine and jacked out the round in the chamber. As I stared at the 9mm round, I could only imagine feeling the deadly metal lodged in my body as I lay dying or seriously wounded. With a deep, cleansing sigh, I threw the bullet and the gun onto the ground far to my left side.

As I approached her, she stared up at me with sad bloodshot eyes rimmed in dark circles, and a voice which was rather raspy.

"Would you have killed me, Mister?"

I took off my hat and slapped it twice on my right thigh, still trying to shake the rain off it. Despite the coldness that had come with the cool nighttime desert rain, I wiped sweat off my bald head.

As I slowly placed my hat back onto my head, I looked down on her, and gently placed my hand on her shoulder, without giving it a conscious thought, I didn't try to lie or even to sugarcoat my reply in any way, since there was no point.

"If you'd lifted that gun, I would have put two or three slugs into you."

Mary Aguilar's vacant eyes that had been staring up at me suddenly opened wide and then she dropped her gaze. It was in that moment that it had finally sunk in, and Mary realized just how close she had come to death.

"Oh - My - *God*," she softly said, almost in a prayer of thanks.

To every person on this earth, death comes sooner or later. In the end, it's how we choose to live that counts. Mary chose to live that night.

Her breathing became very shallow, and she dropped her head to her chest and quietly sobbed some more, as the gravity of it all hit her.

As the tense scene ended, so did the rain; almost as if Mother Nature had decided to return the desert to the way we'd found it, still and quiet under the calm night sky.

I walked back to my car, unlocked the truck, and pulled out my first aid kit. Getting back to Mary, I knelt down next to her, and started to treat her wound.

"I'm just going to treat that head wound."

After cleaning the gash in her forehead, I pulled out an army field-dressing, an absorbent cloth bandage, and wrapped it around her head to stop the bleeding. In the army, field dressings are issued in sealed waterproof pouches to keep them sterile, clean and dry. I always kept several of the pouches readily available just in case I should ever need one. I made sure the dressing was tight, and that no blood seeped through it.

I said, "It should hold till you can get to a doctor."

A half-hour later, after making sure the Chevy was drivable and that Mary was well enough to drive, I told her to go home.

"Be careful, drive safe."

Sometimes, life takes more than it gives.

I watched as the Chevy pulled away from the scene and onto the highway, headed in the opposite direction. It disappeared slowly into the night, until the car's taillights grew smaller and smaller, swallowed up by the blackness of night.

Slowly and quietly, I mouthed, "Adios," genuinely relieved that Mary was driving herself home again.

After Mary had driven off in her wrecked Chevy, I got into my LeBaron and started it up. On the highway again, I headed back toward Tucson, still with ample time to spare before the court's deadline.

A while later, as I drove through the night, Aguilar finally spoke from the backseat.

He said in Spanish, "Hey, I like to . . ."

"The name's Alvarez."

"Okay, Mister Alvarez, I like to thank you for not shooting my sister back there."

I took in a deep breath, and then let out a long, slow sigh. I was feeling relieved that it was all over and that it ended well.

I said, "Hey, it was all on her."

In my rearview mirror, I watched his face; and in a voice that I hoped sounded sincere, still in Spanish, I said, "You know, there are two things we are charged with in this life: living with our mistakes, and endeavoring to learn from them."

He nodded and bowed his head.

"Mmm, Si Senor, you may be right."

My experiences have shown that the taking of a life always leaves an indelible mark; and the killing of another human being will live with me all the days of my life. My dreams are a constant reminder of it. I have taken a life or two in the past, but never the life of a woman. I thanked the good Lord that I didn't have to take Mary's life on that night.

But it never fails, seems like every time I go toe-to-toe with evil I find myself on the winning end. Someday, I won't be so lucky. Someday, evil is bound to find me and there won't be anyone around to save my ass. But, that is what I find so exhilarating and dangerous about this sort of work. Knowing when to stop, now that will be the hard part.

By eleven thirty in the morning, I had Jose Luis Aguilar safely tucked into the Pima County Jail, with a check in my pocket and another job where a bullet hadn't found my body, been kicked or clubbed.

All in all, a very productive hunt; my wife is going to enjoy the payday that's for sure and I, a much needed rest.

<hr>

I ARRIVED HOME AROUND ONE IN THE AFTERNOON, HOPING TO AT LEAST get a couple hours sleep. God knew I needed it.

I was so tired, that I couldn't even remember undressing, washing up some, and crawling under the sheets.

I figured it hadn't been more than an hour since I closed my eyes, when I felt a hand caressing my face. It was Dolores, my wife, waking me up for dinner. I looked over at my alarm clock and saw that five hours had passed since I put my head on my pillow.

I saw my daughter, Carmen-Melissa, standing by the bed looking down on me with a smile on her face.

She said. "It's five o'clock, Daddy. Get up and have dinner with us."

How could I refuse, after being out so late the previous night, I owed them some quality time together.

"Okay . . . okay. See I'm getting right up, honey. I'll be there in a little bit."

After she'd left, and with Dolores sitting on the edge of the bed, I became acutely aware of her scent, of her dark hair parted to one side, combed down past her shoulders. She kept glancing at me, with the most mischievous smile on her lips. With her slim form and pale skin (she hardly ever wore makeup in the house), I noticed she was wearing a sleeveless white top and pink shorts as she rose to leave.

But before she did, I scoped her up in my arms and pulled her onto the bed with me. We kissed rather passionately and after breathlessly pulling away from me, she said, "Not now, Victor. Kids are awake and they want to be with their father. But there's always tonight."

I said, "Can't wait, I'm already excited."

Then she tilted her head down past my waistline.

"I can tell."

Afterward at the dinner table, Dolores had fried chicken and mashed potatoes and gravy, sweet cream style corn and hot buns all set and ready for us to dig into. And she had coffee ready for me.

Halfway through our dinner, Dolores' gazed shifted from the kids to me.

"Victor, you do remember what day this is. Right?" she asked.

No, I didn't, but I didn't tell her that. I was too busy drinking my coffee to think straight, no less remember what today signified.

I peered over the brim of my coffee cup, when as one I saw my kids turned their gaze on me, smiling.

Somehow, I felt I was being ganged up here, four against one. Not fair.

Carmen-Melissa frowned, "Yes, Daddy. Remember?"

I glanced over at Angel my second born, who kept staring at me. He just cracked a smile, and shaking his head.

"Yeah, just like Daddy, not to remember."

Raul-Esteban, my one year old just kept blinking his eyes at me.

I said, "Come on, guys. Give me a break." I was trying to think straight wanting to remember what this was all about.

"Mm-mm-mm," Dolores said, looking over at me shrugging. "It's your daughter's PTA meeting tonight."

"Oh."

"You forgot, didn't you?"

"Yeah, how'd you guess?"

"It's Carmen's big day and she just wants you to take her. And we both decided that it would be better if you took her instead of me. I'll be staying home with the boys; you can tell me all about it when you get home."

I shrugged, put down my coffee cup, and stared at my family.

"Do I have a choice?"

And as one they all said, "No."

Book One

Josie and the Kidnapping

Chapter One

The Call

Two Months Later

I GOT THE CALL AT HOME ABOUT ONE O'CLOCK THAT AFTERNOON.

It was toward the end of July and Tucson was in the grips of yet another hot year, one of its hottest since late in 1913, when the temperatures climbed close to 109 degrees, and it remained sweltering during all the summer months and partially toward the beginning of winter as well.

But today it hasn't gotten that hot yet, still holding to 107. But the weather forecast called for hotter days to come. Maybe topping off at 113 degrees! There was no wind to speak of; the humidity was well below normal for that time of the year, so the outdoors felt like a furnace.

Barely anyone ventured outdoors, with warnings being issued on

TV, radio and the newspapers, about protecting oneself against the harsh sun by wearing sunscreen and sunglasses, to minimize sun exposure and possible skin and eye damage. It didn't lend itself to any possible assignments from my local bail bond agent's, that's for sure.

So, you could have imagined my surprise when I was contacted by Frank Marshall at Triple 'A' Bail Bonds, who asked that I come over to his office in the next hour or so. Frank mentioned that he had a case that could use my expertise and my hunting abilities.

Something in his voice raised my eyebrows a little, and my curiosity was definitely piqued. I kind of sense it was more of a plea than a request, and the urgency of meeting with me caught my attention, too.

I was between some boring cases for some lawyers, so I decided to see what Frank had that seemed so urgent, and made him think of me. Not that he had other hunters at his beck and call mind you, just that he thought of me as more of a friend, of which I felt rather flattered, since I got most all their hard cases. And I suspected this one of being just that — a hard case.

I wasn't wrong.

It was two o'clock that hot July afternoon that I, wearing a pair of black jeans, short sleeve, white shirt and my dark, tinted shades, pulled onto the curb in front of the bail agent's office.

Shutting down my car, I climbed out, pulled my Stetson down over my head, locked the car and slowly walked to Frank's office. I had my gun belt strapped on, with my Colt .45 armed and ready as was my nature, as I pulled open the bail agent's front door.

Once inside I removed my shades, and the first thing I saw was that Frank was not alone. Sitting across from his desk was a narrowly built, rather elderly looking man judging from his gray hair.

The bail agent's office hadn't changed much over the years. It still was a two-room affair. The front was for the main business and the rest of the building for files, storage and a small live-in suite. The portable television was still in its corner. An undersized sofa and a couple of chairs helped make the place cozy. In the other corner sat a Polaroid camera on a tripod. So all in all no changes had been made since my last time here.

As I came in the elderly man turned on his seat, glanced once my way, grinned and turned back around.

In that brief glimpse, I saw a sixty-year-old or so white gentleman, wearing a grey, two-piece suit and a tie-less white shirt. His face was all red and blotchy with bags under his eyes, probably from lack of sleep, with five o'clock stubble, as he maintained a relaxed and cool posture.

Turning away from him, I set my gaze on Frank Marshall. He wore his signature faded blue jeans and blue denim cattleman's type shirt with its snap-front Western pockets. He was sitting behind his desk going over some paperwork.

The air conditioner seemed to be going full blast, and the overhead fan turned slowly, bringing cool air into the front office.

Frank Marshall stopped, and leaned back in his chair. Lacing his fingers behind his head, he glanced up at me while slowly nodding. "Glad to see you, Al. Thanks for coming over so quickly."

I nodded. "Glad to see you too, John, it's been awhile since I've heard from you or Fred." My eyes lingered on John for a moment. "So, not having anything of immediate importance on my agenda, I decided to see why you'd call me over here for."

John went silent for a moment, then nodded kind of absently while his eyes locked on me for a brief second, thinking.

Marshall nodded again. "Hey how's the family coming along?"

"Growing and growing."

"Yeah, I know what you mean. Pull up a chair, Al."

John brought his chair back straight down and placed his hands on the desk. With a hint of laughter in his eyes and a slight grin he glanced once at the elderly gentleman, and then shifted his gazer back to me.

"Let me introduce Mr. Charles Leavitt," he said. "Mr. Leavitt this is Victor Alvarez, my bounty hunter and a licensed private investigator I told you about. I'm very sure Mr. Alvarez can help with your problem."

Nodding once in my direction, Charles Leavitt stood up from his chair. He had the look of a man who has seen death and lived to tell about it. His eyes certainly betrayed himself to me. You can't hide that from a combat veteran. I clearly suspected him of being ex-military. He was tall and muscular and his eyes didn't leave mine nor mine his. I felt him taking me in, maybe sizing me up a little as well.

A narrow stare met my look.

Extending his hand out to me he said, "Please to meet you, I was expecting a slightly taller man from what Mr. Marshall described."

I frowned slightly then grinned as I glanced over to Frank. "Yeah, I get that a lot."

"Mr. Marshall has spoken very highly of you," Charles Leavitt said. He paused briefly before continuing. "He says you're *the* guy who could help with my problem. I truly hope you can."

I looked askance at Leavitt. "I'm just a guy who does a job."

There was a slight pause before I continued.

I shook the proffered hand in turn. "So, tell me about your problem."

He sat back down as I pulled up a chair and sat toward his right. Charles Leavitt went very still and quiet. Then he briefly glanced at me before he dropped his gaze and sighed.

"It's about my daughter," he said, his voice low and unnaturally composed.

Chapter Two

Josie

His daughter was Josephine Leavitt, or Josie as her mother nick named her. She was born in Boston and raised in Tucson, when then Colonel Charles Leavitt had retired from the US Air Force at Davis-Monthan Air Force Base in Tucson back in '75.

Josephine Leavitt was a twenty-one-year old blue eyed blonde. Looking over a Polaroid photograph supplied by John Marshall, I saw she was a full bosomed woman. Not unattractive, but not pretty. She stood five feet two, about a hundred and ten pounds.

The photograph also showed her wearing her short blonde hair to her shoulders and parted in the center, combed to the sides. She had slightly sunken cheeks and bags under her eyes.

John Marshall had mentioned that the photograph was taken shortly after he'd bailed her out of jail, which I would imagine explained the baggy eyes.

According to her father, Josie always had a rebellious side, getting in and out of trouble since turning sixteen when she was arrested for shoplifting. Later it got worse. At the age of nineteen, she'd been arrested for possession of crack and served two years. It was in jail where she met her present boyfriend, Alan Freeman.

Leavitt said, "Freeman was in jail for burglary and possession of a firearm in the commission of a felony when he and Josie got together. They got arrested again, this time for armed robbery and resisting arrest. But that's not the half of it."

He paused and looked away for a second, then continued. "With the help of Mr. Marshall, I bailed out my daughter a couple of weeks ago. She stills lives at home, and works part-time as a waitress while attending Pima Community College. She was to appear in court two days ago but failed to show up for the hearing. The day she was to appear for her court date, I called her from my work to remind her, but she wasn't home. Since then I haven't heard from her."

Another pause.

"I started getting very worried, so I started a search of my own, but couldn't find her in any of her favorite hangouts. Then today I received a call from Freeman, Josie's boyfriend, who said he had taken Josie and was holding her for ransom. If I go to the police, he would kill her. I had nowhere else to turn too, that's why I'm here today. He demanded I come up with twenty thousand dollars to get her back safe and sound. He's given me four days to get the money together."

If I were in his shoes, I too would move heaven and earth to get her back.

Immediately my thoughts turned toward my own daughter.

When my daughter, my first child Carmen-Melissa was born from my second marriage, and as I gazed down on this tiny human bundle wrapped in a blanket looking up at me with the most beautiful dark eyes and a smile that melted my heart, I knew deep down the true meaning of love as it washed over me. I'll always love her and would give my life in defense of her and all my children till death overtakes me.

Thus, I could imagine the pain the Colonel was going through for his only child.

Once Charles Leavitt paused with his story, I wondered why I would even get caught up in this case. Wondered too why the FBI hadn't been called before this.

My attention immediately shifted back to Charles Leavitt, as I noticed he was once again talking to me.

"Mr. Alvarez, please understand my position. I cannot go to the police with this. If I do, I may not see my daughter alive again. I'm a widower and she is all I have left. And I don't want to take the chance of getting her killed if I was to go to the police. Right now, you seem to be the only hope I have of getting my daughter back alive. Can you help me?"

I inclined my head slightly and gently sighed. *Did I have a choice?* I thought. Of course I didn't.

I glanced once at Frank and then back to Leavitt.

"Of course I'll help."

"Thank you."

"John," I said. "I'm going to need everything you can find on Freeman. Colonel, I need everything you can give me on your daughter. You know friends' names, phone numbers and address. I'll also need to go through her room."

Leavitt nodded. "No problem."

I asked. "Will you be able to come up with the ransom in time?"

"Yes, that won't be a problem. I have enough in my savings to cover it."

That takes care of that part, I thought.

"I'll make copies of Josie's bond and all the information I have on her," John said. "I'll place a call to the bondsman who wrote the bond on Freeman get him to cooperate, which shouldn't be a problem."

"Give me a call when you need to see her room," Leavitt said. "I'll make sure I'm home."

Getting up from my chair I nodded absently as my gaze shifted from Leavitt to Frank Marshall. "Okay. I'll do just that."

"So, Al," John Marshall said, just after Leavitt left the office. "How are you going to handle this?"

"Why, you offering to help?"

"Just . . . curious, it's all."

"What I'm wondering . . ." I paused slightly, thinking seriously about my options.

John said, "Yeah . . .?"

"Never mind, John."

Having already negotiated my fees and getting all the paperwork on Josie's bond, I left the agent's office. As I headed back home, I was trying to decide how best to proceed.

I knew time was not on my side. *Would I be able to effectively run an investigation into the kidnapping in just four days?* That thought ran through my mind. But it couldn't be helped. Moreover, experience in this type of investigation showed that the first twenty-four hours of a kidnapping were its most crucial period.

So, I decided to play this by the numbers, so-to-speak, as I used to do when planning and putting together an investigative scenario during my old days as a criminal investigator — dotting every *i* and crossing every *t*.

In this case, I already knew who the players were and it was just a matter of tracking them, pulling surveillance, rescuing Josie and bringing Freeman back to jail. Bing bam boom: a step at a time. Sure. It was a tall order for such a short period of time.

But I'd also come to a decision, if I'd couldn't get Josie back to her father in three days, I'll seek the help of my friends in law enforcement – unofficially of course. I just hope it didn't have to come to that. Also I didn't want the FBI involved; I had to do my own investigation first. See where that leads me.

Chapter Three

The Kids

It was somewhat after four o'clock when I made it back home.

The kids heard the car pulling up to the driveway and all three met me in the garage, with Carmen-Melissa, who was six, right out front of my two boys, Angel, three, and Raul-Esteban who was the baby at age one. And of course, Dolores was there as well.

I've always made it a point, if I'd came home late that I would always bring something for the kids, whether it was toys or food. They knew I would bring them something. I forgot once and never heard the end of it.

While entering the house and stepping into the living room with my family right behind me, I told the kids to look on the passenger seat of the car for a surprise. Then I sat down on the sofa.

After the kids came back in with the food I'd gotten them – hamburgers and fries, Carmen-Melissa took a seat to my right and the two boys went off somewhere in the house. With Dolores seated to my left, we made small talk, laughing and talking about what the future held for us as a family.

Then thinking about the case, I didn't have the heart to tell them I would be going out again tonight. I think she was getting sick of the idea of my working late into the night or through the early morning hours. In fact, there were times she really hated my late night sashays, voicing her dislike on numerous occasions.

I then decided to tell her.

She looked blank for a moment, and then a surprised angry look crossed her face. She took in a deep breath. "I need you back home safe!"

Then surprisingly a more somber look seemed to flood her eyes.

But, there was that something in her tone though which gave me pause.

I nodded. "Don't I always?"

She looked thoughtful at me. "Just make sure you do," she said as she waved her hand in the air.

"Yes ma'am."

I've always said that there is no rhyme or reason to this life. You meet the one love of your life, the one you think will be with you for the rest of your life, and you make it harder than what it seems. But whoever said life is easy? Shit happens no matter what you say, what you do.

It was around six o'clock that I finally made it out of the house, as Dolores saw me out to the front door. Opening the door, I turned back around to say my goodbyes and I noticed a change had come over her. As she lifted her eyes to meet mine, I noticed a faraway look came to her eyes, and in a rather low soft voice she said, "Be careful."

I took in her worried eyes, then held her face in both my hands and gently brought it to mine, and as we kissed, she hugged me tightly almost with an urgent appeal. Then suddenly as we parted she became teary eyed, then turning her back to me, walked into the house and closed the door without another word.

For a few seconds, I stared at the door, and slowly, very slowly sighed, shrugged and turning away, walked toward my car.

Chapter Four

The Kidnapping

Day One

IT WAS HALF PAST EIGHT IN THE EVENING.

The steaming heat of the day disappeared gradually, leaving behind dark shadows into the early evening hours. I had the air conditioner turned on in my car trying to keep the sweating to a minimum on this hot sticky night. The temperature was still in the mid-90s and the humidity was high too. I kept hydrated sipping on some cold water from my ice chest from the trunk of the car.

It was almost an unbearable night. Thank goodness for the air conditioner. The sky was clear and it was a very starry night, while the full moon lit up the desert. It was a beautiful night except of course for the heat.

I'd already made two wrong turns, missing North Sabino Canyon Road. The lack of street lights made seeing road signs that more difficult.

My destination was Colonel Charles Leavitt's residence out at the Catalina Foothills in Tucson, where rows of several affluent ranch style homes were constructed four years ago. They were built for those who could afford the two thousand dollars or more mortgage payments. Some of those homes were going for so much more, all for the rich and famous.

After a ten-minute drive, I finally got onto North Sabino Canyon Road, and one and a half miles further on, I made a left on North Larrea Lane. Then I hung another left onto Brookwood Drive catching sight of the house a minute later.

Earlier, I'd made contact with Charles Leavitt and made arrangements to see Josie's room. He assured me he'd be at home by the time I arrived.

I had a pretty good idea on how to get to Levitt's residence. Although I couldn't find it on my five-year-old map. Guess it was time to get an updated one.

Tucson was growing by leaps and bounds. Soon you wouldn't be able to recognize the old place. Years later when I came back for a visit I immediately saw I'd been right; everything had changed for the better.

His house was nestled away in what I surmised was about a two-acre plot with empty sub-plots on either side. Lights were on throughout the house, and from what I saw as I drove up, it was a well-maintained, split-level ranch home, done up in adobe style.

Parking on the curb just by an old ten-foot Saguaro cactus, I shut down the engine, climbed out and grabbing my Stetson locked the car and walked up to the half-moon shape black tarred driveway.

I came to a stop at a three-foot brick fence that wrapped around on either side of the ranch house. At the center of the fence was a small gate leading to the front door and onto a large veranda.

The main door was massive, consisting of two doors that swung open in the center and constructed in the old Spanish style woodwork design. You could just smell the money oozing out of this place. Wow, very impressive.

And standing at the open door, was Colonel Charles Leavitt, wearing jeans, cowboy boots and white shirt.

Once he led me into the house, I followed him down a hallway to what appeared to be a cavernous family room, then to a small bar located just left of a large wood-burning fireplace. And on either side of the fireplace, were built-in book cases stacked with rows of books with several ceramic figurines dotting throughout.

It seemed like an elegant library and a family room rolled into one. On the fireplace mantel, I saw what appeared to be family pictures; that of a woman standing next to a young little girl. And of a family portrait of both Leavitt and his late wife, who bore a strong resemblance to her daughter, Josie. Getting closer to the bar and on closer examination, I saw they were indeed family photos.

Above the mantel was a very large painting of his wife. She had a warm smile, and long flowing dark hair cascading down to her shoulders. She wore a tight white cuff-off blouse that was pulled back revealing her bare shoulders, and a fair amount of exposed cleavage. The artist painted a light blue background, highlighting a truly beautiful young woman.

The rather generously stocked bar had the feel and look of a person who is used to entertaining. Although for no reasons that I could fathom, he struck me as a man who valued, above all, his privacy.

The house was chilly, quiet and the only sounds breaking the stillness came from beyond the closed windows.

I stopped just by the fireplace, and watched as Charles Leavitt started pouring himself a shot of bourbon at the bar.

"Care for a drink?" he asked.

"Sure. What do you have?"

"Scotch, rum, gin, name your poison."

"Gin on the rocks with a twist of lime, would do."

"A martini man, would you like some vermouth added to your drink?"

"If you don't mind, I'd rather do without."

He shrugged. "Suit yourself."

We both lapsed into silence, each of us with our own thoughts before Leavitt spoke once more. "Mind if I ask you a question?"

I frowned. "Ask away."

Leavitt hesitated. "By the way you carry yourself; you seem like a man who's served time in the military. The way your eyes shift and appear to be taking everything in, also tells me you may have seen combat."

Turning around to face me, and holding a cocktail glass with my gin, and his bourbon, he stopped a few steps in front of me. As I took the glass he offered up, I sat down on one of two leather armchairs by the fireplace, while he sat down in the other.

A brief silence settled in the room.

Taking a sip of the gin, I smiled. "So, what's your question?"

He didn't immediately reply, but sipped his drink. He diverted his eyes away from me for a second, and then as he set eyes on me again, he said, "What branch of the military were you in? Although I'd hazard a guess and say army?"

"Correct army it was. I was in a little over twenty years when I retired. It was a good run."

"What was your military specialty?"

"I was an MP and criminal investigator."

"So that's why you're a private investigator?"

"Among other reasons, but yes, thought I'd fit right in."

"From what Mr. Marshall said of you, I think you have."

"Yeah, guess so."

After a short silence, he asked, "So, are you also a combat veteran?"

"I did two tours in the 'Nam," I said not delving into it.

Charles Leavitt glanced down on his drink then back to me.

"I see."

"How about you, Colonel, see any combat?"

He looked over at me and closed his eyes, as though discussing his thoughts would add more sorrow to what he was already feeling. "A little bit," he said.

Hell, I remember when I lived through my very first ordeal of combat. I felt absolutely lucky to have lived through it all, and thought of nothing else afterward. But it had been a magical time. You can't forget something like that, no matter what some psychologists say to the contrary.

I didn't try to pry. I understood the look. Stories about blood and death are grim reminders combat veterans just don't care to share with friends or loved ones. It was only after constant consultations that some veterans opened up at all to those experiences. It was true for him, as it was for me. His memories were his own, and so were his nightmares.

Changing the subject, I said, "Think I'd like to look over your daughter's room if you don't mind."

"Of course, follow me."

After setting our drinks down, Colonel Leavitt led me out from the library and down a wide hallway, toward the far-left side of the house. Several paintings of Air Force warplanes hung on either side of the hallway. I recognized a few, like the Lockheed F-80s flying in combat formation, a pair of F-82s Twin Mustangs, and a B-52 Stratofortress, plus others I didn't recognize.

"That's a nice collection of paintings," I said as we approached three doors just off the hallway.

"Those are planes I flew before taking on a desk job," he said as he stopped at one of the doors.

He opened the door to a rather large bedroom. "This is Josie's room."

Following him into the bedroom, I stopped half way through and gazed around the bedroom. First thing that caught my eye, was that it was all done up in pink, or what is typically called a mauve shade, a very frilly girly feel.

All four walls were decorated in a dainty style floral wallpaper. On the bed, an iron bedpost frame, from what I could see, were a lot of ruffles. Three pillows and ruffled sheets, and a pinkish colored bed cover drawn back to the foot of the bed that hung down to the floor.

Left of the bed was a built-in book case with several books laid out in an unorganized fashion. A round shaped night stand was on the right, draped with a pinkish ruffled cloth and a night lamp on top.

Right side of the bed was a magazine rack with several copies of the Sears Roebuck catalogues, a couple of Teen Beat magazines and several others I couldn't make out.

On the foot of the bed was a tall wooden trunk stained in a light oak finish with a floral-clear vase on top, with yellow roses in it.

On one side of the room, was an "L" shape student desk and chair with shelves of business college books on top of the desk. I assumed the books were used in her college classes. And a La-Z-Boy recliner was by the two windows on the other side of the room, which completed the furnishings. The windows had pink colored, drawn drapes with gray sheer curtain-scarf on either side, which would let in daylight.

All in all, a very tidy and clean kept bedroom. Looking over to my left, I saw an open door which led into a bathroom. I walked over to it, stopped, stood by the open door, looked in and noticed that it too was clean and orderly.

First thing that crossed my mind on seeing Josie's bedroom was that for the life of me, I couldn't see any signs of a struggle, which would indicate abduction had been perpetrated in the room. The only thing out of place was the books on the shelves.

The abduction could have taken place somewhere else in the house, I thought. But, I started getting a funny feeling about all this; something just didn't sit right with me; couldn't put my finger on it though.

It'll come to me sooner or later.

Chapter Five

Doubts

SITTING DOWN ON THE EDGE OF THE BED, I STARTED RIFLING THOUGH THE drawers, not really looking for anything in particular. I'll know the moment I find it . . . but I didn't find anything. I also went through her chest of drawers, and noticed one of them empty; no signs of any girly stuff.

Getting up, I went through all the drawers in the bedroom, but again I didn't find a damn thing. And that was truly curious.

Then I went through her walk-in closet. There I found several empty hangers, telling me a lot of her clothing was missing, or maybe ready for the laundry.

What I didn't find, outweighed what I did find, and it begged a big question here.

I knew for a fact that the Colonel traveled a lot during his time in the military. Most officers just didn't stay stationed in one place too long. And most everywhere he traveled to, his family was sure to follow — or traveled with him. That's the military family, no matter what branch of the service one was in, the family was sure to go as well.

Which begged the question, where was Josie's passport? It was not in the bedroom. Maybe the colonel had it. Something to ask about, that's for sure.

Throughout my search of the bedroom, Colonel Leavitt had stayed outside of the room, leaving me to my own.

The moment I started walking into the room, he asked, "Find anything?"

"Yes, as a matter of fact I did."

Chapter Six

Suspicions

BUT THE PASSPORT AND CLOTHING WEREN'T THE ONLY THINGS I DIDN'T
find in the room.

I didn't find a diary!

Now, I know from experience that most girls keep a diary. My own
daughter kept one. Although, she's never let on to me that she had one,
nor tell her mother about it. But that's to be expected. Right? Some
diaries can be overly private and highly secretive in scope, and are
often kept hidden away from parents' prying eyes. But as soon as they
get to post-adolescence it gets destroyed; but not all the time.

I was willing to bet she hadn't destroyed it. And if she did have
one, where was it?

We got back to the library.

"Does your daughter keep her own passport?" Or do you hold on
to it?"

He looked at me steadily, but hesitated before answering. "That's
an odd question."

"Humor me please. I'm just trying to get a complete picture here."

Leavitt considered my question in silence.

"I don't know what you're trying to accomplish with her passport. But to answer your question, I let her keep it."

"I see. The reason I ask is that I couldn't find it in her bedroom."

Leavitt frowned. "That's strange. I'm sure that's where she kept it."

I hesitated a little on my next question, probably knowing he wasn't going to like it. "Mind if I go through the rest of the house?"

"Why? What would you gain by looking through my house?"

"Nothing or something, I'm trying to establish the crime scene."

"But she was taken from the house, and I would imagine from her room."

"That's what I'm trying to establish."

"Going through my house sounds farfetched, if you ask me, but very well then, go ahead."

"Thank you. Do you have maid service?"

"Yes, as a matter of fact I do. Why?"

"Again, humor me please. When was the last time your house was serviced?"

"They come in every Monday morning."

"So, that was last week then?"

"Yes."

"Okay."

I left the Colonel in the library and went through the rest of the house alone.

After I'd inspected all the windows and doors, I couldn't find any signs of forced entry. I also noticed the house was protected by a burglar alarm system. After finishing my walk though, I failed to see any signs where a struggle could have taken place.

Nothing conclusive mind you, she could have been taken without a fight anywhere in the house, or taken forcefully at any other place. But it didn't seem likely, considering that the last place Josie was heard from was the house. Also, the alarm hadn't been tripped, which would suggest Jose had let someone in. Someone she knew!

Definitely, something was off here.

Or, I could be dead wrong about everything. I've been wrong

before. But things just didn't feel right. I started believing that the evidence did not support a kidnapping from the house.

So if not the house, where then? That was the burning question.

If it was a kidnapping to begin with, where was the passport? Where was her diary? And most important, why were several articles of clothing missing?

Those were questions that I didn't have any answers to, yet.

I took a deep breath. Part of me wanted this to be an open and shut case of a kidnapping. But the other part of me was seeing too many discrepancies in the crime. In other words, why were those items missing? And again it came back to, why weren't there signs of a struggle?

Things just didn't add up.

I decided to keep my suspicions to myself for now. No use getting the Colonel all riled up about it.

Working my way back to the library and Colonel Leavitt, whom I found sitting down on his leather armchair, sipping on his drink, I thought of a few more questions that needed answers.

I took a seat on the vacant leather chair.

He looked at me rather bewildered. "Honestly, I'm not sure looking over the rest of my house accomplished anything."

I shook my head. "Well that's a matter of opinion. My point is this. Experience has shown me that in any investigation, everything needs to be covered, no matter how weird it sounds to anyone else. An investigator needs to cover all the bases, if he intends to close his case satisfactory with the perp or perps arrested and all parties safely back with loved ones."

"I hope you can do just that."

"Why I'm here."

After a brief silence, I said, "Your daughter, does she have her own checking account?"

"No, not since her troubles started. She was on my account, and I removed her from it. Her spending was getting out of hand, and I thought she was spending it on drugs, and not on school. "Why?"

"Just curious, has she asked you for any sums of money, say, in the last week or so?"

"Why are you asking these silly questions? What does that have to do with anything? Whoa, wait a minute now. Are you suggesting that this may not be a kidnapping . . .?"

He caught on fast. But I wasn't sure yet if I'd go that far. Nevertheless, it sure was starting to look that way.

I cut him off. "I'm not saying anything yet, Colonel. But it's a possibility, something to think about. Look at it from my point of view. I see a lot of things here that don't add up. It could be nothing, but then again, I have to look at everything."

"Okay. To answer your question, she did ask for a thousand dollars a few days before the kidnapping. She said she needed several books and other things for school."

"I see. And did you give it to her?"

"Yes, I did."

"One more thing, does she have her own car?"

"Yes, one of those Japanese cars, a 1986 Toyota Corolla, blue. It's a coupe."

"Is it registered under her name or yours?"

"It's registered under her name, but I seem to be always making payments on it."

I saw the hurt reflected in his eyes, and my mind briefly wondered toward my own daughter.

"I can't promise anything, Colonel. But I'll do what I can to get your daughter back."

He nodded and fell silent.

Colonel Leavitt finally spoke. "Ever since her mother died Josie has taken it rather poorly. In a way, she blames me for it. Her mother and I were at odds on a lot of things. We argued back and forth, and Josie was always trying to defuse the situation. She put a lot on her shoulders because of me. So please bring her back to me soon. She's all I've got left in this world."

Of course, I couldn't make such a promise, I thought; life is full of surprises, and a good cop never, ever promises anything he can't keep.

I just hope I was all wrong about Josie.

After a moment, I rose from the chair and shook his hand. "No need to get up, Colonel, I'll see myself out."

I left a very desperate and distraught man, but I also left him with some shred of optimism. But if truth be told, I just didn't know if I could bring this to a satisfactory conclusion.

Back in my car, I put my head in my hands. This whole thing just didn't sit right with me. I felt like someone's playing with my head, and it ain't me.

Chapter Seven

Dolores

It was late in the evening by the time I got home again.

The house seemed very quiet, and the only lights I saw came from the living room. My children were probably all in bed, and I imagine my wife Dolores, still up reading from one of her favorite books, or watching TV. She usually goes to bed rather late, and she seems to be always waiting up for me during my late-night activities.

I first met Dolores while stationed in South Korea; me with the army and her with her father a civilian working for the army, and her mother, a housewife. We both hit it off the moment we met. You can say it was love at first sight for me, if you believe in those things. Dolores was half Japanese and the other half Caucasian; her mother being the Japanese who was born in Tokyo. Her father was born a Texan. After arriving back State-side, she became pregnant with our daughter, Carmen-Melissa.

My house, which I rent, was a three bedroom, single story with a large backyard, built back in 1977. It had a lot going for it and it was home. Also it was just about a twenty-minute drive to downtown Tucson.

We'd never really discussed buying a house, since in those days, we couldn't afford it. But, years later we did decide to buy, only after assuring ourselves that we were financially able. And that turned out to be a great investment, and it was just about the right time to buy.

Parking my car in the driveway, I killed the engine, and slowly got out of the car, but not before snatching up my Stetson. Locking the LeBaron, I came around toward the front. And as I did, the heat just suddenly hit me, sapping what little energy I had left.

It was eleven thirty and it was still as hot as hell. With the temps still in the 90s and no end in sight until probably mid-October; this searing heat could cause heat stroke, or worse, if you're not careful.

I walked up to the front door and, went to insert my key, when the door was pulled open. A sight surprised welcomed me, for on the other side of the door, was my beautiful wife, with what I gleaned was a most mischievous smile on her face.

She stood there wearing a loose fitting pink Hawaiian Muumuu nightgown that was about ankle length. And it was cut low, and I saw she was braless as her nipples showed right through. Oh my!

With her long black hair pulled back behind her ears, and gathered in the center of her back, with the rest hanging down her back, my heart just skipped a beat. I felt sexually aroused wanting her right there, right then. But that's the way I always felt whenever we were that close to each other; never fails.

I went to hold her and kiss her, when she pressed a finger to her lips.

"The kids just got in bed. They waited around as long as they could before falling asleep, Victor."

I smiled back, also pressing a finger to my lips.

"No problem, babe, sorry I'm so late."

Once in the house, and closing and locking the door behind me, I walked into the living room, and on the easy chair, saw an open book. Just as I thought, she had been reading. And it looked like a Charlotte Lamb novel.

I'd just placed my hat on the hat rack, when she stopped just shy of the easy chair. She slowly turned to me and taking a couple steps stopped just in front of me. Taking my hand rather gently, she pressed it to her breast she said, "I missed you."

I was feeling exhausted, but all that kind of flew out the window, as I drew her into my arms. And as she melted into me, we kissed long and very passionately, feeling our way into each other.

We briefly parted. She took my hand and led me to the bedroom. And as she led us to the bed, I stopped and stood there taking off my clothes.

"No," she said. "Don't take them off, let me do it."

What was I going to say, no? Hell no?

So, I undid my gun belt and let it drop on the floor.

"Whatever you say, honey."

I heard her take in a deep breath and slowly exhaled as she came up to me. She started undressing me down to my last shred of clothing. Then taking a step back, she let her gaze drop slightly and said, "I can't wait to have you."

Then she pulled her nightgown down from around her shoulders, down her body, and let it puddle at her feet. My heart skipped a beat as I saw she had nothing else on.

She was in full control of what was happening, and what was to follow.

Her eyes held on mine as we came into each other's arms once again.

She was breathless and pleading in my ear. "I'm all wet honey, and I need you firmly inside me. Please don't make me beg."

I truly, completely, and with all my heart, loved this woman.

Love, is a basic human need none of us can't go long without; and we both explored that *need* to its fullest.

Later, as we lay in bed, with her body tightly pressed onto mine, she fell asleep with her head on my chest and I taking in the aroma of our love making, fell asleep totally exhausted.

THE NEXT DAY ABOUT SEVEN O'CLOCK IN THE MORNING, THE KIDS WOKE us up.

Carmen-Melissa, Angel, and Raul-Esteban my one year old, who thought he was much older than that, were all trying to get on the bed, yelling for me to get up and make them breakfast.

They were all laughing and having a great time, trying to pull us off the bed. I sat up and drew them close to me, while Dolores held Carmen-Melissa. Then I had a great idea. Or I thought it was. Why not take the family out to breakfast? So, I put the question out to them.

Carmen-Melissa said it was cool, and the rest also agreed. Dolores just looked at me like I was crazy, but she also agreed. "Hmm, that's very sweet of you, Victor," she murmured as she gently laid a hand on my shoulder. "I'll get them ready."

Yep, it was a great idea.

"Okay, then it's a go," and we all laughed knowing the whole family was in on this.

Dolores gently pulled me toward her and gave me a kiss full on the lips, like maybe saying thanks.

Carmen-Melissa made a face. "Mommy, please not in front of us."

The boys turned their heads and ran out of the bedroom. Dolores and I looked at each other and laughed.

Forty-five minutes later, after getting everyone showered and dressed, we piled into our '82 Chevy van, our family vehicle, and drove out to Denny's.

Eventually we all had a lot of fun being out together as a family. Being out like this felt as if nothing could ever come between Dolores and I, and the family. I truly never wanted that to ever come to an end.

But there's the inevitability that eventually things do come to an end – and sometimes, they come way too soon.

So, for the time being, despite my wife's ongoing objections to my work, life was good.

Chapter Eight

Day Two

IN THE EARLY MORNING HOURS, JUST AS THE SUN NUDGED ITS WAY OVER the Rincon Mountain range, she was roused by the sun's beams that were starting to shine down on her face. The beams were peeking through the only open window of her bedroom.

She was wide awake now and alone on the bed, when she realized too that there was someone gently knocking on the bedroom door.

"Come in."

Then pulling the sheets over her shoulders, covering herself completely, she realized, she wasn't wearing a stitch of clothing under the sheets. Remembering what had happened the night before, a slow mischievous smile played across her face.

As the door opened, she sat up in bed and brushed her hair back from her eyes, keeping the sheets over her, and looked over to see who it was.

The door slowly opened to reveal the person behind the knock; she saw whom she'd expected to see.

His eyes immediately shifted to the woman on the bed.

A slow smile played across his face. "Hello there."

Closing the door behind him and making his way to her side of the bed, he finally came and sat on the edge facing her.

"How do you feel this morning?" he asked.

He found that he couldn't take his eyes away from her beautiful eyes.

Before she could reply, he leaned over to her and taking her face in his hands, gave her a kiss full on the lips as she returned the favor, exploring with her tongue.

Breathlessly, she pulled away smiling.

"I'm okay."

She got up wrapping the sheet around her body, and walking a couple steps, stopped in front of her dresser. His eyes followed her. With his mouth slightly open, his tongue played across the top of his lip. He knew full well what she was hiding under the sheet.

She took a pack of Marlboros off the dresser, pulled out a cigarette, lit it and blew a steam of smoke.

"Ah, have you heard from my father?" she asked as she turned around looking at him expectantly.

A sense of weariness crept into his voice. "Nothing yet. If I had, you'd be the first to know. Anyway, it's still too early though."

"Damn, I can't wait till this is all over, and we leave this rat hole."

He nodded. "Know how you feel, honey. I'm getting tired of this shit-hole myself."

For a short time, they just stared at each other, without saying a word. Finally, she asked, "Do you think he suspects anything?"

He didn't reply right away.

"Your father, well I don't rightly know, but how could he?"

She looked away and took a drag of her cigarette, and then slowly turning her head slightly she blew out the smoke. "Yeah, guess you're right."

"Hey, don't worry about it. In the next couple of days, we should be long gone, sitting pretty, and starting all over again somewhere else."

She remembered then, the asshole guard, whose eyes raked her from head to foot, while licking his lips every time he came near her. She felt him undressing her with those evil looking eyes. Each time he came near her, she shuddered to think what he would do if he got her alone. She was sure there wasn't a thing she could do to stop him. She took another drag of the cigarette and slowly blowing out the smoke, locked eyes with him.

"God, I hope so, I don't want to go back to jail."

She watched him hesitate a little before answering. And that little gesture was not lost on her.

"Me too, come on, let's have some breakfast. Our two protectors are out in the kitchen, waiting to get everything rolling."

"Are the two brothers really necessary, Alan? We could take care of everything ourselves you know."

This time there was annoyance edged in his voice.

"We've been through this before, if push comes to shove, I'll feel better if we had someone watching our backs."

"We should talk about this some more. I don't feel safe around those two. They look like thugs, not any better than the guards at the jailhouse. Are you sure you can trust them?"

"No, not entirely, but I've known Ethan and Luke for several years. It'll be alright, promise."

She nodded. "Okay, let me shower and I'll be right along."

"Don't take too long."

"You should never ask that of a woman."

Smiling faintly, he nodded, "Right."

He opened the bedroom door, and gently closed it behind him. But not before he gave her a wink and blew her a kiss.

Chapter Nine

The Plan

It was a little after eleven in the morning that we finally made it back home from Denny's.

Once in the house, the kids had gone off to play, and Dolores started preparing to do some house cleaning, when, over the noise of the children yelling and running around, I heard the incessant beeping of my telephone answering machine; over, and over again. I really hated that machine. But it was a necessary evil. And according to my wife, she wasn't going to play secretary.

A minute later, Carmen-Melissa was yelling out to me, that the answering machine was beeping.

"I can hear it, honey, thanks. I'll be right over."

I'd been trying to avoid the damn thing, and not bother to listen to any of the messages. But the damn beeping was slowly getting to me. I was trying to get a mug of coffee, and wanted to have a pleasant morning with a little peace and quiet, before starting out the afternoon.

Guess it just wasn't to be.

Taking my mug of coffee into the living room, I sat on the edge of the sofa, reached over to the end table, turned the damn thing on, and started listening to the two messages the machine had stored.

As the machine spooled through the two messages, I leaned slightly back on the sofa. I picked up my mug of coffee and slowly blew on it, trying not to burn myself, and took a sip of the strong hot Puerto Rican coffee called "Bustelo" with its dark roast blend. It's what I grew up drinking since the age of five.

Coffee in Puerto Rico is as big as its rum production, maybe even more so. We Puerto Ricans start drinking the stuff early, the coffee I mean, some at the tender age of two.

I then heard the machine turned-over and click on.

First up; from John Marshall, saying he received the notarized bond for Alan Freeman, and that it was ready for me to pick up at his office.

I'll make sure that would be my first stop-off.

The machine moved on to the second message.

This one was from Colonel Charles Leavitt, who said, "Hello Mr. Alvarez. I've got all the money together, and in a travel bag, ready for when Freeman calls. Let me know if you need anything. I'll be home. Thank you." The machine clicked off just then.

Charles Leavitt's message was the important one. Lifting the phone's receiver, I immediately dialed his home number.

After the third ring, Charles Leavitt's voice came on the line, and in a matter-of-fact voice said, "Hello."

"Colonel, its Victor Alvarez. Got a minute?"

The line went abruptly silent.

"Of course," he began. "Did you get my message?"

"Yes, I did. That's the reason for my call."

"Thank you for contacting me so promptly."

"No problem."

Silence again. Short but there.

Finally, sounding genuinely concerned he asked, "Is there something wrong?"

Sensing his concern, I paused, thinking how to phrase my recommendations on the money exchange I knew would be happening in the next day or so.

"No — no, nothing is wrong."

I paused once again, and leaned back on the sofa.

"Soon, you're going to get a call from Freeman, telling you when and where to deliver the money. He'll probably send someone to pick it up. He probably won't do it himself. Nine out of ten times, that's how these things usually turn out. He'll want to know if you have all the money ready."

I waited again, to see if he'd say anything.

Not a word.

Just silence on the other end of the line.

"Need you to make sure," I continued. "To have him put your daughter on the line. We have to make certain she is still alive."

I shook my head. He still didn't say a word.

For a moment I remained silent too. Then I continued once again. "I'll be somewhere nearby. When you make the drop, you won't see me, and I hope neither will they."

I heard Leavitt clearing his throat. Then he spoke, just a little too haltingly. "Do you think . . . Josie will be with them at the drop?"

As I listened, I just couldn't imagine what he was going through. This was a very difficult time for him and his daughter.

"Maybe, then again maybe not, I'll have to plan accordingly though. Wait to see what type of instructions you're bound to get."

"How will we know then?"

"Well, when Freeman calls, you're going to ask that she be at the drop off before you deliver the money. It's a long shot. He may agree to it, and then again he may not. It's a fifty-fifty chance. But one we have to throw that out there."

"I agree."

Not knowing how this will end, I tried sounding as convincing as possible for his benefit and for mine. "So, we're all set then. With any luck, you'll have your daughter back soon."

"Thank you."

"If I think of anything else, I'll let you know." Then keeping my voice low, I said, "Let's hope Freeman brings her to the drop off point."

Another moment of silence passed between us. And then, I heard him sigh. "I hope so too."

I said, "Will be in touch," as with a faint click, I heard the line go dead.

Replacing the receiver back on the cradle, I leaned forward on the sofa, and taking a sip of my still warm coffee, started planning my course of action for the following days.

Chapter Ten

Frank Marshall, Bondsman

Two hours later, I was driving out to meet up with Frank Marshall at his office.

At one-thirty in the afternoon, traffic on the I-10 was rather heavy. So, it had taken me more time than normal to get to the downtown area and the bail bond office on Congress Street.

I could have taken the main streets, thinking maybe it would have been much easier, but knowing Tucson, it could've taken me that much longer. What with all the construction on some of the main roads, traffic was overly congested.

Finding parking on Congress Street can be frustrating, to say the least, and a daunting task most any time of the day during the weekdays. So, my best option was finding an empty space in one of several parking lots in the area. And that was a chore as unto itself. It's why I don't like coming into the downtown area on weekdays, or during the day for that matter.

I spent fifteen minutes of driving around and expending my gas, which incidentally had gone up in price from my usual ninety-nine cents to a buck fifty overnight – I've been trying to keep my gas cost down. But try as I might, I couldn't control gas prices. This economy sucks!

Finally, I found a space, as a fire-engine-red 1969 Chevy Camaro was vacating it just as I drove up.

Parking my LeBaron and shutting down the engine, I stayed in the car for a few minutes, thinking what are the odds of something happening right here, right now? Being careful has been so ingrained in me over the years in the military that I treated it like second nature.

I'd been a cop in the army for several years, and had always been cautious and conscious of my surroundings. After surviving two combat tours in 'Nam, the experience and awareness had paid itself in spades for me, developing a keen sense of apprehension for possible dangers. And now chasing after fugitives those phases of my senses had come alive once again. Or maybe, I' never lost it.

Taking a quick glance in my rearview mirror, turning quickly to the left and right of me, and making sure no one was fast approaching my car, I didn't sense any dangers that could befall me. These are the little things I do rather instinctively which have kept me alive.

So, getting out of my LeBaron, I grabbed my Stetson, blinked in the sunlight, locked the car and from my peripherals searched for any likely ambush spots.

But I couldn't see anything out of the ordinary.

This profession can make a person somewhat paranoid, but those were the facts of life when it came to dealing with fugitives. You know what they say, "You can't have the sweet without the sour." Or so I'm told.

Assuring myself I was in no immediate danger, I walked the intervening two blocks to the bail bonds office.

Couple of minutes later, walking into the offices of Triple 'A' Bail Bonds and closing the door behind me, I noticed a young black female sitting in the waiting area, an older couple sitting with John Marshall processing a bond, and Fred Luna, John's bail bond partner, who was also processing a bond with another couple.

Fred Luna and John Marshall looked up, saw me at the door and went back to their clients.

I nodded, not saying a word. So, it was wait time for me as I took a seat, patiently waiting my turn.

Taking a seat next to the young black woman, I picked up the newspaper – the *Tucson Daily Star* that had been left on the seat of the chair next to me. Front page news, homicides, robberies and suicides were on the rise and a growing crime rate the Tucson police couldn't quite get a handle on.

Gee, nothing new.

But one suicide I immediately remembered jumped to the forefront of my memories.

It happened to be one of my very first cases as a young agent, while stationed at Camp Evans, in Vietnam so many years ago. It was a rude awakening to the field of investigations. . .

Being the youngest agent in the field office, I accompanied Agent Ed Walsh, who was still the on-call duty agent to the scene of a possible homicide. Ed was a six foot one, two hundred twenty-pound white guy, with short blond hair, who wore glasses and smoked like a chimney. A great investigator from whom I learned many things; things one doesn't learn in MP or CID school.

The information was that about 0600 hours, the unit orderly room clerk found the body of their first sergeant lying in a pool of blood, and reported the incident to his unit commander.

At 0635 hours, the MP's were called who immediately secured the scene. We arrived at the unit, the 7th Cavalry Regiment of the First Cavalry Division (George Armstrong Custer's old unit) about 0715 hours. First thing that caught my eye, which turned my stomach somewhat, was the body of a white male lying face-up on his military issue cot with one side of his head blown away by a large caliber handgun. After examining the other side of the head, I saw the entry wound and what appeared to be burned marks around the small hole where the bullet entered, indicative of a close-range shot. Blood and what appeared to be brain matter was spattered on the wall to the right side of the hooch.

A lot of blood had pooled and congealed around the cot's side, under and around the first sergeant's head. He'd been wearing only shorts, and his right hand was hanging over the side of the cot. His army issue Colt .45 lying on the floor within easy reach of his hand. Naturally we assumed to be the gun he'd used.

Walsh made a 360-degree visual inspection of the hooch; top to bottom, side to side while jotting down his observations in his investigative notebook.

I stood to one side, observing, and learning. Waiting, but also doing my own crime scene investigation.

He started to pace a little. Stopped and turned toward me.

"What do you think happened here, Victor?" he queued as he closed his notebook.

I turned to face him. "All indications point to a suicide. But it may be too early to call without an autopsy first."

Walsh nodded, and started pacing again.

He disregarded my last observation, with a dismissive hand gesture.

"You can readily see it's a typical suicide. But you're right. Without the coroner's report, we won't be absolutely certain. First impressions, Victor, always go with your first impressions, until proven right or wrong."

"Yes sir. I'll remember that."

I started walking toward the cot's side trying to get a better handle on the weapon used.

Coming around to the cot, I secured the weapon in an evidence bag, but not before Walsh made sure it was the weapon that had fired the fatal shot.

And on top of the deceased's writing table, that had been made from wood and metal ammunition boxes, I found a letter addressed to the first sergeant from his wife, a "Dear John letter," which mentioned she was leaving him for someone else. It would obviously explain the suicide. Later, we found out that the first sergeant had only three weeks left in-country.

Such were the cases we dealt with in the 'Nam, 'Dear John Letters, the worst of the lot. I've heard mentioned that the Vietnam War claimed more 'Dear John Letters' than any other US conflict. Besides the known enemies of war, soldiers had to deal with family as well, while at the same time trying to stay as focused as one could on staying alive and coming back home in one piece.

We spent another hour poring over the crime scene, taking notes, and photographs, before Walsh released the body to the coroner.

They say war is hell. Not just on the combatants, but family as well.

Nearly an hour later, as the last person walked out of the bail bonds office, and with no phones ringing off the hook, the office back to normal, I got up from my chair.

As I placed the newspaper back on the seat, John Marshall, waived me over as I watched Fred Luna walked into the back of the office. I made my way to a chair in front of his desk. After taking a seat, I removed my Stetson and placed it on his desk top.

I softly whistled. "Hey, John seems you two been busy today."

"Yeah, it's been like this all week. But it's all good."

"Bet. I'm here to pick up the bond on Freeman."

"Ah, right."

Reaching and pulling open a drawer on the left side of his desk he rifled through and pulled out a manila folder. He reached over and handed it to me.

"Here you go."

As I grabbed for the folder, I heard Fred yelling from the back of the office.

"Hey, Al, want some coffee?"

"I could use a cup. Thanks."

"Me too," Frank called.

Fred said, "Coming right up, guys,"

"You know, Al," Frank said, "You really need to get yourself a hobby."

"Yeah," I said. "Why's that?"

"You're in a line of business which can get very stressful."

Fred Luna came back in with our coffee, and sat down at his desk.

Fred said, "Hobbies are good, Al."

Glancing at Frank and then to Fred, I laughed.

"Yeah well, I have a hobby."

"What hobby is that?" Frank asked.

Smiling, I looked over at them again and lowered my voice some, "Shooting people."

They both laughed, shaking their heads.

Frank said, "You're an asshole, Al."

After a short silence and as I sipped my warm coffee, I opened the folder and started reading though it.

Nothing really popped out at me that I hadn't already known about our boy Alan Freeman. But one thing that interested me most was the person who bailed Freeman out of jail. That was new.

Here was a good lead. Not a very promising lead, but interesting nevertheless.

A HALF HOUR LATER, I WAS BACK IN MY CAR AND DRIFTING DOWN Speedway Boulevard, then onto Interstate 10.

It was getting late in the afternoon so I decided to head home all the while thinking about what Fred had said as I was leaving his office concerning our boy Freeman.

"Be careful with this guy, Al," Fred said, looking straight at me, his face flat and serious. *"Things are not always what they appear with him. According to his bondsman, Freeman has a history of mental disorder and given his violent past, he could be very dangerous."*

I thought about that for a while.

Ninety-nine percent of the criminals I have gone after I have always considered dangerous, until proven otherwise. No matter what they were jailed for there was always that element of danger associated with their capture. I have never underestimated my jumpers, male or female. If I'd tried to handle them with kid gloves that would be the day I would find myself in the hospital, or dead in some lonely back-yard or some dark corner of a road. I'm not a cop anymore. I don't have the luxury of being a nice guy when I confront my jumpers. No way.

So, my ultimate goal was to capture them alive, and not to kill. But

I'm not here to play psychic games with them. I'm here to get them back in jail no matter the cost.

I've stayed alive this long because I'd stayed cautious. Given that I have a lot of violence in my past and present life, which was most unforgettable, I took Fred's words to heart and decided, like I usually do on playing it close to the vest.

I kept the LeBaron to just below the speed limit. Since the state police were always setting up speed traps throughout the interstate junction into the city, I kept it as legal as I could. No use getting a ticket on my way home, although, I had some good friends in the T.P.D that could take care of it for me. I also kept thinking of my kids and Dolores waiting up for me, and dinner that she was surely preparing.

But something else was stirring in the back of my mind, as I kept the engine wailing smoothly, putting it through its paces, kind of enjoying the ride as well, and trying hard to focus on the road and my job.

It'll come to me.

Minutes later, it dawned on me what I'd been subconsciously trying to remember. It had to do with something I'd read in Freeman's folder. Suddenly, that bit of information flashed across my mind — it concerned the person that bailed Freeman out of jail! Why I'd nearly forgotten that piece of information was beyond me.

With traffic being heavy on Interstate 10, I decided to pull off the highway. On my next exit, I drove onto the exit ramp. I then eased the LeBaron to a stop on the shoulder of the road, motor running. I put it in park and sat there for a few moments. I then reached over across to the passenger seat, where I had my case folders, and grabbed and pulled open Freeman's folder. Rifling through several loose sheets of forms, I found the information I was looking for.

His name was Jebodiah Hill, Freeman's uncle, and from the information he supplied his bondman, he was a retired railroad worker and a Navy veteran. He had a one room apartment out on Twelfth Avenue and West Virginia Street, at an apartment complex called Mission Park.

Getting my map out from the glove compartment, I opened it, oriented myself as to my location on the map and plotted my route, which would take me about thirty minutes give or take, depending on traffic, to get to the apartment complex.

Stowing the map back and replacing the folder on the passenger seat, I shifted into first gear, eased the LeBaron out onto the Interstate, and once flowing with the traffic, I drove south though the late afternoon sun.

Chapter Eleven

Jebodiah Hill

With the sun slowly fading in the west silhouetting the Tucson Mountains, and temperatures still holding to the upper nineties, and no visible signs of traffic along the route, I turned right onto South Missiondale Road.

I'd just exited South Nogales Highway, when I almost missed my turn-off to South Missiondale. I backed up a couple of feet, got into the turn, and then hung a left to Mission Park apartments just off West Virginia Street.

It had taken me more than the thirty minutes I'd given myself to reach the apartment complex. Once there though, I eased slowly past the closed leasing office, pulled into a parking space and surveyed the complex.

The landscape around the complex with its barren desert hills to the east were fringed by a couple of wrecked abandoned cars just off to left side where I had pulled in. It had an overabundance of large tall trees growing throughout. Driving into the complex there was a sign to

the right side of the entrance which read: Mission Park Apartments —
1978.

The 1978 reference I assumed stood for the year it had been built.
Just a few years old and already needing some good old maintenance
to get it back to some semblance of its old self once again.

I didn't find it appealing. Not someplace I would live. Then again,
I'm quite picky as to where I'd call home, and not an apartment
complex that's for sure. Not my style.

I waited for dusk to find the uncle's apartment.

Finally watching the last of the sun dipping in the west, I put the
LeBaron in first gear and drove out slowly looking for uncle Jeb's
building, and his apartment.

Precisely ten minutes later, I found it. It was on the ground floor,
nestled away toward the back of the complex. The building was very
well lit making it that much easier to see the apartment number as I
slowly drove by.

I didn't see a living soul as I crept past, but the one thing I saw that
brought a little smile to my otherwise uneventful day was a car parked
in front of the apartment. This I didn't expect. But there it was!

It was a Japanese made car, a 1986 blue Toyota Corolla coupe.

I memorized the plate number. I needed to make sure it was the
same one registered to Josie. But I was damned sure it was.

Invariably, the one constant theme in my line of work that has
made me very successful in finding my jumpers is luck. And it hadn't
left me. I still had it. I just hoped it would stay with me, at least until I
closed out this case.

I drove around the building, and came back toward the front
finding a parking space in between two wrecked cars just toward the
left side of the apartment, way in the back. I pulled in and killed the
engine. I had a very good eye on the front door and the car. I could just
make out shadows of two forms by the front window, but nothing
distinct.

I pulled Josie's folder, scanned through it and found the vehicle
registration information supplied by her father. There it was. The plate
number was a match!

How lucky can I get? I thought.

Now to see who comes in or who goes out.

My wife, dinner and the kids went on the back burner. I was working the case, and nothing else mattered just then. Had to stay focused and ready for whatever happens next.

I was clad in a pair of old faded jeans, black short-sleeved shirt, and my cuff-off combat boots I always wore when I'm out hunting. Strapped on my right hip I had my Colt .45, and a small-bore Smith & Wesson .38 detective special, with the small two inched barrel holstered down on my right ankle. I like to be prepared for any eventuality, especially going after some very dangerous jumpers. Better to need the extra firepower, and have it, and not have it and need it.

So, I was locked, cocked and ready to go!

With my car shut down, I rolled down my window. I could already feel the searing heat permeate me. I didn't let that bother me as I grabbed my binoculars from the back seat. Slowly I fitted the binoculars to my eyes, but not before assuring myself no one was anywhere near my car. Feeling confident no one was lurking about, I slowly peered over at the apartment. I could clearly see the front door and the only window on the left side, and I hoped no one could see me.

From my place of concealment, I kept the binoculars level with the front door. I couldn't see any shadow movements at the window. Then I scanned the entire area, left to right, right to left. All was still. There weren't the slightest signs of life. I only heard the sounds from my car as the exhaust cooled down. Then I slowly brought the binoculars back to the apartment's door.

I kept my steady watch hoping someone would either enter or leave the apartment.

My patience was rewarded when after two hours and forty-five minutes had elapsed, I saw the apartment door slowly open letting light filter through into the night. I saw three men emerge from the apartment carrying on a quiet conversation, then stop in front of the Toyota coupe still talking. I was too far away to catch what they were saying.

The older of the three, I assumed was Uncle Jeb. One of the other two I immediately recognized from the photograph — Alan Freeman.

Twice lucky! Someone was definitely helping me out tonight.

Uncle Jeb, or the old man I took to be so, was a tall lanky bearded old man, while the last man was young, perhaps in his late twenties, about five-feet-nine, give or take, wearing jeans, cowboy boots, and a white dirty T-shirt with the imprint of the Confederate flag, with the words in red that read: *'If you ain't Redneck, Ya' ain't shit.'*

He looked rough, with his long dirty blond hair combed back that hung like a limp rag down past his shoulders. He had what appeared to be old scars on the left side of his face.

Yeah, a very rough looking redneck, to be sure.

He said something to the old man, who shook his grizzled head in the negative. Then just as quickly, he reentered the apartment slamming shut the door behind him. I heard it all the way to where I was hiding, like the blast of a shotgun going off in an enclosed place. *Bam!*

Something must've riled the old man, because as soon as the old man had closed the door, Freeman and the redneck broke out laughing.

Then the two of them climbed into the Toyota, and with Freeman doing the driving, backed out. He turned to his right, and drove out of the apartment complex.

Giving them a slight head start, and keeping my headlights off, I fired up the LeBaron and followed at a very discreet distance. But just far behind where I wouldn't be spotted. Once I was safely behind them I turned on my headlights.

Freeman must've sensed what I was thinking, because he drove the Toyota below the speed limit. Getting pulled over by the cops at this stage of the game, I figured, could signal the end of whatever plans he had.

Thirty minutes later, and after driving for about forty miles and stopping once for gas, they left Interstate 10, crossing over Cienega Creek, with the Rincon Mountains in the distance.

As I approached the city of Vail, I looked curiously out the window. I'd never been this far out. I couldn't see much because of the darkness. Maybe I'll come back someday soon and do some exploring with the family.

They drove past the city of Vail, onto some lonely dirt road, then unto Bridle Ridge Place.

Later, I learned that the city of Vail is well known for the nearby Saguaro National Park, and the tourist attraction of Colossal Cave — a large cave system. Vail was named after two brothers, Edward and Walter Vail back in the 19th century who founded the city. They built the Empire Ranch, the biggest horse ranch in the area at the time. I'd definitely need to visit there with the family someday.

City traffic was minimal at that time of night, and then it thinned out once we were on Bridle Ridge Place. I kept back maybe five, six car lengths, not wanting to give them the impression someone was following them.

I looked over toward the west, and saw the tops of the Rincon Mountains silhouetted against the half moon and bright stars on this clear hot night.

Minutes later as the Toyota took a turn I heard it come to a complete stop. I also came to a stop, turned off my headlights shut down my car, and waited.

Moments later, I heard the Toyota start up again.

Making sure my car's interior light was off, I exited the car and walked the intervening few yards. I saw a gravel road leading to a grated gate, and house lights way down the end of the gravel road.

Walking back to my car, I grabbed my binoculars from the passenger seat, then closed and locked the car and headed back to the gate. Climbing over it, I slowly made my way to the house.

Chapter Twelve

In For A Penny

I THINK I MUST'VE TREKKED HALFWAY THERE.

Hell, I couldn't tell for sure, considering the only lights for miles came from the left side of the house. And those lights were much dimmed, casting furtive shadows everywhere.

But to the right side of the road, I could just make out a small rise and so I started walking for it. I was hoping it could afford me a good vantage point to where I could observe the house. I saw it was a small hillock, clear of trees giving me exactly what I needed — full clear view of the land ahead of me.

Crawling up to the rise, and making the top, I laid down and put the binoculars to my eyes, and scanned over to the house, which now seemed about a little more than a "klick" or two down the gravel road. I squinted and adjusted the focus knob.

There were two vehicles parked on the left side of an 'L' shape one story ranch house; the Toyota and a dirty brown Chevy pickup truck. I kept listening and listening, but couldn't detect the faintest sounds of movement anywhere around the house.

Jesus, everything was as still as a tomb, with only a slight breeze coming in from the west, and the howling of a wolf or some other animal far out in the distance, keeping me company. Hell, there wasn't even with an occasional car passing by on the main road.

It was creepy feeling!

I tracked east and west, north and south, but as far as I could see this was the only ranch for miles. I kept a vigil on the only door I saw just left of the house, and on the front window. But I still did not see any movements or shadows to indicate the presence of life inside.

The wind picked up and started moaning through the tree tops, bringing with it the smells of the desert and the dry hot air. And as I focused back to the house, I finally caught some movement of activity, shadows on the front window. Two shadows, one right after the other. I kept the binoculars pinned to the window, staring at it a little longer, but the shadows didn't reappear. Then, rising and shaking the dirt and dry leaves from my pants and shirt, I stood there thinking about my options.

So, the way I see it, I could do this one of two ways; first, stay on the rise and pull surveillance, see who goes in and who goes out, and see if by chance, Josie was being held at the ranch. Second; leave the rise and just go for it. Get to the house and see for myself. One was as sound as the other, I guess.

After thinking it over for a minute or two, I decided on the latter.

So, retreating down the hillock back to my car, I dropped off my binoculars, then closed and locked my car. Drawing my Colt .45, I ejected the magazine, replaced it after making sure it was a full one, and jacked a round in. Making sure the safety was off, I holstered it. I hoped I would not draw it anytime soon. Fat chance in my line of work, but one could only hope.

Now I looked north and south, making sure no one was lurking anywhere near to my location. Then I started off toward the gate and eventually the house.

The wind picked up a little stronger as I heard and felt it blowing, as if someone was crying and moaning at the same time, through the tall Palo Verde trees on both sides of the road. These trees can grow upwards of twenty-five feet or more and as wide. I could also make out tall mesquite too, now these can grow to about thirty feet.

The wind kept to a steady gust as it dried the sweat beads from my face.

I stopped, and for a brief moment there, swayed just a little. Okay, maybe more than a little unsteadily, as the wind kind of pulled and pushed me toward the gate.

I was feeling a little wary of becoming involved in another gun fight. But in this profession, there just weren't any guarantees.

Pulling my bandana from my back pocket and removing my Stetson, I wiped the sweat from about my head. Getting my hat back on, I started walking again. But I started to feel the excitement building up in me. Knowing that soon, one way or another, something was bound to happen. And I confidently knew I was in full control of my emotions, and was prepared to take this to the end.

In for penny in for a pound, or so they say, in control, but a little scared too! I get that way once in a while.

Hell, I'm only human!

Chapter Thirteen

One at a Time

BY MY ESTIMATION, I RECKON I'D BEEN UP SINCE ABOUT SEVEN THIS morning. And now I started feeling slightly exhausted, and from the loud growling of my stomach, remembered I'd not eaten a bite since breakfast.

I stopped once again and took a quick glance at my watch; it was 10:32. And damn but the temperature felt like it was over 100 degrees! Just hope this wasn't another one of those long grueling hot nights I usually find myself in.

"Better get on with it, Al," I said quietly to myself, as I once again took up my trek to the house.

It came on quite unexpectedly. A few drops here and there at first — a light sprinkle. But after a few seconds, it increased to a light downpour. Then in the distance the sky pulsated with lightning, and then some thunder and boom would ripple and cascade through the mountains. I stood in the open for a moment under the rain and soaked in the cool wind. I kept on going; occasionally glancing left and right of me, letting my Stetson protect me from the worst.

Finally, I made it to within several yards of the house. As I came around toward the front, the front door flew open, lighting up the darkness. It bathed the ground in front of the entrance in a yellowish eerie incandescence, just as a male figure walked out heading away from me.

Ah, shit, I thought, — just as I took cover behind some mesquite off to my right — *fun and games were about to start!*

I had to take this guy out first, no way around it. I didn't know how many more were in the house. I figured one less would help in the long run. I had to cut down the odds one way or another.

So, I followed the guy to the left side of the house out to a lean-to shed. The grass grew all around the area almost knee high, which would make my approach rather quiet. I waited to see if he would enter. Sure enough he did. This was my break. No one would see me taking him down, nor would anyone in the house hear me doing it because of the rain.

Perfect.

I drew my Colt and held it loosely at my side, ready if this got ugly.

I'm not a violent man, nor do I have a violent behavior, although I've been on both the giving and receiving ends of fist fights, shootouts, and knife fights. I seem to sense that violence has always found me, ever since my days in gangs growing up in New York City's tough Spanish Harlem. So, what I was about to do, was in my defense; take them out hard and fast, before they knew what hit them, and before they could do me any harm.

So, walking slowly but with even strides, and very stealthily keeping as quiet as I could, I came to just a little over an arm's length away from him.

Then the improbable happened!

It could've been some sixth sense or something that may have warned him of danger close behind him, because I was sure I hadn't made a single sound.

Suddenly, I saw him stiffen and start to slowly turn around.

"What the fu. . ." he began to say, as his voice died in his throat before he could complete his turn.

I'd taken a quick step toward him, brought my gun to bear, and struck him a hard blow to a point just below the back of his neck, way before he could even complete his sentence.

As the guy swayed backwards a little, I took a quick step to my right side just as he dropped as if he held an anvil in his arms — straight down in a heap onto the plywood floor. He was totally out for the count.

Not taking any chances, I searched the shed and found what I was looking for — rope. I tied his hands behind his back, and also tied his legs together. Even if he woke up, he wasn't going anywhere.

Looking down on him, I noticed the guy was about my height, heavier and bulkier than me, blond hair. I learned later that his name was Ethan, and brother to Luke.

Stepping out of the shed and closing the door behind me, I turned toward the still open front door leading into the house, which no one had bothered to close.

Slowly making my way to the house, I made it to the right side of the door. As soon as I'd flattened myself against the side of the house, I heard above the patter of the rain fall, the faintest sounds of movement like unhurried footsteps of someone approaching the door.

The footsteps were getting louder by the second. Then I saw a big tall son-of-a-bitch of a man framed against the door. He must've been at least six feet and maybe a hundred ninety or maybe two hundred pounds, with long dirty blond hair flowing down to his shoulders, in a grey T-shirt and dark jeans.

"Hey Ethan!" he yelled. "Where the hell are you? We're waiting for you, brother."

Then he stepped all the way out the door. If he turned my way, he would spot me. Couldn't let that happen.

So gathering myself up, and still holding my Colt by my side, I stepped up behind him before he could turn around.

"Hi there," I said.

He quickly turned, and without missing a beat, once he was facing me and seeing the surprise come over his face, I used my gun once again. I struck him across the side of the jaw before he knew what was happening. He must've had a glass jaw, because I heard bone shattering as blood came flying from his mouth. The blow made his head snap hard to the side, and his body made a half turn to his left. I took a step back before he slumped to the ground landing on his side, completely unconscious.

Immediately I ducked back into the shadows thinking maybe someone may have heard the slight commotion from inside the house. But after a couple of seconds, I didn't hear anything.

Getting back to the guy on the ground, I raised him by his shoulders and dragged him to the shed. Man, was he heavy! Once there and finding some more rope, I tied him up too. I noticed the second guy bore a strong resemblance to the first guy. This must be Luke, the brother.

Two down, and no telling how many more were in the house.

Chapter Fourteen

Caught by Surprise

The rain stopped.

Just as quickly as it started it died out, leaving a steady cool breeze coming in from the west. But it remained cloudy, and not even the moon could brighten up that dark starless night.

Once again, I found myself on the left side of the house, by the front door. I took a very slow and deliberate count to ten. Not hearing any sounds from within, I slowly made my way from the darkness to the light emanating from the inside, as it showered the entrance.

Slowly leading with my Colt, but keeping it close to the chest, I entered and found myself in the living room. Or what I thought was the living room. There was a small love seat, and a round dining table with three chairs off to one corner. On a table stand by the love seat, was a Motorola TV with a rabbit ears antenna sticking up from the top. A small shag rug completed the furnishing. The lights came from a four-bladed ceiling fan with four lights. The fan was slowly blowing cool air throughout the room.

Off to my left side were two doors; one maybe leading into a bedroom, and another door that was half open. The second door I saw led into a bathroom, where the light had been left on. The first door was slightly ajar with no visible lighting coming from within.

I turned my back away from the two doors and started walking through a small hallway leading into the kitchen proper.

Mind you now, I don't usually make mistakes, not when it comes to life and death situations. But that night, I neglected to do what I'd been trained to do, and was a little overconfident. That alone could get you killed faster than a bullet! What I did wrong, was to completely neglect to check and clear the bedrooms! And I almost paid the price for my negligence.

I've always done a lot of things out of plain habit. Like making sure my guns are loaded, cocked and ready to fire; keeping my back away from doors while in a restaurant or in a bar. But the most important one was to check and clear rooms while searching an unknown house — before turning your back on them.

Yeah. I sure enough fucked up pretty bad that night, and it nearly cost me my life!

As I walked toward the kitchen, and keeping my Colt close to my chest, I didn't hear what was coming up behind me, or the danger I was in till it was too late.

Then *bam*, I felt it. A crushing blow from behind with a stick of some kind!

It hit my shoulder blades just missing the back of my head by inches. The strength behind the blow jerked me forward a step or two, but I maintained consciousness. And for a split second, I didn't know whether I was coming or going. The blow had also knocked my Colt from my hand, as I watched it drop on the floor a few feet in front of me.

I felt anger and surprise for almost being taken out, and angry at myself for acting like a stupid rookie.

Recovering from my shock, I directed that anger toward my would-be assailant, whoever it was. Immediately, I turned and saw Freeman holding onto a baseball bat. He just kept staring at me with a stupid look on his face, maybe thinking, *why the hell didn't he go down?*

Just then, Freeman's shock had worn off. And setting himself up again, brought the bat behind him, and with a loud yell like a man possessed, viciously brought it down attempting to strike at my head.

He didn't get the chance!

I caught the fat part of the bat as it came down, aimed at my face while at the same time, I balled my right fist. I was so damn mad, that I struck him a hard, savage blow that caused his face to jerk backward then back down. As he staggered backwards, I rushed in before he could regain his footing. His lips were a mess, and his mouth was full of blood. Once I was within arm's reach, I struck him again, this time to his abdomen, and as he doubled over with pain, I was about to deliver an elbow strike to his neck when I heard a woman's voice yelling something from somewhere behind me.

Quickly turning to the sound of the woman's voice behind me, my eyes fell on her.

She was standing in the middle of the room, looking uneasy, worried and scared all at once. It was Josie, no doubt about it. Just like in her photograph. But her hair was a mess, and she had no makeup on. She was wearing light colored slacks and a blue blouse and her arms were wrapped around her bosom. She started yelling again.

"Stop it!" she cried at the top of her lungs. "You're hurting him. Please, don't hurt him anymore!"

I could hear the shock and fear in her cry as I kept my gaze on her.

Finally, I released Freeman, who dropped onto the floor in a fetal position grasping and moaning in pain as he started to puke and retch as he clutched his stomach.

Oh Christ, I said to myself, good thing I'd let go of him when I did. At least he wasn't going anywhere anytime soon.

Josie rushed over to Freeman, who was now crying and knelt beside her boyfriend wiping the blood oozing from his mouth. And at that moment I knew there had been no kidnapping. The ransom was probably for their use, maybe to escape the country.

Freeman tried to stand.

I glanced at him. "Sit still, asshole, just stay right where you are."

He tried to say something, but changed his mind as he locked eyes with me.

Taking my bandanna from my hip pocket, I wiped the blood from my hand. Not seeing any cuts or abrasions on it, I pocketed the bandanna. I then reached down to my right leg, and pulled out my Smith and Wesson .38 and kept them covered till I recovered my Colt. I found it, just where I'd dropped it. I returned the .38 back to its holster, and came back to Freeman and Josie, who were still on the floor where I left them.

Recovering her composure somewhat she stared up at me, while also locking her gaze on my gun, maybe thinking I was there to shoot her boyfriend.

"Who the hell are you, mister?" she asked.

I looked back at her, and as I locked eyes on her, a slow smile briefly played across my face.

"I'm from the bail bonds company. Here to take you back to jail, and your boyfriend too."

Josie just stared up at me with a quizzical look on her face.

"So, you're a bounty hunter?" she asked, rather incredulously and surprised at the same time.

"Yes, I am."

"Well I'll be damned!"

I said, "Some of us are."

"I'm not afraid of you."

"You should be, young lady."

I believe she was starting to get confident about her situation, and I could just hear the wheels turning in her head, going round and round thinking, and maybe evaluating her present predicament.

Then, still looking up at me, her eyes opened wide as if she'd just had an epiphany.

"My father sent you, didn't he?"

I slowly glanced away from her, fell silent for a few seconds, then glanced back again and shrugged. I could see she was growing impatient with me, but I didn't give a damn.

"In a matter of speaking, it doesn't really matter who sent me at this point. I'm here now and just about ready to take the both of you back to jail."

Josie was still staring at me, still confident calculating maybe on how to get out of this, once and for all.

"There are two big men outside. And when they return you're going to wish you never found us."

"Is that right?"

"You bet your ass, you son-of-a-bitch."

"Oh, you mean the two guys outside? They're taking a long rest out in the shed."

"You didn't kill 'em did you?"

"Ah, no, I don't kill people anymore."

She opened her mouth to say something to that, but thought better of it.

Taking a quick step toward them, I got behind Josie and knelt down right behind her and Freeman, handcuffing both of them together. This would ensure one wasn't going to run away from me without the other, in this case Freeman, being the burden.

I noticed that Freeman's mouth had almost swollen shut, but the bleeding had stopped. That was good for me, didn't have to take him to the hospital before getting him to the jail.

Standing back up, I told them to stand. I helped them along by grabbing their cuffed arms and pulling them up onto their feet.

Once outside, I pushed and prodded them along out to where I'd parked my car. Once there, I cuffed them separately to the center bar in back of the LeBaron.

Before closing the door on them, I rolled down the window just a little, enough where they could get some fresh cool air.

"Don't go anywhere," I said. "I'll be right back."

"Fuck you, wetback!" she said. "Hope you break a leg out there."

I just shrugged. "Christ, lady, be nice."

I then closed the door on her before she could reply. Just didn't want to hear anymore from her. I'd probably get to hear more from her on the trip to the jail, for sure.

First, I had one other important chore I needed to take care of.

Walking back down the road, I returned to the shed. Once there, I opened the door, and saw the two brothers were still in the position I had left them in. Albeit — awake.

They both stared up at me as I came in.

"Hey," the one called Ethan said. "You the asshole put us here?"

I cracked a smile. "I'm the asshole all right."

He glanced at me with fear in his eyes as his gaze dropped to my Colt pointed down on them.

"What you planning on doing with us?"

I didn't say a word.

Looking through the shed, I found an overturned wooden stool. Strolling over to it, I picked it up, set in down on the floor, and sat facing the two brothers.

Resting my Colt on my lap, I stared down at them, letting a long silence come between us.

I kept pointing my Colt at them, as I put an edge to my voice letting my next words sink in.

"What to do, whatever to do."

They both followed the path of my Colt, and as they stole a glance at each other, I started to sense fear, as their eyes grew bigger. It was the fear of knowing what could happen in the next few minutes. They both had a miserable look to them.

"Mister," Ethan said shrugging. "We got no quarrel with you."

A pause.

"I don't see it that way," I said.

"We'll do whatever you say."

His brother Luke nodded his head in agreement. "Just let us go."

I gave him a quick brusque shake of my head. "Yeah, I could do that, then what? Although, I could put a bullet into each of you, then say it was self-defense."

"Wait, uh, you wouldn't kill us."

Still I kept staring down on them. I looked to Luke then back at Ethan.

"Don't tempt me, boys. Here's the way I see this. You two have one of three ways to go. One, I let you go, and you forget ever seeing me, and everything that's happened here tonight. I mean everything. Two, I call the feds, let them arrest you two for kidnapping, aiding and abetting in a federal crime, and maybe other charges added on later. You'll be looking at six to ten years easily. Or three, I can take the easy way out, and put a bullet into each of you. Wish would suit me just fine."

I let that sink in, as they looked over at each other.

"You guys better think long and hard on my offer, because I won't make it again. You have a minute to decide."

It took them half that time to come to a decision.

Luke and Ethan glanced at each other. Luke nodded and Ethan returned the gesture.

"All right," Ethan said.

I looked at both of them. "All right what?"

Ethan nodded, swallowed. "Okay, let us go. Don't call the fed's, and we forget everything."

I cracked a wan smile as I stared long and hard at them, not saying a word for a couple of seconds. Then slowly holstering my weapon, I stood up from the stool.

"You guy's renege on the deal, and I'll come back and finish up what I started in doing. Understand?"

They both nodded.

"Yes sir," Ethan said.

After untying Ethan's hands, I slowly backed out of the shed.

I never heard from them again. Apparently, they kept their word. Guess my threat paid off. But if either of them had known I wouldn't go through with killing them, the outcome would have been different.

Chapter Fifteen

County Jail

We made it back into Tucson about one-thirty the next morning. It was an uneventful ride. No one said so much as a word, for which I was truly grateful. I wasn't in the talking mood anyway, at least not with the likes of those two. Most of my jumpers would be talking my ears off offering me large sums of money to let them go. But do I concede to their wishes? Hell no. I'm an honest hunter.

Finding a vacant space wasn't all that hard. All seemed quiet and peaceful at the Pima County jailhouse, with just three to five cars parked out front.

It must be a slow night, I thought.

At times like these one starts to wonder what the rest of the night would bring. And here I was delivering two prisoners. Someone's not going to be very happy with me.

Just prior to getting back into Tucson, I'd stopped at a gas station to use a pay phone and called Charles Leavitt. Told him I had both Freeman and his daughter, and was heading to the Pima County jail.

"Is it okay to see her at the jailhouse?" he asked.

"I don't know. But if you get there before I hand them over, you could at least see her for a few seconds."

Making it to the front desk with my two prisoners walking ahead of me, handcuffed to each other and being as quiet as can be, I was met by a female jail guard whose name plate read E. Gutierrez. She was a pretty good looking thing, a dark eyed, black haired beauty that stood no more than five-feet-six, if that. She kept her hair combed back tight in a pony-tail, but she kept flicking back several loose ends over her right ear, in a very sexy and provocative gesture. Yeah, she knew she was sexy!

Upon seeing me in front of her, she didn't return my smile, which deflated my ego just a little.

"What'ya have for me?" she asked in a rather strong Mexican accent, as she glanced over at my two prisoners, but she kept her stare onto Freeman's jaw, waiting to hear my report.

She reminded me of my time in New York City, when I had a Spanish accent I'd gotten rid off. I felt it just wasn't cool. So, I picked up on the New Yorker's accent, which I thought was more appropriate at the time.

I pulled out the bonds. "I'm surrendering the bonds on two prisoners."

"What 'a hell hap 'in to the guy's jaw?"

"He ran into my fist, and I couldn't pull it back in time."

She gave me a hard look. "Yeah right," she said.

I didn't say anything, but just gave her a nice wide smile. Just then, I turned slightly to my right and there was Charles Leavitt waiting right there at the jail, just off to the right of the guard counter. He got up from his seat, just as I came in, saw his daughter and started walking toward her.

Josephine Leavitt on seeing him, turned immediately away from him without saying a word.

He stopped, and I saw the look of hurt come over his face as he turned to retake his seat. No crying or tears from him, just a stoic stare straight ahead.

I then placed the bonds on the desk counter, wherein Gutierrez picked them up. She looked through them making sure they were notarized, and then called over to a male guard who was sitting behind a desk in another room down by the holding cells.

"Hola Harr'y, I gott'a two for booking and hold'en."

"I'll be right there," Harry said.

Harry was Harry Weiss, a Texan, and a fellow veteran I've known for a couple of months.

Just then Gutierrez stepped away from the desk and walked into another room, but I couldn't help notice how her hips swayed in a gentile to and fro. I also noticed that the hips were attached to a trim waist line, a most vivacious Latina. Her uniform didn't do her justice though.

I took in a slow breath, let it out slowly. I briefly closed and opened my eyes and thought about Dolores, and feeling a little guilty, as I met up with Harry Weiss.

"She's good to the eyes uh, Al?" Harry asked.

I nodded. "She is that and more."

"So, Al, what's new?" Harry asked.

A slow wry smile crossed my lips.

"Yo, Harry, I see you're working hard."

"Hell no, real quiet till you came in."

I smiled. "You got to earn your keep somehow."

"Screw you," Harry said grinning.

As he unlocked the gate, he took hold of my two prisoners, and uncuffed them. Returning my cuffs to me, he used his cuffs on both of them, and walked them to their holding cells. But not before closing the gate behind him.

Then taking my cue from Harry, I strolled over and sat at a patrol officer's desk and prepared to write my report of the capture. I left the account of the kidnapping and my encounter with the two brothers out of my report, leaving only the most pertinent information as to their re-arrest.

Just as I was about finished with my report, Charles Leavitt came over and sat across from me. "Thank you, Mr. Alvarez for getting my daughter back. So, it was just as you suspected all along, it wasn't a kidnapping at all."

"No, it wasn't. I suspect they planned to use the money in order to leave the country."

Leavitt hesitated then nodded. "I see."

I didn't say anything.

"What's going to happen next?" he queried.

After signing my report and placing it in the case folder, I looked over at him.

"One of two ways the courts will see this. At the bond forfeiture hearing, they can declare your daughter a flight risk and deny bond based on my report and that of the bondsman. Or they would release her to you on bond once again."

"How would you handle this situation, if she was your daughter?"

For a short time, we stood there staring at each other. I was thinking of how to respond to his question, since I'd never been in the situation he was in. Then I stood up with the folder in hand and walked around and stopped a few feet in from him.

"You're asking for my advice?"

Charles Leavitt was nodding. "Yes. Yes, I am."

Gathering myself up I stared directly into his eyes.

"If she was mine, I would just let her stay in jail until her court appearances. That way, I wouldn't have to worry about her running away again, and putting me through all the hardship. But all in all, it's a delicate situation, and a decision not to be made hastily, one way or another."

I saw him thinking about that. He took in a long slow breath and slowly exhaled. Cocking his head to the cell block where his daughter was being held, he seemed to have made up his mind. "Thank you, Mr. Alvarez for everything."

Nodding I said, "Just doing what I'm paid to do."

I spun around, and walked over to the main desk and placed my case folder on the counter. Harry Weiss looked up at me but didn't say a word. I looked blankly at Harry, then out of curiosity turned back around. I then saw Charles Leavitt walk out of the cell block. Slowly shaking my head, I silently wished him the best, for himself and his daughter.

I MADE IT BACK HOME ABOUT THREE O'CLOCK.

Tired, sleepy and hungry, I couldn't decide which one was worst. Christ! My hunger won out though.

Rummaging through the refrigerator, I saw a dinner plate with three pieces of fried chicken and a bowl of potato salad off to one side.

Gathering those up, I headed to the dining table and commenced to attack my hunger, and with a large bottle of apple juice to wash it down with. Man, it was good.

Then, after devouring the last of the chicken, I looked up from the plate, and saw her standing on the door jamb leading into the kitchen — my wife, with a tired look about her. She was wearing nothing but a pair of sheer panties, and one of my white T-shirts that clung to her every curve. And man was she ever a sight for sore eyes. Wow! And a whole lot better looking than E. Gutierrez.

"Hey there," I said. "How long have you been standing there?"

"Not long."

She looked groggy and sleepy and maybe a little mad.

"Glad you made it home in one piece, Victor."

I merely smiled.

Dolores kept looking over at me. "I see you found the food I left for you."

"Yes, and it's good too. Like always. Thanks."

"Are you coming to bed? I need you next to me."

"Yes ma'am. I'll be right along."

As she turned to go back into the bedroom, I saw her nice rounded rear posture, and felt myself getting all aroused.

Just then, I forgot all about the rest of the food, as I pushed away the plate and made my way into our bedroom with thoughts of my beautiful wife waiting there for me.

And maybe, just maybe I'll get lucky.

Book Two

The DEA and the Crack Head

Chapter Sixteen

The Crack House

October, 1987

I was in South Tucson, Arizona, a city within a city, and well known for being heavily populated by mostly Hispanic's. It is governed by an elected mayor, a city manager with six council members, and a small police department founded in 1943.

It was late in the evening and I'd just exited the off-ramp to Highway 10. I then drove past the Veterans hospital, and after a short ride made the city of South Tucson.

My target was a house on Fifth Avenue.

Arriving ten minutes later, I saw the house I needed to pull surveillance on.

It wasn't what I expected.

The one-story adobe family home on the corner of South Fifth

Avenue and East Twenty-Ninth Street, had the feel and look of a crack house. But appearances could be deceiving — though something told me, not this time.

The two visible side windows which overlooked Twenty-Ninth Street, were spaced about fifteen-feet apart, with three overgrown blue Palo Verde trees visible, two on the front side, one right dab smack in between the windows, and one toward the back side of the house.

It would make surveillance tricky, if not impossible.

The windows were completely covered over by dark curtains. It afforded no visible way to tell what was behind them and who was inside the house. Again, making surveillance that more difficult for those *watching* the house. The main door leading to the house was facing Fifth Avenue, with a back door on the opposite end.

And just about a foot away from the door, were two six- foot-tall black thugs, who made a living out of others' misery and hardship. They appeared to be in their middle or late twenties, bulky guys. Menacing in all extremes, real tough looking. They wore black sleeveless T-shirts, and dark pants, with black bandanas wrapped around their heads, Indian style. They had what appeared to be gold chains around their necks as well. They were smoking and having a quiet conversation. These were the lookouts. There in the event of approaching cops or anyone else who came too close to the house, or them.

I couldn't wait till they were busted and safely locked up behind bars where they belong.

The *watchers* knew instantly, as did I, that these two for damn sure were packing heat!

The area around the outside was in complete disarray. Grass hadn't been mowed in months, which was growing about a half a foot high. Three city trash cans were piled high and overflowing with garbage. More rubbish was lying on the ground beside the trash cans, and two skinny black cats were ripping open the bags, looking for something to eat. The stench was nauseating to say the least.

There was a four-foot high chain link fence wrapped around the house. And facing the front door was a small three-foot opening and a gate that was wide open. And another three-foot high opening, this one without a gate, was located toward the back.

Two street lights just at the corner of Fifth Avenue were the only visible means of lighting in the area. Two other street lights over by Twenty-Ninth Street were both burned out.

The lamps emitted a monochromatic yellow colored dim light, which cast dark shadows everywhere. As in any surveillance, lighting was very important. And the occupants of the house knew that, that's why no outside lights were on the front porch, as well as in the back.

There were watchers all right. I could just make two of them out. But what I didn't know was — who *they* were. It was too dark to make them out. Cops maybe? If they were cops, they were using advanced tactics usually reserved for SWAT. They could be Feds, DEA on a stake-out. That seemed the more logical alternative.

Then, I immediately spotted their surveillance vehicles — three cars; Chevys by the looks of them, with local plates. One car parked across the street facing the north end in toward the house, and the other two on either side of the Twenty-Ninth Street and Fifth Avenue corners.

This was a typical tactical formation, affording the perp's very little leeway of escape out of the area. And in each car, there was a driver, trying their damnedest on keeping a low profile. It wasn't working. But what gave them away, were the antenna array on the back of their cars.

In toward the back of the house, parked in a dark shaded area, was a 1984 black Lincoln Town Car, possibly a getaway car. And just to the right side of the car well back in the shadows was a figure of a man, dressed in dark clothing, trying hard to stay well hidden.

"Shit," I muttered under my breath. I may have just stepped into a can of worms. Federal worms to be exact.

Jesus H Christ! Now what?

It was the crack house that gave it all away for me. They had to be DEA agents on a stakeout.

But, I wasn't sure. Not yet. Still, it was quite an unexpected turn of events, to say the least.

Chapter Seventeen

Angel Serrano

I t was later on that I was proven right.

It was at times like these, I hated being right.

So, I was in a sticky situation here. Should I stay or should I go? And maybe try later when I didn't have the Feds breathing down my neck.

"Well, shit happens," I finally said to myself shrugging. But then, I decided to stay and get in on the action, and maybe just maybe pick up my jumper in the bargain.

Sitting in my LeBaron, I took it all in.

Plan for the worst — hope for the best. Oh yeah.

And just in case, I'd come prepared for a long surveillance with some goodies, you know, coffee and donuts, cops' best friends.

Parked behind several cars, I tuned off the headlights, shut off the motor, and just sat there in my driver's seat. I was hoping to catch sight of my jumper, either going in or coming out of the house.

It became apparent to me, after several minutes had gone by, that maybe I hadn't been spotted coming in or setting up my surveillance point, or no one really cared. Considering no one had paid me any visits yet.

So, I was in the good, so far.

Reaching into my bag of donuts, I pulled out one of my favorites, a lemon-filled and taking a bite, I took a sip of my warm coffee.

Once I'd finished with my snack, I pulled out my binoculars from my bag of tools laid out open on the passenger seat, and surveyed the area. That's when I saw them. And that's when I knew that somehow, I wasn't going to get my guy!

The guy, or my jumper, was Angel Luis Serrano, age 48. Born in the Dominican Republic to an American service man, his mother was a naturalized US citizen of Dominican birth.

Piecing together the information from his rap sheet and his biographical information sheet, supplied by the bondsman, I came away with a clear picture of my jumper.

Angel Luis Serrano had served three years in the U.S. Army as an infantryman, but had been court-martialed out of the service during his last year. He received a dishonorable discharge and sentenced to eight years on two counts of sale and distribution of a controlled substance — heroin. He served six of those years at the U.S. Military Prison at Fort Leavenworth, Kansas, before getting an early release for good behavior.

But Serrano had slipped right back into his old habits, and soon after getting released from prison, he was off and running — selling crack on the streets. Seems Serrano had hooked up with some new shakers in South Tucson.

For several months, Serrano had been the subject of a DEA investigation. And after a long drawn out surveillance, the Feds had enough to make an arrest.

Serrano was eventually pulled over leaving an apartment complex and arrested. He was caught with a hundred grams of crack, and six thousand dollars in cash.

At his arraignment and bond hearing, bail was set at five hundred thousand dollars. Days later his bond was posted by relatives. Where they had come up with the money, was a matter of speculation. A week later Serrano went FTA, failed to appear for his initial court date, and disappeared without a trace.

Just two weeks after Serrano went FTA, Lupita Shestko-Montiel of Montiel Bail Bonds had me out chasing after his ass all over Tucson.

IT ALWAYS PAYS TO GO *SOFT* INTO SURVEILLANCE, INSTEAD OF *HARD*. GOING *soft* provides you with a greater sense of what to expect, if anything. As opposed to the hard approach — no knock, no identifying myself, just bust-right-on-in-approach. Most times the hard approach usually gets me my jumper. But I only take the hard approach, if and when I know for a fact, my jumper was to be found where I suspected him or her to be. So, I came upon the scene in a soft approach.

Good thing I did. If not, I would've walked into a shit storm.

So here I was in surveillance mode, waiting for the appearance of my jumper.

All was silent and strangely still, except for the two look outs. But they too stopped in their conversation, furtively casting glances up and down the street, like they were expecting something to happen, which wasn't too far from the truth.

It was 11:32, heavily overcast with a light sprinkle of rain that had just started. Traffic was very light, and no pedestrians could be seen anywhere throughout the neighborhood. Then, as the dark rain clouds thickened, hiding what was left of the half moon, and bathing the scene into even more darkness, I tried to focus more on the two lookouts.

They were showing signs of restlessness. And as yet, I was unable to locate the other watchers I knew to be hiding in the dark. They were doing a very good job of staying hidden.

Something was going to happen, and soon!

Chapter Eighteen

Family Plans

Earlier that morning

It was a cool, gray Wednesday morning, just a little after ten when I got the call from Lupita Shestko-Montiel, of Montiel Bail Bonds.

I was home with a long honey-do list I was just getting around to. And first on that list was mowing the lawn, raking, and then painting the fences came next. Besides that, I still had several chores my wife, Dolores needed done inside as well.

Married life is bliss. But it can also be a struggle, a journey with no predictions of the outcome. The only things I can control are my choices which define who I am. I enjoy married life, but there are times it can be pretty difficult, if not downright frustrating, even more so when they hand you their 'honey-do-list.'

I hadn't had a job since back in July with that so-called kidnapping case, and Dolores was so happy to have me around the house that the excitement of it all showed through in her eyes. She didn't have to say a word though, the huge smiles she gave me, the hugs and little kisses were all an indication of her excitement. And I just ate it all up, returning those hugs and kisses too whenever I could. But she was overly happy that a lot of the chores were getting done as well, and happy to have me home during the nights and having me all to herself, and of course with the kids.

Earlier that morning, my wife let me know in no uncertain terms, that she had already made plans for the family. We were visiting her parents that afternoon. My wife's father and mother, Jack and Akemi Darby, wanted to spend some quality time with the family. So, it was grandparents' day with barbecue and a movie. I was well looking forward to it, since Jack Darby was warming up to me and I was feeling the same toward him.

But it was short lived. I didn't know it then, but I was going to have several long days ahead of me.

Dolores and the kids were going to be mad at me that was for sure.

After I'd finished mowing, I saw Dolores at the back door, as she shouted out to me that I was wanted on the phone.

I started walking toward her. "Who is it, honey?"

"It's Lupita."

And just like that, I saw the hurt and frustration flash across her beautiful eyes.

It was frustrating for me as well, but right now I needed the paycheck that went along with the job, whatever it was. Dolores behaved exactly like I knew she would, I guess. She put herself and the kids ahead of everything, but I couldn't do that.

And therein lies the rub; I needed the income to support the family. And this is the only job I had at the moment. She had always wanted me to quit and get an eight-to-five job somewhere, for no reason than to have me around on weekends and those lonely nights I wasn't around for her. I wasn't blind. I knew it was very frustrating for her and the kids as well, couldn't be helped though. We all need to live with our choices. But sometimes, we make the wrong choices to get to the right place; only time will tell if I'd made the right ones.

But times were bad. Jobs were hard to come by, and P.I. and bounty hunting were a very lucrative profession. I knew she still had some faith in me — faith in providing for the family at all costs. I had to believe that or else, it was all for naught.

As I walked toward her, she looked angry, and somewhat heartbroken. She had made plans, and I was not going to keep my promise.

"She wants you for a job. Every time she calls you is for another job. This sucks. I made plans for today."

"I'm sorry, Dolores. Maybe it isn't a job. Let's not jump the gun just now."

"Wha'ever. I knew this wasn't going to last much longer."

I stopped by her side, looked into her eyes, and knew nothing I could say was going to change the way she was feeling.

"Well, I'll tell you what," she continued. "With or without you, I'm taking the kids to see their grandparents."

She then turned away from me, and walked back into the house, with me following close behind shaking my head.

It's hard not to get mad. But that's the thing; I never let anger enter my mind when it came to her. If I did, I could not do what I needed to do in such a state of mind. Nonetheless, I kept seeing a growing awareness of her negative attitude toward my work. I saw it with my first wife when I was an army investigator, and now as a bounty hunter I'm seeing it again with her.

Women, you could never understand them. Nor did I try.

Making it into the house without another word from Dolores, I picked up the phone.

"Hello Lupita." I showed no the excitement in my voice, just in case Dolores was listening. Secretly, I was hoping it was a job.

Seconds after Lupita Montiel's voice came over the receiver, she didn't spare any time and went right into the heart of the matter.

"Victor, can you come over right away?"

No other explanations were necessary from either of us. I knew I had a case.

I didn't know it then, but I wouldn't make it back home till the next day.

Chapter Nineteen

Montiel, Bail Bondsman

It was almost twelve o'clock.

The skies were clear, or mostly clear with the temperatures somewhere in the upper 70s, normal for this time of the month. And it was October, when the weather pattern usually shifts between thunderstorms, light to moderate rain, depending on the probability of precipitation in the air. And so far, we hadn't any rain since the beginning of the month, which was a blessing.

But otherwise, it was turning out to be a good day, as I made the Congress Street exit just off Interstate 10. Then straight up past Pennington Street, Church Street then at North Stone Avenue where I hung a left. After a mile and a half on Stone Avenue, I saw the old gas station that was Montiel Bail Bonds on the right side just getting to the intersection of Fourth Avenue. I turned onto Fourth and found a parking space.

I was feeling a little saddened for my wife and the kids, as I parked my LeBaron, but at the same time happy as hell. I could be getting back into another hunt and a paycheck to top it off.

Just wish it would be a quick snatch 'N' grab affair. A few hours work, in-and-out. But sometimes, we hardly ever get what we wish for. Fate is a bitch! And right now, she was snarling her ugly face at me.

I just didn't know it then.

I climbed out of my LeBaron, and stood in the cold for a few seconds. I let the cool breeze blow on my face and bald head, waking me up a little as it was. Just taking in the scenery and watching for tell-tale signs of danger in or about the area. One never knew when danger would come out of nowhere wanting to cause me harm. Always pays to stay alert, no matter where you were. One thing I've learned in this business — you were never truly safe anywhere.

Assuring myself all was clear, I pushed the door shut, locked it and walked the few intervening feet to the bail bonds front door entrance. As I opened the door and walked inside, I noticed that Lupita's front office staffers were not around. So, I turned left and headed to her front office. But I stopped just at the glass plate door, when I saw she was with another person, whose back was toward me.

The guy was a suit. Maybe a cop or lawyer couldn't tell from his backend. Tall though, five-feet-ten or maybe six feet, about one-hundred-ninety pounds, with a lot of hair on his head, turning gray, maybe in his late forties to be on the conservative side.

He stood about a yard from Lupita's front desk, just a little to the left side of it, gesticulating with both of his hands, much like Latino's do to emphasize some point in their conversation.

From where I was standing, I saw Lupita had a stone cold steady stare as she looked up at the guy. She said something I couldn't make out. Then she stood up from her chair, again said something else. The guy stood there for a second or two, then threw up his hands, turned and started walking out of the office. Opening the plate glass door, the dark-skinned Latino passed right by me without as much as a look, and proceeded out to the street, closing the door behind him.

With the door wide open, I stood on the threshold of her office.

"Hello Lupita. Mind if I come in?"

"Hello Victor. Come on in. I've been expecting you."

I looked at her meaningfully and cocked my head to the side, indicating the guy who'd just left her office.

"Was that trouble?"

"Nothing I can't handle."

We met halfway into her office, and exchanged a warm hug. I gave her a tiny peck on her cheek, which seemed to give her a little solace, at least for the time being maybe.

"So, you got a problem needs fixing?"

Her face turned a little grim. "Damn right I do."

She then turned without a word, and returned to her desk. As she sat down, she pulled a file folder from an open drawer on her right side and held it in front of her, waiting for me to take it.

I came around to the chair in front of her desk, pulled it out and sat down across from her. I removed my Stetson and placing it on top of her desk, reached out to take the proffered folder.

As I opened the folder, Lupita was explaining the case, way before I even had a chance to go through it.

Angel Luis Serrano was the subject of her story to me. A Dominican-American arrested by the DEA for drugs. She pushed over a photograph of Serrano to me.

Lupita-Shestko Montiel looked over at me as I picked up the photograph.

I noticed she had her black hair cut short to her shoulders. She had pale skin with heavy eyeliner, light red colored lipstick, and gold earrings; loose fitting black ankle high skirt, and a girly white button-down blouse that accentuated her firm robust breasts, which was held on with a wide Mexican diamond studded belt. At fifty-seven, and not showing her age whatsoever, she was still a very attractive woman.

I once asked her what a woman of her stature was doing in the surety business. She mentioned it all started back in '84 when she worked as a Fiscal manager, then one thing led to another. When friends asked her help in legal matters, she decided to open her own surety business and her bail bonds business took off after that. To this day, she is still in business.

I looked over the photograph. The profile I saw of Serrano was of a tall six-foot-two, dark skinned man, about a hundred and seventy pounds. A skinny Latino, with wide set small squinty eyes, tight set jaw, small ears pulled back to his skull. But the most prominent feature was a scar that started below his right cheek bone and stopped just below his chin. According to his rap sheet, the cut came from a knife fight while in a bar at an overseas duty station with the Army. Not a good-looking perp.

Once Lupita had finished with my jumper's story, I leaned back on the chair, dropped the photograph on top of the folder, folded my arms across my chest and with a slight smile, stared over at her.

"My usual cut right?"

"Yes of course, Victor. But. . ."

"There's a *but*?"

"Yes. But I need him back in jail by tomorrow afternoon."

"So, what's the hurry?"

"A bench warrant will be issued then. I don't want to lose this one. He's a local guy, so you shouldn't have any problems tracking him down."

I nodded. "I see. So, then. . ." I stopped for a second or two thinking about it. "You do know most times these jumpers head out of town, looking for someplace to hide, can't say it's going to be a midnight run."

"I know, Victor. Please, just get him back before then."

"I'll try my best."

I watched her raise her eyebrows.

"God, if anyone can bring him in before then, it's you. That's why I called you."

Chapter Twenty

The Indemnitor

I didn't head straight home after leaving Lupita's office. Instead, I called Dolores from a pay phone booth at a local Shell gas station on the corner of North First Avenue and Speedway Boulevard.

Letting it ring several times, the answering machine kicked in. Seems she wasn't home. Or maybe she was out in the back yard with the kids. But more likely than not, she was at her parents' house. So, I left a message saying I wouldn't be home till late that evening. I knew it wasn't going to sit well with her, but it couldn't be helped.

I shrugged it off. Although — I'd be totally honest about it — I felt somewhat gloomy considering.

Hanging up the receiver, I walked back to my car, pulled up at a pump and topped off the tank. I figured I wouldn't get a chance later.

Boy was I right!

Since it was somewhat after one o'clock, I decided on some much needed lunch. And somewhere to look through the reports and all the information Lupita had given me about my latest jumper, besides home.

I wanted something fast, and somewhere I wouldn't be disturbed. I decided on a Denny's restaurant I knew of down on Speedway Boulevard, between Dodge and Richey Boulevards, if I wasn't mistaken. Shouldn't be too packed considering the time.

By the time I made the Denny's, I noticed it had taken me about twelve minutes, give or take. Traffic was heavy and a light rain was starting to fall. As I drove into the parking lot, I wasn't disappointed. There were only three parked cars in evidence, and plenty of room for me.

Pulling up in front of the entrance, I sat in my idling car for a few seconds watching the rain fall as it swept in sheets against the windshield. There's something quite blissful about rainstorms that can interrupt one's routine in life. It was either pleasurable or sad, it all depended on one's outlook and it can let you go from expectations of sorts. But I wasn't going to let it get to me.

Then shutting down the engine, I reached into the back seat, pulled out my knee-high rain jacket and got it on. Also taking the case folder from the passenger seat, I tucked it into my jacket.

With the rain picking up steam, I climbed out of the LeBaron. I made sure the flap of the jacket concealed my Colt strapped on my waist, and settled my Stetson on my head. Outside, the city was wet and sodden and slowly turning dark. Then pushing the door shut, locking the car, I turned my collar up and shrugged down into my jacket and walked toward the front entrance. As was my nature, I carefully observed if any avenues of danger were open that could cause me harm, as the rain and wind whipped against my body stinging my cheeks and hands.

I walked in and immediately took it all in at a glance. It had the feel, charm and smells of any other Denny's I've found — the same deco, and the same kind of clienteles, and waitresses.

The place was virtually deserted except for two guys at the counter enjoying their pancakes and coffee, and a woman in a booth toward the front, waiting on her order, or already finished and was waiting on her check. It was hard to tell, since there were no plates on the table.

I didn't see a waitress, so I bypassed the sign telling me to wait and be seated, and headed out towards the back and a booth.

I found one to my liking, and once I had taken a seat, I was careful to keep my back to the wall, facing the main entrance. As soon as the waitress came over, I immediately went straight for the coffee and OJ, and then decided on a cheeseburger with fries.

It was ten minutes later, when the waitress came with my coffee and orange juice, and as I sipped on my black coffee, I waited for my order to arrive, before going through the file.

"Well, would you look at that!" I whispered to myself, looking out one of the windows. The rain was falling in sheets. The sound it made resembled hundreds of bullets as it hit the pavement. Mingled with it, was the roar of the storm as it passed directly above us, darkening the day. Just hope it stops soon so I could get back to work.

Sitting there watching and listening to the thunderstorm, I remembered how much I loved the rainfall. Remembered too, of so many years ago, of how my mother and I would sit by the front window in our one room shack home in Puerto Rico. She in a chair, and I on her lap with Greg my older brother sitting on the floor, as she would hum some little old Spanish tune I didn't recognize. It was a soothing but at the same times a haunting melody, as it brought tears to her brown eyes. I once asked her about the tune, and she said it was something her mother used to sing to her.

The memory of her tear-filled eyes, and the saddened look on her face, made me close my eyes for a second. And as I did, I wiped at some tears that were about to fall from my eyes.

Memories; it's truly amazing what little things like rain could bring back from the depths of one's subconscious mind.

The rain continued unabated for over an hour.

My burger and fries came, and it didn't take me long to empty the plate. I washed it down with a glass of water, then another. The waitress came back around and filled my cup with coffee. I pushed the plate away from me and sat back, totally satisfied with myself.

Several minutes later, after taking my last sip of coffee, the waitress came back around to refill my cup once again. But I placed my hand on the cup. Two cups were good enough for me.

She hovered over me for a few seconds and smiled down on me.

She was smiling. "Didn't take you long to chow that down."

I nodded. "Well it was that good. And I was hungry enough to eat a cow, if you'd placed it in front of me."

"I believe you."

After she left, and removed the plates, I opened the folder, and laid out most of the important pages flat on the table.

Forgotten were the rain, and my mother's sad tune. It was time to get back to work.

I skipped his rap sheet. Already knew his past encounters with the law, and his military history. So far, that was an open book. What interested me most was the Indemnitor, the person who had posted the bond on Serrano.

In this case it was one person. And there was a check mark on the relative box on the form I was reading; it was an uncle, a relative on the father's side of the family. Checking out the address, I saw he lived way out in Tombstone. I saw a phone number for the uncle, but I decided not to call ahead. I wanted to check out the residence first, just in case my jumper was being kept there.

The uncle was named Roberto Angel Serrano, sixty-two. An Arizona driver's license photo taken a year ago, and clipped to the form, depicted a gray-haired man, dark skinned with long hair coming down over his shoulders, with piercing brown eyes. He was unsmiling to the camera. The license showed him to be a two hundred pounds, six feet tall individual.

Next was a brother, named Hector Jesus Serrano, no description was indicated on the form, married, living in Tucson on East Maguire Hill apartments.

And last a sister, named Alicia Serrano-Martinez. I assumed Martinez being her married name. No other information about her was indicated on the form, other than she lived way out in Sierra Vista.

Well, as I took it all in, I wondered whom should I get to first.

Interestingly enough, I had several leads I could follow. Haven't had this many to follow up on in a long while. But ultimately, I decided that the first ones I should visit would be the parents. More often than not, they could provide me with information as to the whereabouts of their son, either directly or indirectly.

The information on the parents was sketchy though, with only their names and place of residence, no phone number or any other information I could have used. It would do for now.

With the rain completely stopped, I picked up all the forms and tucked them back in the folder. Leaving a five spot on the table for the waitress, I paid my bill and walked outside to my car.

Stepping just outside the entrance to Denny's, there was a strange smell in the air. It was a clean but sharp fresh and almost sweet fragrance. Scientists call it "Petrichor." Whatever it's called, it felt very invigorating to my senses. The city street smells were completely washed away with it. It was rather nice for a change.

Once back in my car, I turned on the ignition and sat there for a few seconds listening to the humming sounds of the air conditioner, and deciding on my next move. So, I opened the glove compartment, pulled out my Tucson city street map, checked the address for Serrano's parents and decided on the best possible route there.

Chapter Twenty-One

Serrano and the Ford

About half past two, I was crisscrossing the city on Interstate 10. My destination was on West Ethan Crossing Lane, thirty minutes away, give or take.

Once getting off I-10 onto North Travel Center, it was a matter of several minutes and several right and left turns, when I came upon the house on the right side of West Ethan Crossing Lane.

I made a slow brief pass of the house and noticed a brown 1984 Chevy pickup truck parked on the curb directly across the house, and a white 1982 Toyota Corolla coupe, parked in the driveway. Neither of the two vehicles belonged to my jumper, who had a red, two-door 1981 Ford Mustang registered under his name.

I continued driving slowly up the street, then hung a U-turn at the dead-end street, drove up to the intersection, and hung another U-turn and came to a stop. I parked by the curb just three houses down from their house, and sat down to wait.

Thinking maybe it was going to be a long surveillance, I rummaged through my glove compartment and found what I was looking for — a cassette tape. I popped it in the car's cassette player and listened to some Puerto Rican Salsa music, by El Gran Combo, which was one of my favorite Latin Groups. Turning the volume real low, I sang along with Andy Montanez to the song entitled *'Don Goyo'*:

Encontraron a Don Goyo,
Muerticito en el arroyo...

It was a catchy little song.

I remembered too, that my mother had nicknamed my father Don Goyo. So, every time I played that song, it reminded me of him.

My father, being a Merchant Marine didn't spend much time with us as a family, being out to sea ten to eleven months of the year. We obviously didn't get to see much of him. But the moments we did, they were happy times my brother and I cherished. They say history repeats itself. I find the irony in that statement, because here I am being away from my family for an extended period of time, even days on end — funny how that works.

I waited about thirty minutes, and getting nothing from my surveillance, decided on another tactic. Removing my Colt's holster, weapon and cuffs from about my waist, I placed them under the driver's seat. Then leaving my Stetson on the passenger seat, pulled out my private investigator's badge with my credentials and placed it in my back pocket. Then I removed a clipboard from my bag and placed it on the passenger seat alongside my hat.

My objective in this was simple. I didn't want them thinking I was a cop or bounty hunter out after their son. Impressions were very important in this line of work. I've never dressed or looked like a cop or SWAT team member, wearing all sorts of equipment on me, as if I was going into battle; not likely. When I go on a hunt, I dress very lightly, with no outward signs I was a hunter, always trying to keep my jumpers guessing and off balance, till it was too late for them. And keeping the parents off balance is precisely the impression I was after.

Sometimes being a police detective or in my case, a private investigator, is much like playing poker — you hold on to your cards and try to bluff your way through to a winning hand. But sometimes you lose. Just hope I win out with my bluff.

So, putting the car in gear, I drove over to my target's house and parked behind the Chevy pickup.

I waited about a minute or so, wanting to see if anyone had noticed where I'd parked, and come out to see who it was. But no one did.

I then rather slowly opened the driver's door, grabbed my clipboard and swiveled on the car seat, and again slowly stepped out of my car. I tucked the clipboard under my left arm, and closed and locked the car. Then I took a step forward and walked toward their driveway, past the Toyota coupe, and up to the front door.

Still, no one ventured out.

There wasn't a screen door, and the front door looked solid, heavy looking with a fish-eye lens. I rang the doorbell on the left side of the door, but after several seconds, I didn't get any type of response. I hesitated a moment then rapped my knuckles and knocked three times rather loudly.

Then I heard a lock being pulled, then another, probably the upper and lower locks, maybe. Then the door was slowly being opened. As it was swung in all the way, I saw standing there a light skinned, gray hired slender figure of a Latina woman, of average height in a gray dress and white blouse. She appeared to be in her mid-sixties.

I said, "Hi. Are you Mrs. Serrano?"

She took me in with those nice brown eyes.

"Yes, I am. How can I help you?"

I detected a slight noticeable Caribbean accent. Her eyes had that kind of look that lingers and made you feel good to be a Latino — an inviting look, with happy smile lines. In my estimation, she was the type of woman who made you smile just by her looks alone. She must've been a knockout when she was younger, because she still retained her beauty, even at her age.

I caught myself smiling at her.

Then I reached into my back pants pocket and pulled out my credential case. Flipping it open exposing my badge and laminated identification card, I briefly let her see it. Then I slowly returned it back to my pocket, and stared at her.

"My name is Victor Alvarez," I said. "I'm a private investigator working for a law firm of Reynolds and Mark. I'd like to talk to you and your husband about your son Angel."

Suddenly, I saw her stiffen. And for moment she just stood there unblinking, hesitating, suspiciously.

"What about my son?"

"Can I come in and discuss it, please?"

Then I heard a male voice coming from somewhere inside the house. "Honey, who is it?"

She looked over her shoulder, slightly to her left. "It's a private investigator, asking about Angel."

"Well, invite him in," the voice said.

Returning her gaze back to be, she grinned slightly.

"Please come in."

As I entered an archway, she held the door open and stepped back a pace or two. Closing the door behind me, she took her place in front of me, and led me into a foyer, and to a living room furnished in modern motif. It was painted in a bright white color, lending a feel of warm, cool and a relaxing atmosphere. My wife would love to have this color in our kitchen.

I stepped into a modestly furnished living room; television and stereo toward a corner, a love seat and sofa in the center of the room. There were two side tables on either side and table lamps on top of both. Two tall bookcases on the opposite wall were stacked full of hard bound books and there was a rifle cabinet off to one side. I noticed three shotguns and four small-bore weapons locked inside.

Four very nice colorful oil based paintings hung almost on every wall depicting Caribbean landscapes. I would imagine from her home island of the Dominican Republic. I couldn't tell if they were originals or prints from where I was standing.

In the center of the room stood an older version of my jumper, Angel, who was about the same height, a little more heavyset than Angel Serrano, gray-haired with a small, round pot belly. This was the father, no doubt about it.

"Please, have a seat," he said. "Can we get you something to drink?"

"No. No, I'm fine, thank you."

He took a seat on the sofa, with his wife on his right. I sat down on the love seat, facing them. I opened my clipboard and took out a pen, ready to jot down any information I got from them.

"So, please tell us what this is about." he said.

I glanced at him then his wife. "Yes . . . yes of course. I've been hired to find your son, Angel. . ."

"Has something happened to him?" Mrs. Serrano asked cutting me off.

I stared at her shaking my head.

"Not that I'm aware of. We believe your son may have witnessed an incident while he was in jail. And I was hired to see if in fact he had some information pertinent to our investigation."

They both looked at each other for a second of two.

"Oh, I see," Mrs. Serrano said.

Her husband nodded, clasped his hands together and leaned slightly forward.

"What type of incident are you talking about?" he asked.

We locked eyes, and for a moment thought I detected nervousness and uncertainty in his.

"I can't discuss that. All I can say is that your son hasn't done anything wrong. I have tried locating him, but according to his last listed address, he hasn't lived there for a while."

"And you thought he'd moved back with us?" he asked.

"Or that you could tell me how to contact him."

He looked at me for a matter of seconds, and glanced over to his wife, then looked back at me.

"You're not Mexican, are you?"

I paused before I answered.

"No, I'm not."

I wasn't going to give any other information about myself. They didn't need to know. But I was sure he was going to ask anyway.

"Where're you from?" he asked.

Figured he'd ask.

Slowly I said, "Puerto Rico."

"So, you know that family comes first. Right? And that we as a Latino family, we take care of family ourselves, no matter what."

I thought about it for a second.

By our nature, we as Hispanic's or Latinos consider ourselves first as Latinos independent of origin or place of birth, and having the strongest ties to family values. Hence, we treasure and hold to a higher sense, the traditional morals of family togetherness. If one falls into serious problems, the family steps in, immaterial of someone asking for the assistance or help. It's family first. The same can be seen, in lesser degrees in other cultures.

Growing up in a totally traditional Spanish family, I saw it first-hand, as with my mother struggling to make ends meet, never once asked for a handout, or spoke of the hardships our family went through. But family came in to take care of us.

Thus, I figured Mr. Serrano either knew the whereabouts of his son, or was himself hiding him out. My next question then wasn't totally out of place.

"So, you know where he is?"

He turned slightly to his wife and said, "Honey, can you get me our address book please."

She looked over at her husband with a questioning look, but slowly got up, and walked out of the living room. She disappeared into another part of the house.

A couple of minutes later, she came back, sat down and handed over a small book to her husband.

He opened it, and flipped over a few pages.

"He may be staying with his brother. Here is the address."

He read off the address, as I wrote it down. The brother was named Hector Serrano. But I already knew the address. Mr. Serrano also gave me a phone number and his number as well.

My bluff seemed to work quite well.

Now it was time to go pick his ass up!

I got up, thanked them both, and turning toward my right, noticed out of the corner of my eye, a door slowly being closed on the far right side of the living room. There was no light coming through, so I couldn't see who was behind the door.

That's odd, I thought. *Wonder what that was all about?*

After shaking hands with Mr. Serrano, he led me to the front door, again I said thanks, and started walking back to my car.

I'd just reached my car, and standing by the driver's door, was attempting to unlock it, when I heard a car start up. The sound it made was like the roar of a race car *Vroom, vroom*! It sounded like it came from behind Serrano's house.

Then, quickly things got out of hand.

Suddenly, from around the back of the house, I saw a red Ford Mustang slowly move away from the corner of the house. Coming onto the street, it slowly picked up speed. Then I saw the driver as he swung the wheel hard to the left, leveled it out and peeled out burning rubber, leaving a trail of white smoke behind.

Accelerating faster, the car sped out right in front of me, that's when I glimpsed a side profile of my jumper behind the wheel!

Chapter Twenty-Two

Good and Bad Luck

SECONDS TICKED AWAY, AND IT SEEMED LIKE TIME HAD STOOD STILL FOR ME.

A scowl formed across my face. I'd been taken completely by surprise, caught momentarily off balance, which rarely happens. But there it was. There's always a first time for everything. And if you were in my shoes, you'd know exactly how I was feeling.

Ah, hell, I thought. *Son-of-a bitch was in the house all this time.*

I can't worry about that now.

Getting into my car, I fired it up, hung a quick U-turn, and peeled out trying to catch up to him. Driving with my left hand, I reached under the seat with the other, and got a hold of my Colt. Then, clicking off the safety, I placed it on the seat between my legs; he wasn't going to take me by surprise again!

I reached the intersection, stopped and looked right and left and faintly saw the Mustang on my left side, as his brake lights came on momentarily.

"I got you, fucker!" I said out loud.

But he was still too far off in the distance, just hope I can catch up. Stomping on the gas pedal, I turned the wheel hard over to the left, and peeled out of there.

Knowing we were closing up to the I-10, I needed to catch up before he turned onto the interstate. There were the added possibilities of losing him in some possibly heavy traffic on the interstate. I couldn't afford that right now.

I kicked it into overdrive, feeling the big car respond to my needs. I sensed the four-barrel carburetor opening wide, drinking up the gas. Sixty turned to eighty, then ninety miles per hour, all in a few seconds time.

I came to the intersection and sped through, barely missing a car that was slowly getting into the intersection from the left side. I saw it as it came to a complete stop, and watched as the guy's eyes lit up and his mouth hanging wide open.

"Sorry," I muttered, as I tried to keep in visual contact with my jumper's car.

I checked my speed — one hundred and two miles per hour! *Christ,* I thought, *how long can I keep this up?* I hadn't been this fast before. I was so pumped! While a voice in my head screamed Go, go, go!

Through right and left turns we went, still I caught faint taillights up ahead — the Mustang, had to be. Then I lost sight of it on one of those turns, but I kept on going. Still not making visual contact, I made the intersection leading to the I-10 interstate and slowed, then came to a complete stop. Looking both ways, I couldn't see if he went east or west.

"Garr," I growled, knowing I'd just lost him!

I slammed the steering wheel hard. So damn hard, I may have hurt my hand. I ignored the pain, but felt the anger building up inside me for losing the asshole so quickly.

It's not every day I lose on a chase. But don't get me wrong here. Having twenty odd years of law enforcement behind me, it's bound to happen — just not that often.

I tilted and rubbed my bald head, feeling some perspiration. Then wiping at it with my hand, I dried it on my pants leg. Rubbing both my hands together, I tried to get some feeling back from my hand that was starting to throb some.

Feeling my pulse rate gradually slow to its normal rate, I closed my eyes. Then leaned my head down slightly, shaking it side to side. I struggled with my disappointment, but I'll get over it.

Shit happens. No use crying over spilled milk.

I stared out my windshield with half closed eyes, but I saw nothing at all; just the face of my jumper materializing right in front of me, laughing.

There'll be a next time.

"If at first you don't succeed . . ." I mused aloud.

Chapter Twenty-Three

The Brother

Ten minutes later, I was back on the interstate driving east heading back into Tucson, and Hector Serrano's apartment on Maguire Road.

Now that my jumper was truly on the run, and knowing someone was after him, I suspected his next move would be to find a place to lay low. So, working under that assumption, I decided to hit all the relatives' residences, common enough places where he would turn to ground. Sounded exhausting and time consuming, but it needed to be done.

Getting out on Kolb Road, I hung a right and headed out to Speedway Boulevard. Fifteen minutes later traveling on East Maguire Road, and up a slight hill I saw the complex on the left side of the road. Making the left turn, I drove onto the complex and following the main road I passed a sign that read: Office and Directory.

I found the building and the apartment adjacent to the office on the same side of the road.

The apartments were two stories, adobe style structures with front stairs leading to the second landing, where Hector Serrano and his family lived.

The complex area was full of parked cars on the other side of the street, so I decided to setup a surveillance point there. But first I needed to do a drive through, see if my jumper wasn't already there. I drove around the building, but didn't catch sight of the red Mustang. Getting back to my surveillance point, I got behind a beat up, green colored 1972 two door AMC Gremlin that had seen better days, and prepared to wait and see what developed, if anything.

A half hour into the watch, two small kids, a boy and a girl, about six and seven years old, both wearing sandals short pants and colored T-shirts, and a woman, unmistakably Latina, with slightly dark skin, black colored hair, wearing tight jeans and a white blouse, which I took to be the mother, came out of Hector's apartment.

They walked down to street level, where the kids started playing some sort of game, enjoying themselves. I imagine happy to be out in the sun. The mother sat down on the lawn to watch them. She had an open book flipping through pages maybe looking for her last place in the story, while at the same time keeping a watchful eye out for her two kids.

Reaching over onto the backseat, I grabbed my gym bag, where I kept most of my investigative tools. I decided it would be a good idea to bring out my parabolic microphone, and wait to see if Hector Serrano came out to be with his family.

Ten minutes later, he came down the stairs and joined them on the front lawn. I recognized him immediately. He had longer thinning hair with a slight bald spot, but otherwise he was very similar to his brother.

I had the microphone all set up and my earphones on. Then what transpired between him and his wife, brought on a little cheer to my otherwise disappointing day.

Sitting down next to his wife, they started conversing low in Spanish, like they were trying to hide something from someone.

"Yeah, you got that right. Me," I muttered under my breath.

"That was my dad on the phone," he said, matter of fact, staring over at his wife.

She stared back at her husband, and dropped her book on her lap.

"Oh, what did he want this time?"

Momentarily looking away from his wife and glancing over at his children playing, he was very glad that it wasn't him in trouble. Then he glanced back at his wife.

"It was about Angel, someone is after him. Dad said it was a private investigator."

"Madre de Dios, but why would someone be after him?"

"Something about Angel not making his court date."

"And someone is after him for that?"

She sounded incredulous that someone would even do that.

"Yeah, it's the law here, Angela. You don't show up for your court date, they can put you back in jail."

Angela, keeping her eyes on her two kids, simply nodded.

She said. "So, what's going to happen to him?"

"Dad told him to go to Uncle Roberto's house and stay there till they stop looking for him."

Angela paused for a moment, not knowing what to think about that. She glanced over to him, then back to the kids, then back at him.

She shrugged.

"Think he'll go there?"

For a moment, there was silence between them, and then he glanced away from his kids.

"Don't know, but it's safer there than here or with our sister."

"Well, I hope it works out okay for Angel. He hasn't had any good luck since getting out of jail."

"Yeah, me too," he said.

Silence.

He said, "Want to go take the kids to the park?"

"That sounds like a good idea."

Picking herself up from the lawn, she called the two kids, and they all went back to their apartment.

I'd heard enough.

Storing the microphone back in the bag, I started up the car and backed up slightly. Then, putting it in first gear, I pulled away from the curb and got out onto the main drag as I contemplated my next move.

Chapter Twenty-Four

Tombstone

I wasted ten minutes at a convenience store on the access road leading onto the I-10. I purchased a soda and some crackers to munch on for my drive to Tombstone, and my visit to Roberto Angel Serrano, the uncle's residence.

In my car, I munched on the crackers and sipped on the Coke, while reading my two maps of Tucson and Tombstone. I plotted my routes, both to Tombstone and the uncle's house. Once I had my bearings, and the streets I needed, I fired up the engine, then turned onto I-10 heading east.

Tombstone, Arizona was about a seventy-two-mile drive, and it should take me about an hour's time, more or less, depending on traffic. It would take me past the city of Vail, then onto Benson, where I would switch onto Highway 80 all the way south to Tombstone.

Tombstone is a historic city in itself, located in Cochise County and founded in 1879. It was one of the last wide open frontier boomtowns in the American Old West. But, it's best known as the site of the Gunfight at the O.K. Corral.

I wasn't headed there for a sightseeing tour though. I had business to attend to.

It was fast approaching early evening. Only have about two hours before sundown. The dry air was still hanging on. A cool wind blew through my open driver's window, and with it, it brought a nice flowery sweet smell too. It reminded me of the Creosote bush growing in my back yard, as the sweet swell hung over the yard after a rainfall.

Hurriedly passing through Benson, after getting onto Highway 80, I arrived shortly before seven o'clock into Tombstone proper. From there it was a simple matter of following East Fremont Street down to South Landin Parkway where it intersected with Old Bisbee Highway.

I came to a stop and parked just off Bisbee Highway, and saw the house I was looking for.

It was situated up on a ridge overlooking South Landin Parkway. It had two structures, the house proper — a one story brick home, I'd say built back in the 1960s, and the other which I suspected to be a detached garage. There was a gravel road that led up to the house.

Getting off Bisbee Highway, I drove onto the gravel road. I wasn't going to hide who I was to him. He was the one that bailed my jumper, so he had much to lose and all to gain from his nephew returning to jail.

Or so I hoped.

Driving up a steep incline which led to the front of the house, I saw an older looking white male standing on the veranda, staring over as I drove up, casually holding a shotgun in the crook of his left arm.

Pulling up parallel to him, driver's side facing out, I shut down the engine. Then, slowly undid the button on my holster — just in case I needed to pull quickly. Opening and climbing out of my car, I closed the door, walked around toward the front and turned to face the old man.

Dusk had settled in, and the last of the sun's rays were slowly dipping away in the west darkening the area, as shadows deepened, bringing a surreal feel to the landscape.

I slowly walked up to him, keeping sight of his posture, waiting to see what he would do with the shotgun. He didn't move it as I walked to within two yards of him.

"Hello, sir," I said extending my hand out to him. "Are you
Mr. Roberto Serrano?"

He nodded slowly as he lowered the shotgun and leaned it on the railing off to his right.

"That's right, sonny."

I dropped my hand, as he declined to extend his.

Serrano took in a deep breath. I didn't think he liked me being on his land.

"Who are you, sonny, and whaddya doing in my land?"

"I'm a private investigator. Montiel sent me."

"Aha, so ya be the bounty hunter looking for Angel?"

"Yes, sir, I am."

"Well, matter of fact ya just missed him. He was here earlier. He wanted to stay with me, but I told him he couldn't. Didn't want the responsibility and the problems he has."

So, okay, he was here alright, now he wasn't, I thought.

"You know where he may have gone to?"

Serrano thought for a second.

The old man hesitated for a moment. "He said something about going back to Tucson and about staying at friend's house."

"Do you have any idea where that would be?"

"Yeah, I guess. I drove him there once about two months ago. Let me try and remember where."

The old man dropped his head low, desperately thinking.

I didn't say anything, waiting for the guy to remember and hoping his information would help me out.

The old man glanced to his left, like trying to put it all together before he spoke.

"If I remember right, I think his friend lives out on Twenty-Ninth Street, somewhere by Fifth Avenue somewhere. Sorry I couldn't be any more help."

"Hey, no, you did fine, thanks."

"Wish I could help more."

"Well, I was wondering . . ."

"Yeah . . . What about?"

"Did he give a name for his friend?"

The old man scratched his head. "You know, I think he did. I think it was something like Evert, no, Evans."

"Is that a first or last name?"

"Don't know."

"Thank you, sir."

There was something else that was bothering me ever since I accepted this job. I stared at Serrano for a second.

"Something else. . ."

Serrano said, "Shoot. . ."

"Okay. Can I ask where you got the money to bail Angel with?"

Serrano scratched his head again and nodded. "Oh that. Well, I'd just come back from visiting some friends, and a paper bag was left on my doorstep. It had a lot of money in it, and a note. The note said that the money was to be used for Angel's release. I didn't know Angel was in jail, till I got a hold of his father. Also, the note wasn't signed so figured it came from the family. But it didn't."

"You have any ideas where it could have come from?"

Serrano crossed his arms across his chest. "Maybe it was his friend. I remember Angel once said his friend was into drugs."

I made a face, and I asked myself: *Yeah, okay, but how did they know to leave the money here with the old man? And how did they get the address? Also, why not leave it with relatives living in Tucson?* But the fact of the matter was I thought I already knew the answers.

And somehow, I also knew I'd never get confirmation of those answers from anyone involved. But I wasn't a cop anymore, so it wasn't all that important then.

I shrugged and noticed old man Serrano was trying to get my attention.

"Hey sonny ya still here?"

I quickly looked over at him.

"That help ya any?" he asked.

"Yes, sir, and it does."

Chapter Twenty-Five

Jeff and Anna Nichols

Once back in Tucson, I brought the LeBaron to a stop just outside one of my friend's home on Twenty-Second Street, down by Golf Links Road.

It was getting late in the evening, so I decided not to go home and disappoint the family by staying a short while and then taking off again. That would have been cruel of me. So here I was looking up an old friend. But, the person I really wanted to talk to was his wife.

I'd known Jeff and his wife Anna Nichols for about two years. He worked as a security officer and his wife was a Tucson police patrol officer. They were good friends with whom I played poker off and on. I met Jeff while working on a case, and we hit it off very well. He was a Vietnam vet, who also served as an army military policeman.

Once inside the house, Jeff offered me a beer and said he'd be right back with it.

I parked my butt in a chair facing their fireplace, and waited for his return, just as Anna, came into the room and sat down on the sofa facing me.

"Hello, Victor," she said. "Glad you could come around."

I swung around to face her. She was wearing slacks and a white blouse and was holding a beer.

"Hi Anna, you're looking good as ever."

In answer, she raised her beer, nodded slightly and took a quick sip. Just then Jeff came back with our beers, and we lapsed into talking about old times.

Then after a few minutes, the point of my visit came up.

"So, Al?" Jeff asked. "We haven't had the pleasure of your company for a while. So, what's up?"

I noticed he had a bemused grin spread across his lips when as he looked at me.

I leaned forward and rested an elbow on my knee, lifted the beer bottle and downed half of it, as I watched Jeff light up a cigarette.

I smiled. "Well, you two are hardly the answer to my prayers, but as a beggar, I can't be too choosy."

Jeff stood about my height, a hundred-ninety pounds worth of all muscle and brains to boot. He was a blue eyed, blond haired white guy and with an easy going smile. I really liked him, and we got along very nicely. He'd always wanted to come out with me on my hunts, but his wife always put the stop to that. She just wouldn't let him do it. Anna was about my height as well, a slender blonde, awfully pretty too, with deep blue eyes.

I offered up another smile and leaned toward them. "Want to see if Anna and you could do me a favor."

Anna raised her eyebrows. Jeff glanced at Anna in a knowing smile.

"What kind of favor?" Anna asked.

I glanced at Anna. "Hey, Anna, relax. I'm not going to ask Jeff to go out with me, just in need of a little information."

Jeff mashed his cigarette into an ashtray and looked over at me. "What kind of information?"

"I'm working on a case, and I need to verify an address and of those who live there."

Anna nodded. "Give me what you have, Al. Let's see what I can do with it."

Just like that, they just up and helped.

Friends can't do without them, even if I did get to use them once in a while. I looked up quickly, expectantly. And with a smile on my face, I passed Anna the information. She stood, quickly turned her gaze toward her husband, like looking for approval. I saw Jeff shrug his shoulders, and watched as she walked away to some other part of the house.

Exactly an hour after I'd arrived, I was back in my car, driving the fastest route to where I hoped my jumper was hiding out. Just hope the information Anna had given me was solid. But knowing her, and considering it came straight from some of her contacts at the TPD, it couldn't be anything else but.

Chapter Twenty-Six

Knife Fight and Take Down

Back at the Crack House

It was 12:30 a.m. and yet no action by the Feds, or from those inside the crack house.

Munching on the last of my donuts and drinking what was left of the cold coffee, I too kept up my vigil.

The rain had died out completely and a light humidity was moving in fast, starting to warm things up a bit.

All was silent. But, then I heard a car or truck approaching from the Fifth Avenue side, breaking the still quiet of the night.

I saw headlights first as they broke through the darkness, lighting its way. Then I saw it rounding the corner leading onto Twenty-Ninth Street; it wasn't a truck, it was a Ford Mustang, my jumper's car!

It had to be Serrano driving. It couldn't be anyone else. I kept my hopes up that it was. Then, whoever was behind the wheel drove up and stopped in the front of the house.

As the driver climbed out of the Mustang, I saw who it was, Serrano! Just as old man Serrano had said. And here he was. If he's allowed to stay in the crack house, it will make my job difficult or nearly impossible to root him out and arrest him. So, I didn't need that to happen.

The situation appeared dour.

Angel Serrano walked up to the two ugly looking black guys. He said something to them; they shook their heads in the negative. He started looking around, when one of the lookouts said something else to Serrano.

They fell silent for a few seconds. Serrano was probably trying to figure out his options and what else to say. He had come looking to hide out in the house, and the lookouts said no. It was a possibility.

The three parted with Serrano heading back to his car, and the two lookouts back on the watch. As he started his car, I started mine and with my headlights off, I slowly drove out of the used car lot and waited to see in which direction Serrano would take.

Didn't have too long to wait.

Serrano eased his Ford just past me. Giving him at least a three-car interval, I turned the steering wheel over to the right and decided on following instead of giving chase. I needed a nice quiet place to take him down.

Up ahead of me I saw police strobe lights flashing, and heard sirens wailing, as three patrol cars speed down Twenty-Ninth Street. They were moving very fast, obviously ready to join in the bust at the crack house.

I didn't slow down, just pulled off slowly to the side of the road, letting them past me on the opposite side.

So, it was going down. I didn't want to be near any of it. What was going down was not my affair. I had a bigger fish to fry. And, I was glad I'd left just in the nick of time.

As the cops flew by me, I pushed it into overdrive. If the need for speed had been vital before, I truly had a need for it now. The cops' presence had run down the minutes for me, but seconds later I caught up with the Mustang staying well behind it. I then followed Serrano onto Speedway Boulevard, and caught myself smiling. I knew where he was taking me — his brother's apartment.

I stayed back, not letting him catch sight of my car, didn't want to spook him. Hell, I already knew where he was taking me. No sense tipping my hand, and letting him know I was tailing him.

Five minutes later, he proved me right. He made a left-hand turn onto the Maguire Hill apartments. I stayed back and watched him drive up to his brother's apartment building.

Then, two things happened; the first was my fault, the second his.

I stopped and parked my car way back about four cars behind the Mustang. Serrano had parked across the street from his brother's apartment, and I had the feeling he wasn't going to overstay his welcome.

Serrano found an empty space, shut down the engine, and climbed out of his car. He came around toward the front and walked up the stairs leading to his brother's front door. He walked like a man with purpose and determination, but I imagined, a little misguided, considering his family problems.

I waited long enough to see him knock on the door. Then seeing the door opened, I caught a glimpse of his brother as he stood by the open door. As soon as the door was closed behind him, I made my move.

Leaving my Stetson in the car seat, I climbed out leaving it unlocked, and stood by the trunk almost in darkness, waiting patiently for Serrano's return.

I knew my jumper was looking for some place to hide, and his brother's place seemed the logical alternative. Considering his uncle didn't want anything to do with him, and his parents' house could conceivably be the next place where he would turn to if his brother turned him down.

Fifteen minutes later, my jumper walked out of the apartment, stood by the open door, angrily yelling at his brother in Spanish. But I couldn't hear clearly what was being said. Then the door was slammed shut on his face, apparently by his brother. I couldn't be sure. It could have been his brother's wife though, but I doubted it. From my vantage point, I was unable to see clearly.

He started down the stairs, talking to himself with his head bowed low, oblivious that I was close by. Then he shrugged and blew a long sigh. Apparently, he didn't get what he wanted from his brother.

It was bad news for him, excellent news for me.

I watched him as he walked down the stairs. Then, I came around my car and slowly started walking toward him. I had the advantage, and I wanted to take him by surprise, hopefully without any bloodshed.

But, life is always full of surprises, and it didn't quite work the way I expected.

Coming to the end of the stairs, he took two steps toward his car, and stopped. I kept on walking slowly closing the gap between us. I didn't want to rush it, not just yet.

He turned his gaze on me, in a vague manner. Then his eyes opened wide in recognition, as if he'd just seen a ghost. He knew who I was. My mistake!

I kept on coming, slowly though, wasn't totally sure if he knew who I was. But his next move told me he most assuredly did.

He made the first of his mistakes!

He looked about, but there wasn't anyone else around — just us two. Turning, and looking directly at me, he reached in his back pocket and pulled out a switchblade. I heard the click of the blade locking in place. Damn, I'd know that sound anywhere. Had the occasion to use the blade myself once or twice back in my gang life in New York City.

I was still too far to try and rush him. I could've taken my gun out and shot him, or had made him drop the knife. And from my point of view, this guy needed shooting. But, I wanted to take him without getting him to a hospital. I needed to return him back to jail before a warrant was issued for his arrest. If that happened, Lupita would lose, and I wouldn't have a pay check as well.

After gaining a distance of about four feet from him and instead of taking my gun out as any self-assured cop would have, I decided to have some fun on his account for losing him before. It was a dangerous game I was playing. But hell, he had it coming.

He had the blade pointed in my direction, while he stared straight at me.

"Stop right there!" he screamed.

But I didn't stop. Kept on coming very slowly though.

I didn't say a word, just stared at him.

He must've been debating what to do. He took in a deep breath and blew it out yelling at me once more.

"Don't come any closer, or I'll cut you up, man."

He sighed loudly, apparently frustrated at not getting his meaning across. He was just screaming. Not very loud just enough to be heard by anyone walking around close by. He knew he was caught. It seemed as if he was weighing his options, which weren't that many, and none too good.

I needed to get a little closer. As I took several more steps, I kept my eyes on his knife hand.

I remained calm, not letting his screaming get to me, especially in the face of danger.

Seconds ticked by.

"You know who I am, right? You're coming with me, walking or dragged. It's your choice, Angel."

He stared at me, glanced away to his left over to where his car was parked, and maybe was considering running to it. But, I figured that wasn't an option for him.

He took a small step back. "Fuck you, asshole. I'm going for my car, you try to stop me and I'll put my blade in your chest!"

He probably thought I wasn't armed. So, I flipped aside the tail end of my raincoat, showing him my holstered weapon.

Staring into his eyes, I smiled. "Go ahead try it. I've been keeping tabs on how many men I've shot. You could be my next number."

He looked over at it, and smiled.

He laughed. "You ain't gonna use that on me, asshole."

I didn't say a word, just kept staring at him, waiting to see what he'll do.

Then before he could make his move toward his car, I'd finally gotten to within three feet of him. He was hoping I'd get closer to him, and I obliged. That's when he made his move.

Not to his car, but at me!

He stared at me stupidly for a split second, opened his mouth screaming before he charged. He led with the point of the blade aimed squarely at my chest. It was a good straight move except for the screaming bit, but it was something he'd done several times before, no doubt. I've even used it myself on occasion.

He could have run to his car, but then I would have pulled and shot him. He probably knew that, that's why he charged me: Take me out and he'd have a clear unobstructed getaway.

It was another mistake on his part.

I didn't hesitate nor did I stop to think on ways to defend myself. It came rather natural to me. So, I kept on eyes on the blade, not him.

He lowered the point of the blade just a little, drawing back his knife hand, hoping for more power and speed in the lunge.

I moved quickly into his attack, letting his movements carry him forward. Just as his blade was inches from me, I suddenly shot forward in a burst of speed, leading with my left hand. Grabbing his knife hand at the wrist, I twisted to his right, came in around his back, twisted his hand again and taking the knife out of his hand, let it fall to the ground.

Then I swung him over my back and threw him heavily onto the ground. He landed with a loud *thump* hitting his head on the pavement, knocking him out. It gave me ample time to secure his hands behind his back with a set of cuffs. That's when I saw the blood running down from the back of his head.

Then as quickly as it started, the fight was over.

I was breathing hard, caught myself and slowly regulated my breathing, slowing down my heart rate, feeling a little better. Serrano was laid out flat on his back, unconscious, but I needed to stop the flow of blood. So, I ran to my car, opened the trunk and pulled out one of my large bandages I kept in there, just for occasions such as these.

Getting back to Serrano, I saw his brother standing on the second floor landing with his wife next to him, yelling down at me, wanting to know what was going on. I ignored him for the moment.

Kneeling down next to Serrano's inert figure, I lifted his head, and as I did, he slowly started coming around. Then gently I got him to sit up, while I wrapped the bandage around his head, stemming the flow of blood.

Serrano was sitting up and holding his own, but I saw he was still woozy from loss of blood. He tried twisting his head, but the task was too painful to accomplish. His mouth was opening and closing, trying to work, as blood still gradually spilled down his back.

I'd figured with a blow to the back of the head, he's going to be laid up for a few days while he's in jail, at least till he's brought up in front of a judge.

"Whoa!" Serrano said, "My head it hurts like hell."

His eyes were dull and empty as he opened his mouth to say something else, caught himself then went silent.

"It doesn't look that bad, but I'm no doctor. They'll take care of it once I get you back in jail."

"What you hit me with?"

"I didn't."

"Ah Christ, you didn't hit me?"

"You don't remember?"

"No."

"The pavement . . . .?"

"The what?"

"You know, when I threw you on the ground."

He looked at me, and then turned away, and slowly he said, "Oh . . . yeah, now I remember. Damn."

"Hey, what's going on?" Serrano's brother, Hector Serrano asked.

He'd come down and was standing just to my left side. Immediately, I pulled out my credentials, and flashed him my badge. I told him who I was, and what I was going to do.

"Is he going to be alright?" he asked, sounding worried about his brother. "He's bleeding."

"Yeah, he'll be ok. But he'll have a terrible headache for a day or two."

Chapter Twenty-Seven

Federal Lockup

By the time I pulled up in front of the Federal Correctional Institution, or FCI, it was about two o'clock in the morning.

The FCI is a medium security level prison. Mainly housing pretrial inmates from Federal court proceedings in the district of Arizona. And since Serrano was a Federal jumper, this was where I needed to surrender the bond and my prisoner too.

The FCI was built in 1982, and is located about ten miles southeast of Tucson on Wilmot Road. It is a most imposing structure. The complex itself is a long low row of buildings, two stories high, with all the usual precautionary barriers associated with prisons worldwide.

I parked in back. I got out of my car, and grabbed a pair of leg irons from my bag. Setting my Stetson on, I opened the back passenger door, and noticed Serrano asleep curled up in a ball.

"Hey, wake up. We're here."

Once he was awake, I instructed him to put out his legs. Once he did that, I set the leg irons on.

"Okay, let's go. Get out of the car."

Once I had him standing in front of my car, I grabbed his hands that were cuffed behind him, lifting them just enough to let Serrano know he couldn't possibly try to escape. The leg irons added to that assumption.

Closing and locking the car door, we started walking toward the high iron gate and the prisoner cell block proper.

He was still groggy and as yet not in full control. His balance was off, as I helped him along.

Serrano tilted his head sideward to his left, and then gazed over at me for a moment. He smiled rather menacingly, maybe trying to frighten me, I think. "You know this ain't finished between us, right?"

I sighed. "Oh, what exactly are you getting at?"

But I already knew exactly what he meant, just wanted to hear it.

He slowly turned his head toward the front once again and clenched his teeth.

"I'm be getting out soon and you can bet I'll be coming for you. Is that clear enough, asshole?"

I shook my head.

"Listen you piece of shit, when you do, I'll be waiting."

I was fighting hard an urge to kick him in the balls.

Calming myself down, I pushed him forward.

"If you decide on gunning for me, you're gonna find a bullet and a body bag with your name on it. That's a promise. Now, *is that clear enough for you?*"

He smirked and shook his cuffs.

"I'm still not afraid of you."

But I detected a slight tremor in his voice, which I took to be fear, and maybe a sense of false bravado thrown in.

"Most aren't, till it's too late. Keep walking and keep quiet, or I'll find other parts of you to hurt."

Giving me a lopsided smile, he just grunted.

I wasn't worried about Serrano's threat. I get that a lot. It's not the first time, nor will it be the last. It goes with the territory. But if he did come for me that would be a grave mistake on his part.

An hour later, after turning over the bond with Serrano safely tucked away in a cell, and getting my copy of the bond, signed and sealed, I headed home. I needed to get back in my wife's good graces once again.

I had a promise I needed to make good on.

"So, let's talk about broken promises," I said.

It was one in the afternoon and Dolores and I were having a little quiet time together. We were sitting apart from each other on the living room sofa; I with the newspaper and Dolores with a book. The kids were all out back in the yard playing.

Dolores sighed. If that sigh was any indication, I could be heading for trouble. This wasn't going to be easy. Then she shook her head, dropped her book on her lap, and clasped her hands over the book.

Oh boy, here it comes.

She stared straight at me. "What broken promise are you talking about?"

And there it was.

She knew full well what I was talking about, but it was her way of annoying me to no end. I didn't take the bait.

"I don't like your coy manner honey. You know quite well what I'm talking about."

She shrugged.

"So, what?"

Oh yeah. She was still burning over the whole affair. But I had an idea that could get me back in her graces once again.

I returned her stare and smiled.

"So, maybe I can make it up to you and kids. Like maybe going over to your parents and having a makeup thing, you know, with a movie and barbeque for today."

She opened her mouth to say something, thought about it for a second, and leaned back on the sofa.

She gazed at me. "I'll see what my father has planned for this afternoon."

And without another word, she returned to her book.

It was later during the day that she finally caved into my plan, but still not completely forgiving me. That same afternoon, we as a family met with her parents, Jack Darby and Akemi Darby — a barbeque with a movie. Dolores chose a VHS 1984 movie titled *Romancing the Stone*. The Darby's enjoyed it, and she saw her father in one of his rare moments — he laughed, as he enjoyed his time with his grandkids and his daughter.

It wasn't till we got back home, that Dolores finally forgave me.

We were in bed. And before turning off the lights, she raised herself on an elbow, and looked over at me as if I'd just won the lottery.

"That was one of the most wonderful times that I've spent with my father and mom in a long time. You made me very happy. Thank you, Victor."

Then she gave me a warm loving smile.

And her smile was all the thanks I needed.

Book Three

The New Mexico Jumper

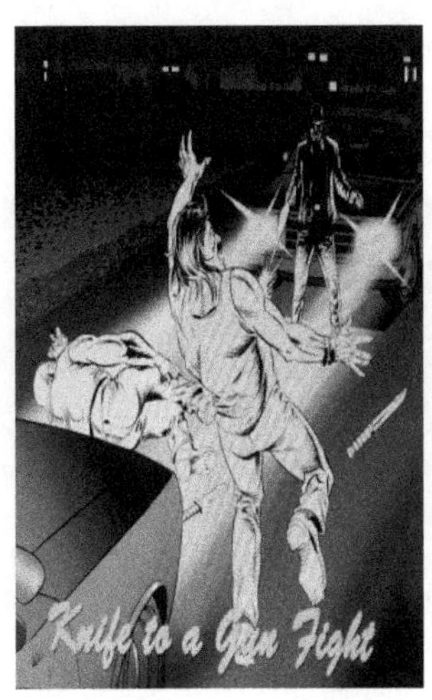

Chapter Twenty-Eight

Andrew Starr, Bondsman

November 1987, Albuquerque, New Mexico

"I was told if I needed someone back in jail, in a certain amount of time, you ask for the best. . ."

The man curled his lips into a slight grin, rather pleased with himself in offering the opening salvo, trying to impress the hell out of me. I wasn't biting.

Andrew J. Starr was the sole owner of the Albuquerque Bail Bonds Company. He's been operating the business for the last year or so, out on Fifth Street in downtown Albuquerque.

"So I did," he continued, as he looked up from behind his desk. "And your name was at the top of list. They said to ask for the Puerto Rican bounty hunter, a guy who's called the huntsman."

I was in Albuquerque on the request made through Frank Marshall at Triple 'A' Bail Bonds. So, without so much as a job since last month, I took him up on his offer, that of tracking, capturing and returning one of his jumpers back to Albuquerque.

It had taken me six and a half hours driving time, and four-hundred-and-fifty miles. It was a Sunday when traffic wasn't as heavy on the interstate. And driving cross states, I knew it would have taken me much longer doing peek driving days.

It was a cold windy afternoon. I had no idea how cold it was, only that I wanted to get back to Tucson soon and feel the warm air once again. And to compound my situation, my car's heater was on the fritz; I knew I should have gotten it fixed before I left. Piss poor planning on my part. I had on my black leather jacket, black colored shirt, blue jeans and my combat boots and of course my Stetson.

Prior to leaving Tucson, I called Starr at the phone number given to be by Frank Marshall, one of two partners at Triple 'A' bail bonds. Starr wanted to meet up with him at a place of his choosing. Then, I was supposed to follow him to his office.

So, right about noon, we met up at the appointed place, a gas station just off State Highway Twenty-five, and exit 224. And as the cold wind slowly nipped at my face and hands, going all the way to my bones, I struck my hands in my pocket, looking for a little comforting warmth. Apparently, I hadn't dressed warm enough! After exchanging pleasantries, Starr asked me to follow him to his office.

Andrew Starr was a square jawed, well-proportioned man about five-foot-eleven, maybe six feet tall. He had a ruddy complexion and dark black eyes with a full head of hair. He was wearing a light brown coat and dark slacks and brown colored cowboy boots. He looked young and tough. I'd say a man well suited for the job of a bondsman.

We drove for about six miles almost due east and after some fifteen minutes and a stop off for gas for both our cars, we finally arrived.

Christ, I couldn't have found the place on my own, without getting lost. He led me to a one story building set back about fifty yards from the main road. It had two large glass case windows on both sides and in the center was the main office door, also glass cased. There was iron grating on the windows, and door. And above the door was a neon sign that said:

Albuquerque Bail Bonds
Since 1985
Andrew Starr Owner/Agent

WE PARKED SHOULDER TO SHOULDER, AND AS I CLIMBED OUT OF MY LeBaron. Starr climbed out of his 1987 black Mercedes Benz coupe. I noticed it was a 550SL. He must've been making easy money to own such a pricey little car.

And it was a beauty!

Locking our cars, we both met at the office's front door. He fiddled with a set of keys, found the one he wanted and unlocked the grating fence and the front door.

Once inside, I was greeted with a warm office environment, with heat from a central furnace, keeping it at a nice warm comfortable level. And it was a most welcomed heat, after being in the cold so long. His office was painted out a cool white. The floor was of light oak wood planks. Up along the front of the office, was a row of several office type cushioned chairs — his visitor lounge area. On one wall were four shoulder high filing cabinets. There was a Coke and candy machine on one wall over to the left side of the main entrance. In the back wall was a two pedestal, dark oak wooden desk, clotted over with file folders and papers, a telephone, answering machine and an in-and-out baskets. Both were brimming over with papers. Behind his desk were two wooden book cases, jammed full with books. And there was a Polaroid camera sitting atop a book — within easy reach; ready to be of use at any given time.

On the wall directly behind his desk was a photograph of a group of individuals in police uniform with Starr being the last one on the left. There was another door on his right side. Later I would learn what was behind that closed door.

So, an ex-cop turned bondsman. Mm, sounded vaguely familiar.

Chapter Twenty-Nine

James Echols

With a fresh pot of hot coffee ready, he offered me a cup.

Ah, black neither cream nor sugar, just the way I like it. Taking a sip of its sweet aroma, I tasted a strong dark French roast cup of coffee. The man certainly had good coffee sense, for an ex-cop. So pulling up a chair I sat across his desk waiting to hear what the details of this bounty entailed.

I smiled and raised my eyebrows slightly at the reference of me being *the best*.

I let out a small cough.

"Thank you. So tell me more about your jumper. On the phone, you were vague about the details, only that the bond was for seventy-five-thousand dollars."

The guy stared at me and sipped at his coffee. Then he smiled and placed the cup on the desk to his side.

"I knew that would get you here."

Starr had what I believed to be a mid-western accent, which I couldn't place. I didn't ask. But it sounded cool.

I eyed Starr with some appreciation. Man after my own heart.

I returned his smile.

"That certainly got me here alright. I've never turned down that kind of money."

"I can see why you're called the huntsman, whoever gave you that moniker, knew what he was talking about. Guess it suits you just fine, hunting after bail skips."

"Yeah, well about that. It was given to me by an old friend."

"Was the friend a cop?"

"Yeah, he's a fed."

He smiled, nodding.

"Yeah, I guessed as much."

A minute later, Andrew Starr, reached over and sorted through his outboxes and found a manila folder full of papers and passed it over the desk to me.

I rose from my chair and took hold of the proffered folder noticing how thick it was. I sat back down and started scanning through it.

"This is a thick file."

"Yes, yes it is. Everything you need to know is in there. Plus there is a certified copy of the bond all signed and sealed. All I ask is that you return the bail jumper to me, not the jail. Can you handle that?"

"I don't see a problem with it."

"Great. Why don't you read over the folder and if you have any questions, I'll try and answer them."

After finishing the last of my coffee, and spending fifteen minutes of reading and scanning through a photograph of my newest jumper, I laid down the folder and stared at Starr.

I frowned and turned to Starr. "Eh, this isn't everything."

Clearly not *everything* was in the folder. I was pretty sure some things were left out. Maybe not intentionally, but left out nevertheless.

Starr nodded.

"Damn, you are good."

"So, what's his story?"

The guy stood up. Fluid and graceful all in one movement letting his confidence show through. He walked around his desk and stopped in front of me.

"I still have more coffee in the pot. Care for another cup? I need a refill."

"Yeah, don't mind if I do. Never turn down a damn good cup of coffee."

After refilling both our cups, Starr sat back behind his desk, and taking a long sip of his coffee, he eyed me.

I stared back. "I'm listening."

Starr grinned, placing down his cup.

"Sure."

The guy leaned back on his seat and folded his arms about his chest, and stared up towards the ceiling. He was apparently gathering his thoughts.

I waited, not saying a word.

He dropped his gaze on me, and took a sip of his coffee. He spoke in an even, unhurried tone. "In a nut shell, James W. Echols was a family man and an addictive gambler. He lost a lot of money to his addiction, even though he had a plush job as an insurance adjuster. But he constantly played the ponies, losing more so than wining. Consequently he owed a great deal of money to his bookie. After being laid off his job, his wife of three years served divorce papers on him. The story goes that Echols became desperate, unable to make ends meet, and with his bookie gunning for him — hell, you can see where this is going. Well one thing led to another, and he ghosts his bookie, with two shots to the guy's chest. This was eight years ago."

I look over at Starr with a perplexed look.

"Interesting story. And he's out already?"

"Yeah, the guy was sentenced to twenty years for the shooting. But six months ago his case was overturned on an appeal."

I took a sip of my coffee. "That's our great justice system at work. Ah hell, give me the good-old days when the law wasn't as complicated and convoluted as it is today."

"Yeah, you got that right."

I shook my head. "So he was sprung from jail, and then committed an armed robbery. Didn't wait long to get into trouble with the law again."

Starr nodded.

"It was an armed robbery of a jewelry store. He was later identified through mug shots by several witnesses. A month later during a traffic stop, he was arrested."

"So, who posted his bond?"

"It was his grandmother."

"Nice."

"According to the grandmother, she believes Echols won't be keeping his next court date. She overheard him talking on the phone about skipping out and heading to Arizona, a place called Apache Junction to be exact. It would seem there's a cousin out there who's willing to take him in for a while."

"So you're turning in the bond?"

"That's why you're here."

"And you have the name and address of this cousin?"

"Sure do. Got it from the grandmother, it's in the folder."

"And do you think Echols knows his grandmother is tuning in the bond?"

"No, I'm pretty sure he doesn't."

"That will make my job that much easier."

Starr shrugged. "I figure it that way too."

"So," I said. "He's a killer and an armed robber. Nice combination."

"Yeah you can say that."

"How much time do I have to get him here to you?"

"Three days. Any more than that and we both lose out."

I quickly looked at him. "My fee is ten percent of the face amount of the bond."

He didn't flinch.

Starr picked up his coffee. He sipped it once, and looked straight at me.

"Yeah, John Marshall told me that's what you charge. You bring him back to me, and I'll have an envelope full of cash ready."

I nodded. "Sounds like a plan."

I got up from my chair ready to leave, and Starr followed suit. We shook hands and stood there in silence for a few seconds. I saw him glanced down at my weapon strapped on my waist.

"What type of weapon you carry, if I may ask?"

Instead of replying, I flipped the end of my jacket, exposing the weapon. I pulled it out, ejected the magazine, and jacked the slide back ejecting the live round in the chamber. Then I reversed my grip on the Colt and handed it over to him.

He said, "I like your 1911. It's a great weapon for close combat shooting. As a matter of fact, I also carry a 1911."

As he said that, he returned the colt.

"Thanks. I see we have the same taste in weapons,"

"Guess so."

I jacked the magazine back in, and chambered a round in my Colt, clicked on the safety and returned it back to its holster.

"So . . . Apache Junction, you know of it?"

"Not really, but I shouldn't have too much of a problem finding it."

"Hey, thanks for coming all the way over here, and taking the case."

"No need to thank me, the money will do nicely." My fee of seven grand will make my wife very happy.

There wasn't any more to say. I finished up the rest of my coffee, and walked out his office to my car. The cold wind was blowing steady as I tucked in my chin against it, and unlocked the LeBaron. Getting in I fired her up. I drove out of the parking lot and tried to remember how to get back on the interstate.

Chapter Thirty

The Watchers

There were two of them.

They were sitting in a red 1984 two-door coupe Dodge Charger, both smoking a 'joint. As they passed it back and forth, they kept a steady surveillance over at the Triple 'A' Bail Bonds office in Tucson.

The weed seemed to mellow them out, not getting them overly high, because they had business to attend to. Once they finished out their 'joint' they both switched over to regular smokes.

They had arrived shortly after ten o'clock that morning. They eased the Charger behind a Chevy pickup truck parked on the other side of the street, about a half a block north of the bail bonds office.

It was a Sunday, and it was their second day of watching. The weather called for a cool day, with temperatures in the mid-sixties. It was cool enough to keep watch for a few hours at a time. They had nothing else better to occupy the day, so they were hoping they could meet up with the asshole sorta . . . Rican; whatever the fuck he was.

They were brothers. They did things together. This was no different. But it wasn't for them. They considered this a big favor for their friend. Knowing once their friend got out of jail, the brothers would stand to have better business with him. They were good at what they did though — bouncing, enforcing and collecting on debts for their boss.

The driver, the older of the two, raised his binoculars keeping a careful watch out at the bail bonds office. There was a white colored four-door Ford sedan parked at the front of the building, probably owned by one of the bondsman, he figured. With the sun's rays shining on his eyes, he could only maintain visual contact for seconds at a time, just till the sun moved away from his field of vision. Then he could spend more time with the binoculars. They were far enough from the office, that they wouldn't rouse suspicion from passing motorist or cops.

Flipping his half spent cigarette out his window, the brother sitting on the passenger seat turned and faced his brother.

"So, you reckon the *wetback* will show?"

His brother thought about it for a second and dropped the binoculars on his lap.

"Well little brother, Serrano did say the bounty hunter does some jobs for them there bail bondsman, time to time."

"Yeah, he says that alright. But ya think he'll show?"

"We're gonna have to wait and see, won't we?"

"Betcha' twenty he don't come today."

"You got yourself a bet, little brother."

They shook hands on it, and then the driver turned back to watching the office.

"Yep, we're gonna be mending some fences here come right, soon enough."

Chapter Thirty-One

Love and Interruptions

Six and a half hours and four-hundred-and-fifty miles later, I arrived home at about 9:30 p.m.

Forty-five minutes later after a late hot dinner with Dolores and our children, I was in the shower getting all the road dirt off my body, and brushing my teeth. I got out of the shower, and grabbing a towel started drying off. Then naked, I walked over to the dresser and grabbed a pair of boxer shorts and pulled them on.

As I turned around, I saw Dolores leaning against the closed door to our bedroom. She had just tucked the kids into bed a moment before. Now, as she leaned on the door with her arms crossed at her breasts, wearing a pink colored opened shower robe, I caught her staring at me with a little smile and curled up lips. She then pulled back loose strands of her black hair that had fallen over her face.

Still staring at me, I started walking toward the bed, and stopped.

I smiled. "Who are you looking at?"

Unmistakable she was looking at me, but it was the way she was doing it that begged the question.

"You, my sexy husband."

She sounded slightly raspy, with a slight husky catch in her sexy voice. Wow!

I gently tilted my head to the side, and winked at her smiling as my eyes widened. I let my gaze drop to her lean strong body, and took a quick peek through her half opened robe. I saw she only had her pink laced panties on, and no bra.

My gaze kept going lower to the mound between her legs, and her long silky legs. The robe she had on wasn't flattering her at all, failing to show the outlining of her curves and of her hips, and the way it perfectly hugged her well-proportioned rounded formed breasts. I didn't need my imagination to know what lay underneath the robe – I knew!

I just stood there, hands on my hips, trying to act cool, which I wasn't. My heart was beating way too fast as I sucked in my breath, trying to stay in control.

She abruptly leaned away from the door, and slipped off the robe dropping it on the floor by her feet, exposing her almost naked body to me.

I inhaled, and slowly let it out as I removed the only piece of clothing I had on — my boxer shorts, exposing myself fully. Without a word, and in a most appreciative manner, I extended my hand to her. She reached out and taking my hand, I led her to the edge of the bed.

We moved into each other, and as our bodies melted into one, we kissed passionately, lovingly and long, exploring our mouths with a hunger born of a deep seated emotion and desire.

We parted and I gently laid her on the bed flat on her back. Then as I pressed my own body onto hers, she spread opened her legs wide . . .

Suddenly from our bedroom door, came a low insistent knocking, which grew louder with each passing second.

My eyes opened wide and so did hers, and as I came off her, I bent to pick up my shorts she quickly crawled out of bed. Finding her robe by the door, she patiently waited till I had on my shorts before answering the door. As she opened it wide, we saw our son, Raul-Esteban my one year old, standing there.

He was rubbing his eyes. "Mommy, I can't sleep."

She picked him up in her arms and gently rubbed his head.

"What's wrong, honey?"

"I'm scared, Mommy."

"There's nothing to be scared of, honey. Mommy will come and stay with you till you fall asleep. Okay?"

Raul-Esteban snuggled closer to his mother and rested his head on her shoulder, and closed his eyes.

Dolores turned and faced me, smiling, maybe reading my mind.

"Sorry, Victor," she said.

I just shrugged and smiled back, "You're going to owe me for this later."

Then still smiling, she turned away.

And there went our moment and the mood.

Chapter Thirty-Two

Apache Junction

Apache Junction, Arizona

NORTH-EAST OF PHOENIX, ARIZONA, ON INTERSTATE 10; CUTTING EAST ON State Highway 60, and further on to the South Goldfield exit through some blacktops and gravel roads, I drove my LeBaron.

I followed it north to the intersection of Apache Trail, then east of that to Old West Highway, which intersected right through to my destination — Apache Junction.

The area teemed with history of the Old Wild West. It has long been the subject of varied stories, mystery, Indian lore and tales of lost treasures of gold. According to what I've read, seems that in the 1860s gold and silver were discovered in the old Superstitions Mountains, and in 1864 at Skeleton Canyon, Arizona, the enigmatic Apache War Chief Geronimo had surrendered to the US Army.

Apache Junction is bounded by the Superstition Mountains on the east, said to be the home of the Lost Dutchman's mine — or so the story goes, and the Goldfield Ghost town toward the north. Today, it roughly has a population of around nine thousand souls.

It was hard going, what with a used street map of the area which I'd purchased at an old Shell gas station, just after getting off the inter-state. The map had some ripped off corners, and it was the last one he had left, the old geezer behind the counter said. I paid two dollars for it, but eventually it got me there.

Five minutes later, I slowed to a stop at the side of the road, and opened the map once more. Finding what I was looking for, I laid the map on the passenger seat, slid the LeBaron back on the road, and started looking for South Phelps Street and West Fifth Ave.

Once I arrived at the intersection, my next point of reference was South Higo Circle. And there it was the second two story brick house on the left, right off of South Higo Circle.

The trip hadn't taken me more than four hours, tops. I left Tucson right around one o'clock that cool Monday afternoon. Packing what I felt was needed into my tactical gear bag was my pistol-grip Mossberg twelve gauge shotgun, extra ammunition, and an extra set of hand-cuffs. Then I kissed my wife and kids, and said my goodbye's. I didn't tell them how long I was going to me, because I really didn't know how long it was going to take me, which honestly, was the truth.

I slowly rolled past the house noting a Toyota four-door sedan and a Dodge pickup truck parked on the driveway and also noticing the absence of life on or near the home. And seeing that in was late in the afternoon when most families were sitting down at the dinner table, it probably would explain the absence of life in the area.

But the most interesting thing about the house was the Toyota. It was the same Toyota registered to my jumper.

That was easy enough.

It was ten minutes later when I pulled onto the curb on South Sierra Vista Drive. I was directly across the roadway about two-hundred yards south of my target house. This is where I've decided to setup my surveillance point. All the other places that I've seen, just didn't give me the visibility or the concealment I was looking for.

And it certainly was a good spot.

I parked behind an old white colored 1969 Volkswagen Karmann-ghia. There were tall trees on both sides of the road affording me some concealment from those at the house. I didn't know how long I'd be there, so I had mentally chosen a secondary spot just in case this one got compromised.

Once settled in, I pulled out the case folder given to me by Andrew Starr. Opening the folder, I casually flipped through all the sheets. He had a lot of pertinent information listed. Plus some that I didn't really need. But, it's always better to have more than mere scant information to work with.

In particular, there was a state property information sheet listing the owners of the house that was the subject of my surveillance. It was owned by a Michael and Corry Newcomb and purchased five years ago. Michael, being *the* cousin that was said to had offered James Echols, my jumper, a safe haven from which he could hide out in.

Skipping through more of the sheets, I came across a photo copy of the registration certificate showing ownership of the Toyota to my jumper.

Yep, it was the same Toyota parked in the driveway.

Then I pulled out a color Polaroid photograph of Echols. The front profile showed a male Caucasian, with long curly black hair that grew past his shoulders, light blue eyes and unshaved stubble of beard and mustache. He had a bodybuilder's physique. And he had a slight narrow three inch scar that ran down his left cheek. Not new, maybe a year or two old. Not an imposing figure, nor dangerous looking either, but still a killer and an accomplished thief nevertheless.

I replaced the mugshot back in the folder, and dropped it on the passenger seat. The outside temperature was dropping, getting colder by the minute. I put the heater dial over to the hot position, and plucked out my binoculars from the equipment bag.

From behind the windshield of my car, I aimed the binoculars over to the house and surveyed it, and also the area surrounding it. All that was visible through the trees was the side of the house and the two parked vehicles.

I was yet to see a living soul.

A few minutes later, I saw a young couple walking out of a house directly across from my target house. They slowly started walking hand-in-hand down the street approaching the crossroads. They seemed to be lovers out for a stroll after partaking of their dinner.

The sun was rapidly setting, and as I took a glance at my watch noticed that it just struck the eight o'clock hour. So, I've spent two hours of steady surveillance without anyone coming out of their homes trying to check me out, or having police cruisers spoiling my fun.

So far so good, I thought.

But, the night was still young, and anything could happen.

Chapter Thirty-Three

Target House

Fifteen minutes later the Newcomb's, front door opened bathing the main passageway in light. Two women walked out. And as one of them closed the door behind them, they slowly walked toward the Dodge pickup truck. The older looking woman climbed in the passenger seat. The younger of the two climbed in the driver's side. Twice I heard it cracking up, trying to catch, and on the third try, it caught starting up with loud exhaust pipes. And as it backed out of the driveway onto the street, the Dodge's headlights came on.

Seconds later, it came directly past the crossroads. As they drove past me, the driver didn't even glance once in my direction, which was a good omen.

I was in one of those interesting predicaments once again. I get those from time to time. Sometimes it works out, but most times it doesn't.

So here was my predicament; I could approach the house, now that the woman had given me a little leeway to work with, break in and arrest my jumper. I figured there was one other person in the house, besides my jumper — the cousin. So those odds were good if I decided to storm the place.

Or, I could wait it out; wait to see if my jumper came out of the house, then take him down before he made it to his car. This option seemed the best course of action. Ultimately, it was the one I went with. Also I didn't want to go chasing him up and down the streets, where I could easily loose him in traffic. Or get pulled over by a patrol car for speeding. No, this had to go down the easy way — no cops nor anyone getting in my way.

A quick snatch-N'-grab was what I was hoping for.

But my decision necessitated moving from my present location, and being closer to the house. Time was of the essence if I wanted to bring him down by his car. And the moment he opened the house door and I identified him, that was the moment I had to move quickly and decisively.

Plan for the worst and hope for the best. So, thinking along those lines, I decided on bringing along my shotgun for close up shooting if it came to it. But I also had my trusty Colt strapped on for backup.

Earlier during my drive through of the area, I noticed a *For Sale* sign on one of the homes close to my target's house. It appeared to be unin-habited, so I noted it as my secondary surveillance spot. What better place to pull a short-term surveillance from, I figured.

I waited about ten minutes before making my move. Once I had the car started, I put it in gear and slowly pulled away from the curb, heading toward the crossroad then up through it toward my next surveillance spot.

Approaching the *For Sale* sign on the house, I veered over to it, and backed in onto the driveway, almost touching the garage door, and killed the engine. I didn't notice anyone coming out to inquire, so I thought I was okay, for the time being.

While the cooling of the engine ticked quietly on, I kept my silent vigil. I was hoping against hope that my jumper showed before someone became suspicious and called the cops on me. That was always a distinct possibility. Something I'd always lived with when it came to pulling surveillance.

Chapter Thirty-Four

Plan B

It was a little past midnight, when a set of headlights approached from the crossroads. It slowly reduced its speed and rolled up onto the driveway of my target house. The Dodge pickup had returned, but with just the driver — the young woman.

Before she climbed out of the cab of the truck, the front door opened. With the light from inside the house, I saw my jumper framed against the door, waiting.

He was wearing a pair of blue jeans, white T-shirt under an untucked long sleeved red checkered shirt. No doubt about it, he was James W. Echols, my jumper! Seconds later, they stepped into the house closing the door behind them, once more bathing the area in darkness. So now I had direct confirmation that he was in the house.

Sitting in my car gave me time to think. Predictable, I thought over my options once again.

Occasionally it pays to go into a situation with a well laid out plan of action. But most times, most plans just don't work out the way you want. That's why you should always have a back-up plan. A plan B, sort of speak.

Just in case.

I didn't have a plan B.

But I needed one.

My mind revolved around the timespan it would take me to reach my jumper, once he came out of the house. *Did I have enough time to get to him before he slips into his car, starts it up and pulls away?* I asked myself. Maybe — maybe not.

So I needed a more viable plan.

Then it hit me.

I had the makings for a plan B.

Of course I had to admit, there was also a timing element involved here as well. My plan wasn't infallible, some unknown complication would force me to alter plan B. But if I'd been careful enough, it should go down without a hitch.

A couple of minutes later, I took my shotgun from the back seat, made sure I had a round down the rabbit hole, then clicked on the safety. Leaving my Stetson on the passenger seat, I exited the car, being careful to quietly close the door.

With only the lighting coming from some of the homes, I waited in the darkness, trying hard to stay as alert as I possibly could.

I stood standing in front of my car for a few seconds longer. I did a quick scan up and down the street, making sure no one was up and about that could conceivably spot my, what they would think, suspicious actions.

Then I slowly walked away from the driveway. Moving silently I veered over to my right and made my way to my target's house. I held my shotgun down on my right side, ready in case I needed it.

Through the darkness I inched my way past one house, than another, finally arriving at the side of my target's house. I wasn't sure if anyone had spotted me. I couldn't afford a mistake at this point. Although this side of the house was in total darkness too: Ready-made for hiding.

And it was utterly quiet and still.

Then, thick clouds came rolling through; obscuring what was left of the half moon, bathing the area in total darkness. Now, I was positive no one could see me there.

Placing the shotgun across my lap, I slowly bent at the knees and squatted down, and resigned myself to my waiting game.

Surveillance is all about standing back and finding out what could happen next. Just as in the military, this game is the process of 'hurry-up and wait.' A game all military and police officers are use to.

So, not even ten minutes had past, when I heard the front door opening. I carefully took a look around the edge of the wall I was up against. Not taking any chances, after seeing someone closing the front door, I slowly stood up keeping my shotgun held loosely at my right side, ready for action.

I took another look. That's when I saw him, my guy, Echols slowly making his way down the driveway.

I let him get half way to his car, when I made my move. Quickly stepping out of my hiding place, with my shotgun at the ready, I rounded the edge of the house. Stepping onto the driveway, I quickly noticed that I was just a few yards behind Echols.

With his back toward me, I slowly approached keeping my shotgun pointed center-mast of his back. Then I stopped.

It is at this junction point where anything could happen. This was all on him. He only had one option — surrender. Anything else would not end well. It was his choice.

"Echols turn around slowly. Keep your hands at your side." He stopped and very slowly turned. Facing me head on he kept his hands loosely at his sides. And with a surprised look on his face, his eyes centered more on the shotgun than at me.

Echols raised his eyebrows.

"What's going on?"

"I'm a bail bondsman, going to take you back to New Mexico. You make any sudden moves I don't like, and I fill you up with buck shot. Understood?"

He didn't say a word, just kept looking at me and the shotgun. He had the look of a man who showed all signs of submission which was what I was hoping for.

"Do you understand?" I repeated.

"Yeah, I understand."

"Good then. Slowly walk toward me and keep your hands where I can see them."

Taking a few forward steps he stopped about an arm's length away, still keeping his arms at his side.

He took a deep breath staring straight at me. "Why are you doing this?"

Apparently, the guy still just didn't get it.

I withdrew a set of cuff. "Buddy, just turn around slowly."

Keeping his hands in sight down by his side, Echols slowly turned his back to me. Suddenly, he broke away making a mad run for it. He thought he would catch me unaware, but I was ready for him.

Ah shit, I thought. *Here we go!*

Acting quickly and decisively, and not letting him get too far, I quickly took two steps and got to within half an arm's length from him. Then before he could take another step, I struck him a blow to the side of his back with the butt end of my shotgun.

Echols went sprawling to the concrete, head first, completely stunned. After his initial shock of being struck in the back, he tried to rise on his wobbling knees. But by the sounds of his coughs and moans, he was in pain.

As he stumbled backwards, I was on him. I placed the barrel of the shotgun up against his face.

I was thinking: *Did the guy really think he could get away when he was so close to me. Not really!*

Just then I felt an involuntary flow of adrenaline kick in. I breathed in breathed out, slowly getting myself back to normal.

"Go ahead try that again, asshole."

Echols stared up at me. His mouth opened, but didn't say a word. And as he laid there on his back, he didn't give any indication he was going to run again.

"Turn on your stomach."

When he didn't comply fast enough, I kick his side once. With a loud howl of pain, he immediately rolled over.

I knelt next to him and finally cuffed his hands behind his back, and patted him down. My hand felt the contours of a gun handle. I wasn't surprised with what I found tucked in his belt, a Smith &

Wesson 357 Magnum. I transferred the gun to the front of my belt. I'll take that as a keepsake, never knew when it could come in handy.

I was completely happy with myself; I didn't give him the time to draw his weapon. The situation could have been turned very ugly, very quickly. That's for sure.

Helping him to his feet, still a little stunned, I pushed him toward my car. Getting there without further mishap, I opened the passenger door.

"Get in, Echols."

Once he was safely tucked in the seat, I came around the car, opened the passenger door, and leaned in. I got his hands to the iron bar and cuffed him to it. He wasn't going to give me any further trouble after that.

Getting behind the wheel, I started seeing people outside their front doors. They were looking over at me, so the curious ones were out. I knew then that I had to leave very quickly before the cops eventually come to investigate.

I turned over the ignition and started up the LeBaron. Once I had it in gear, I took my foot of the brake and slowly pulled away.

Then once onto the street I saw a couple of people in their pajamas staring my way as I drove past. I turned left at the crossroads and as I did, I saw in the distance the flashing lights of a patrol car as it slowly made its way behind me. I knew where it was going. Oh yeah. Luckily, I was going in the opposite direction.

I felt rather safe enough after that.

Chapter Thirty-Five

Ten Percent Fee

With several nature calls behind us, and once to tank up for gas, we finally made it to Albuquerque without cops pulling me over.

Along the way, Echols kept complaining about his back: *You should've run, and then you wouldn't be hurting, jerk.* I was thinking.

He then asked the most inevitable of questions. He asked, "What am I under arrest for?"

"I'll let your bondman tell you all about it, once I get you back to him. Till then just shut up, sit back and enjoy the ride."

At our last stop, I placed a call to Andrew Starr and had him meet me at our last meeting place, because, for the life of me, I wasn't going to find the place without his help.

An hour later, I made the meeting place. And there was Starr's car parked just off to the side. I stopped behind his car, and saw him climbing out of his, as I too stepped out to meet him.

We then met half way.

"I see you made it back in good time."

"I try to oblige."

"Want to see him?"

"You bet."

Once at my car, I opened the door and Echols turned to face us.

He took a deep breath and looked up. "You're my bondsman. Why am I back?"

"All in good time, James, all in good time."

Closing the door, we walked back to his car.

"Let him stay in your car," Starr said. "And you can follow me to the office."

"I'll be right behind you."

Once we arrived at his office, I secured Echols into a makeshift holding cell Starr had in the back of his office. It was the room I noticed the first time I was there. I now knew what was inside. We went back to the front, where he handed me an envelope with my ten percent fee that he picked up from the top of his desk.

"Thanks. It's real kind of you to pay me in cash instead of a check."

"It's what we agreed on. Oh, can I call you if I'm in need again?"

"Anytime, I'd be happy to work with you."

"You do good work."

"It's what I *do*."

We shook hands and said our goodbyes. I got in my car and headed back to Tucson. It was a good payday, and it didn't take me too long this time.

Yeah, a quick snatch-N'-grab.

And a good payday added in.

If I'd known what was waiting for me in Tucson, I would've stayed another day or so.

Chapter Thirty-Six

The Brothers

It was a cool windy November morning, typical for this time of the year.

They've been on watch for the last two hours. They had it all planned out. But they had to make contact first. So they sat to wait.

They were parked on Congress Street, behind a brand new, blue-colored, four-door Volvo. It was their setup point. And they were positioned to wait for as long as it took, until making contact with their intended victim — the Puerto Rican.

Congress Street teemed with heavy vehicular and pedestrian traffic, early morning commuters on their way to work. A few minutes ago Alan Miller saw a coffee shop down the street which had opened for business.

Alan Miller, a skinny guy about one hundred sixty-five pounds with a five-foot-nine frame, wearing jeans and a dark colored jacket over a white T-shirt and sneakers, occupied the Dodge Charger's passenger seat; he was the younger of the two brothers. He appeared agitated, but mostly bored.

He turned to face his brother Richard, the driver who at six-foot and two-hundred pounds, drew a sharp contrast to Alan. He wore a long sleeved checker shirt over a black colored T-shirt, jeans and cowboy boots. Alan was the brains behind the two. They were used to the waiting, both being ex-military, infantry man in the army. Both draftees who'd seen combat during the closing years of the Vietnam War. They now worked as "collectors" for a local bookie, and getting paid better than the army ever did, with better medical benefits to boot.

Two weeks ago Alan Miller had received a call from his friend and business partner, Angel Serrano who was currently in jail. Serrano had offered the brothers a job along with a large sum of money. They were to find and take down a local Tucson bounty hunter.

So after their watch on Sunday didn't go the way they planned, they skipped Monday's altogether. Their boss had pressing business for them, and he couldn't be kept waiting.

But on Tuesday morning bright and early they were back, keeping up the vigil on the bail bonds office down the road. They knew sooner or later they would make contact with the bounty hunter.

Richard Miller sighed. "So, what time is it?"

It had only been ten minutes since the last time he'd ask.

"It's time for ya to buy a watch."

"Come on, what time is it?"

Alan Miller didn't answer.

Richard Miller playfully jabbed Alan in the side. Not hard, just enough to get his attention.

"Well?"

His brother Alan slowly turned facing him. When he did, Richard attempted another jab, but Alan used his arm to fend it off, giving him a wicked little smile.

Alan shook his head. "If you weren't my brother, I'd kick your ass."

"Sure you would. So what time is it?"

"It's eight o'clock exactly. Happy?"

"How long ya thinking of staying here?"

"You know you're a pain in the ass, right? But let's say till five. Then we call it quits, and come back tomorrow morning."

"Good, Susie wants to go shopping this afternoon."

"Hey little brother, you know this comes first."

"Yeah, I know. But I promised Susie."

Alan Miller gave a single brusque shake of his head.

"She's got you wrapped up in her little finger, you know."

"Well, if I don't take her, I don't get any."

They both cracked out laughing.

It was then that Alan remembered the coffee shop, and remembered too that he had not eaten breakfast or had his coffee. He gazed over at his brother.

"Hey, why don't ya head on over and get us some coffee and something to munch on."

"Yeah, I could use a bite to eat myself about now."

Chapter Thirty-Seven

Easy Come, Easy Go

It was a Tuesday morning and just a little after eight.

I'd just finished my shower, dressed and slipped on a pair of warm slippers and walked down the hallway into the kitchen.

Dolores was busy making breakfast. She had coffee on. Coming up behind her, I snuggled up close and gently gave her a kiss on the cheek.

"Good morning, beautiful."

I detected a tinge of agitation in her voice.

"Well, I see you finally woke up."

She turned around after placing the last of the pancakes on a plate. Now we were facing each other staring into each other's eyes; patient, quiet. I didn't say anything waiting on her to start it.

"You came in late last night. Is everything alright?"

The agitation in her voice was gone, replaced with a little alarm and concern.

I didn't say anything.

With our oldest child, Carmen in school and with our two boys who had just finished their breakfast and slipping off to their rooms, it just left me and Dolores to finish our breakfast. She waited for me to wake and have breakfast together; a very thoughtful woman. It was those little things that endeared me so to her.

After placing the plates on the dining table, and pouring coffee for the two of us, I looked over at her.

"It's nothing."

She just closed her eyes for a few moments. Opening them again, I felt as if she was staring right into my soul. She had that effect on me.

"You're not a good liar, Victor."

"It's nothing really, just tired. It was a long drive to New Mexico and back. Guess I'm road weary, nothing more."

"Honey, I know you never want to discuss your cases with me, I'm here whenever you need me. You know that, right?"

"Yeah honey, thanks means a lot."

After a brief silence as we finished up our breakfast, and once I had the dishes cleaned, we sat back to finish our coffee.

"Anyway, I have cash from my last case. All the bills will be caught up. So how you want to spend it?"

She looked at me with a twinkle in her eyes. Then she set her coffee cup down.

She smiled. "I know exactly how to spend it."

Oh my.

Did she ever.

Easy Come, easy go.

WE WERE BACK HOME FROM OUR FAMILY SHOPPING TRIP, AFTER SPENDING A large chunk of the cash on clothing, groceries and what I thought were other inconsequential items.

So, after playing with the kids in the backyard, and having a cold beer, I decided to take a ride over to Montiel bail bonds, then a trip over to Frank Marshal's office to see if they had any cases I could start on. Plus, I needed to get out of the house for a while. I was growing a little restless, and felt I needed to get back on a case soon.

Chapter Thirty-Eight

Knife to a Gun Fight

I arrived at Lupita's bail bonding office in the middle of the afternoon. The sun was just starting to slowly descend in the west, as the northeast winds became colder with each passing minute.

I did a quick drive around the block, which was my nature and didn't spot any unusual parked cars. There wasn't anyone that could pose any immediate threat.

I finally parked in front of her office. Slipping out of my car, I locked it and slowly walked toward the main entrance. Once inside, her receptionist told me that Lupita was in court on a bail hearing and wasn't due back for a couple of hours. Well, that was that. No business here, at least till she returned.

Getting back in my car, I made a slow U-turn coming out onto Stone Avenue. Straightening the LeBaron, I then took a left and headed out to Triple A Bail Bonds. Maybe my luck will change and I'll grab a case with Fred Luna or Frank Marshall.

Fifteen minutes later, driving on Broadway Boulevard I made my way onto Congress Street, with Triple A's office toward the left side of the road about a hundred yards up ahead.

I live a life unlike that of most police officers, where at any given moment I stood to be shot, knifed, gunned down in an alleyway, or just followed by anyone wanting to do me harm, as was now the case. And God only knew how many enemies I've made in my run. I have bagged some very deadly mean men since becoming a bounty hunter. Some of them feared me, but most hated me. And those that hated me wanted me six-feet under.

With twilight fast approaching, the evening was turning into a cold November night. Plus, traffic was still slightly heavy. A lot of commuters were starting to head home after a long day, so I had to keep my speed down to about fifteen miles per hour.

Before approaching Triple A's offices, I decided to circle the block once. Then about a hundred yards into Congress Street, I saw what appeared to be a red Dodge Charger. It was parked on the right side of the street, with the engine running, smoke blowing out of the exhaust. As I drove past it, I saw two men in the front seats. The driver casually looked my way as I drove by. It was a quick glance, but I also saw several cigarette butts lying on the ground by the driver's door. It could be nothing, or then again. They had surely aroused my suspicion and it set off alarms in my head, which is why I decided on a second pass.

Coming around the block on my second go around, I didn't stop. Instead, I drove slowly past letting them get a peek at me. As I quickly glanced their way, the guy behind the wheel looked over at my car then stared straight at me. What I saw flash across his face was some sort of recognition. It became apparent to me that he knew who I was.

Jesus H. Christ! How what, I thought. Were they here for me? I thought so, since the look the driver gave me said it all. Or was I being paranoid?

Damn right I was. I didn't think these two guys were acting on their own; no way. Someone had given them my description and that of my car. And someone was playing a deadly game with me.

I felt that this could well be connected to one or two of my prior jumpers. Guy's who promise to get at me for hauling them back to jail. Someone was trying to keep their promise — had to be.

No use thinking about that now. Now I needed to know their intentions, which I surmised weren't going to be good.

I smiled, thinking that earlier in the day I felt restless and bored; now here I was back in the fray, in action mode once more.

I kept on going. Checking my rearview mirror, I saw their car pull out of the curb, get into the flow of traffic staying about three car lengths behind me.

I continued to drive as if I didn't have a tail. I had to know if it was me they were after, before I was forced to show my hand.

So I started taking some evasive maneuvers. At the next intersection, I turned left and a few moments later so did the Dodge Charger.

Okay then I said to myself, let's try this once more. So I hung a right at the next street and sure enough, the Charger stayed with me.

Okay, I now had confirmation!

Now I needed to find someplace quiet. Somewhere I could force my hand, get them out of their car and see what they were made of. But it wasn't going to be easy. I needed just the right place to try and stage a showdown.

And I knew just the place.

I got back on West Congress Street. I took it all the way under the interstate, past South Cuesta Avenue, with the Charger still tailing me about four car lengths behind me. And as the road curved around toward the south, I saw exactly where I wanted to go. A few yards ahead I made a left turn onto North Congress Terrace, a dirt road. I slowed slightly, letting them catch sight of my car. I didn't want them to lose me.

And it was a good spot. There were several abandoned homes, two alleyways and an empty dirt parking lot, completely away from prying eyes.

I came to a stop, turned off the LeBaron, and waited for the Charger to stop behind me before climbing out. And they came rather slowly, maybe expecting an ambush.

Stopping about two car lengths behind my car, I saw them both exit the Charger. As their doors closed, I too exited my car and drew my Colt. It was chambered and ready with the safety off, hammer pulled back. I held it behind my back. As I faced them, they slowly started walking toward me, one on either side about two yards apart.

They looked like the cold hard professionals types. They knew what they were doing, and it showed.

Yeah, professionals!

But, so was I.

You would say that stuff like this only happens in the movies, right?

Think again.

As they drew nearer, I saw they both held what appeared to be military Ka-bar knives. These were ugly looking knifes. It had a blade length of about seven inches if memory serves me correctly. It was designed primarily for the military as the main fighting knife. And these two hoods held a knife each. Apparently, they didn't want the sounds of gunfire to attract the cops, or maybe the knives were their favorite killing weapon.

So they came for a knife fight then. Alright, I meant to disappoint them. But I didn't show my Colt just yet.

Slowly and very deliberately, I moved away from the side of my car still with my gun held behind my back.

"You guys looking for someone," I said. "Or did you lose something here?"

The bigger of the two smiled at me.

"Me and my brother here, we want you asshole."

I sighed and took a deep breath, but didn't say another word. They didn't waste time talking either.

Slowly they spread themselves out some more. Apparently they had some experience in this kind of fighting. Once they saw I was stepping away from my car, they looked over at each other.

Suddenly and without a word, they charged me from both sides. The closest to me was the tall heavy set brother. The moment he came swinging his Ka-bar in a figure-eight motion — up and down and around movements — and as his blade made its upward movement, he was almost on me. From the corner of my eye I saw his brother momentarily halt his forward charge, apparently to let his brother draw first blood; that was my opening.

Without a moment's hesitation, I withdrew my gun hand from around my back. Holding the Colt by my side, I took a step back raised it and aimed toward the lower part of his body, and shot him once in his right leg.

With a howl of pain he dropped to the ground, forgetting the blade as he clutched his right leg trying to stem the flow of blood that gushed out of him, which was starting to soak his pants leg.

I took a quick step forward, wanting to put my boot to his face. But just at that precise moment, his brother recovered from the initial shock of seeing his brother getting shot. He rushed me with a loud yell.

He came at me in a straight thrust maneuver intended to stab me in the side of my body. But just as the blade reached me, I did a quick 360 degree turn at the same time deflecting his blade with my left arm, and came round behind him. Taking a step back from him, just as he tried regaining his stance, and holding my Colt with both hands, close to my mid-section, I put a .45 caliber bullet in his left calf too.

Yelling and howling with pain and the shock of getting shot, he too fell on the ground grabbing his leg, trying desperately with both hands to stop the flow of blood spilling out of him onto the ground.

I did my best not to kill them. Just wasn't my style anymore. Also I needed some answers.

As I holstered my Colt, I walked over to the first guy I'd shot. He was moaning and groaning with pain, but not as loudly now. Bending down I picked up his Ka-bar. I leaned in and held the point of the knife inches from his face.

"So, I know you two?"

Defiant to the end the guy was, even as his eyes lit up at the sight of the tip of the blade, just mere inches from his face. He clenched his teeth. He said, "Fucked you wetback."

I grabbed his hair, none too gentle, twisted his head to the side and slowly slipped the tip of blade into his neck. It was just enough to draw a tickle of blood.

"I need answers, now!"

"Okay, okay, stop okay. I'll tell you what you want to know."

As I let go of his hair, I withdrew the tip of the blade from his neck, but held it close to this eyes.

"That's a good boy. So, who put you up to this?"

"A guy called Angel Serrano said he wanted you dead."

"How you get on to me?"

"Angel told me what kind of car you drove and gave me a description of you."

"Yeah, okay, but how you know where to make contact?"

"Angel, he said you worked with Triple 'A' bail bonds. So we decided to wait it out for you there."

To my left side I heard his brother still moaning with pain. Turning toward him, I saw he wasn't going to get up any time soon.

I returned my attention to his brother. I shot him a violent look and raising my trigger finger.

"Consider this a warning. You come looking for me again, I won't be thinking of just a leg shot. You understand?"

"Yeah . . ."

"You go to the cops, and you'll find me on your door step. Got it?"

"Yeah, I got it."

I searched them for weapons, and not finding any, I pulled out their wallet, and removed their driver's licenses.

I waived the licenses in my hand.

"Now I know where you guys live."

Getting back up, I started walking back to my car, and threw the Ka-bar away. As I opened the driver's door, I paused for a minute trying to listen for police sirens out in the distance. But I didn't hear any. Doubtless, this had been a good spot.

Getting behind the wheel, I turned on the ignition and heard the roar of the engine coming alive, and putting it in first gear I drove straight out onto West Congress Street and headed for home.

Like my car coming alive, I felt the same way.

I'll handle Serrano later.

Book Four

Alfonso Luis Chavez

Chapter Thirty-Nine

Attempted Murder

December 1987, South Tucson, Arizona

TWO SHOTS RANG OUT LOUD CLEAR AND UNMISTAKABLE!

It came from a small caliber handgun, slightly louder than a .22 caliber, maybe a .38. But certainly nothing larger than that, he guessed.

He froze momentarily, immobile, listening as he motioned for his wife to be quiet.

She asked, "What was that?"

"Shut up," he mumbled irritably.

When the next door neighbor, a tall lean middle-aged man, with long, thick white hair wearing pajama bottoms and matching long sleeve shirt heard the shots, he immediately knew what they were. Hell, he should know, he served in the army once with a tour in Southeast Asia. And it happened at night, when sounds carried further and louder. Shit! And he was just about getting ready for bed and had turned off his TV after watching his favorite series *WiseGuy*.

Several minutes before hearing the shots, there'd been a loud continuous commotion coming from the occupants of the apartment on his left; the same apartment where the shots originated, as if they were having a very heated verbal and physical altercation.

He and his wife heard yelling and things crashing against the other side of the paper-thin walls. He banged on it a couple of times to get them to quit, but no dice. They just kept it up. A few moments later, after the gun shots, he heard a door slamming shut. And as he ran over to his window, he saw someone, maybe a Mexican, slowly walk out of the apartment and stand by the railing just staring down, looking shocked and disoriented.

He then saw the guy slowly shaking his head, talking to himself maybe in Spanish. He couldn't be sure though, then gathering himself up he started to run. The stairs were just four doors down the hallway and no one was in or about the landing walkway to impede his getaway. The guy suddenly came to a stop at the top of the stairs, and just stood there for a moment or two, like maybe trying to decide what to do next.

The neighbor, trying to get a better look at the man opened his front door and calmly stood by the entrance. He looked over at the guy, who quickly glanced over once at the neighbor. Then taking the steps two at a time he bounded down the stairs.

The neighbor later stated to the police, that he saw the man holding a gun in his left hand. And as the guy made the last of the steps, the neighbor saw him tuck the gun into the waistband of his pants, and cover it up with his jacket.

Police responding to the shooting, discovered the occupant of the apartment, a Mexican male, who was slumped over a chair, with life-threatening injuries. He had sustained two gunshots to the chest, fired at close range, but survived his injuries.

The shooter was later identified as Alfonso Luis Chavez, a Mexican in the US on a work visa. He had a full-time job as a truck driver. Further investigation disclosed he had no past criminal history to speak of, just a minor speeding ticket. Days later, a felony arrest warrant was issued for his arrest. Two weeks later, US Marshals acting on a tip, arrested Chavez at a relative's home without incident.

During his initial bond hearing, bail was set at seventy-five thousand dollars. He was not considered a flight risk. But two weeks later he failed to appear for his initial court date and disappeared without a trace.

A day after Chavez went FTA, Lupita Shestko-Montiel, of Montiel Bail Bonds, offered me the case.

Chapter Forty

Rosy the Prostitute

I was doing the guy a favor.

Well not so much a favor since the bounty money was good, for a guy named Jacob Knowles, a local bail bondsman with whom I hadn't worked before.

Knowles wanted me to find a prostitute named Rosalinda Garza, who went by the nick name of Rosy. She was a twenty-three-year-old brunette, with a low cost bond of ten-thousand dollars, which Knowles posted a couple of weeks ago. Now she'd gone missing and no one seemed to know where. To make matters worse, she was FTA (Failure to Appear) for her initial court appearance.

He could've just let the courts issue a bench warrant, and let the cops pick her ass up. But he wasn't about to lose ten grand that easily. No way.

Rosy promised Knowles and had signed a sworn affidavit, stating that she'd show up for her hearing. But when she failed to do so, and not bothering to make any attempt to call him, she left him with no alternative but to put her back in jail.

That's where I came in.

Knowles had appealed to me on two separate occasions, but both times I'd refused his offer. One, I just didn't know how trustworthy he was. Two, the bond was so damn small I would be wasting my time and my own expenses.

On his last call though, he tried to soften me up. He said he'd heard about my 'rep' and my uncanny knack of getting jumpers back in jail before warrants could be issued; it didn't work. But what did it for me was the three thousand dollars he offered to get her back in jail quickly within a set time frame. Not being the type to shy away from three grand, I finally accepted.

Arriving at his office located out on Silverbell Road and West Congress Street, we met at the front double doors leading into his office.

I said, "So tell me a story, Mr. Knowles."

Jacob Knowles looked to be in his late fifties, about five-foot-six, stout with a plump body, and a full head of grayish-black hair growing down over his ears and parted in the center. He wore a pair of thick, wire-rimmed glasses over his black eyes.

He introduced himself as he handed me over one of his business cards that read, *Jacob R. Knowles, Bail Bondsman*. I looked it over, but wasn't really impressed.

Entering his office, I paused and stopped at the threshold for a moment. As I did, I glanced around the place. It was an old nondescript office with a couple of chairs up against the left wall with a half-filled water cooler standing alone on the other side of the wall. Two four-drawer metal filing cabinets were to the right of his metal desk, and a chair on the left side of it. A two-foot-tall wooden divider rail stretched from one end of the wall to the other, with a swing-open gate in the center.

Knowles walked around his desk, and sat down behind it in an old cracked leather swivel chair that had seen better days. He immediately opened the left top drawer, and pulled out a half empty bottle of Johnny Walker Red whiskey, and two ten-ounce whiskey shot glasses. Pouring two fingers worth of the whiskey, he offered me a shot, but I declined. I don't touch whiskey, I'm a gin man. But I wasn't about to ask him for any gin. As I sat in an old armchair, he quickly downed the drink, and just as quickly, returned the glasses back in his drawer, along with the bottle.

Sitting in his one room smoke-filled office, with two ash trays brimming over with butts and ashes, across his grey metal desk, Jacob Knowles was just about to light up a cigarette, when I shook my head. He looked at me, then his unlit cigarette.

Glancing at me again Knowles said, "You don't . . .?" He stopped himself and stared at the unlit cigarette, then glancing over at me again dropped it on the desk.

He kept looking at me funny, waiting to see if I'd change my mind.

I said, "No, I don't."

Nodding a couple of times with a glance of disapproval my way, he proceeded to open a file folder on his desk.

As he read through the profile he had in his case file, he described Rosalinda Garza as a slim and curvy light skinned Latina, of Colombian descent. The color photograph he gave me, showed her with heavy eyeliner, red shiny lipstick, wearing gold earrings. A tight black sleeveless top that came down to her belly button with a possible "B" cup and size thirty-two, well-rounded breasts. She had a colored tattoo of a butterfly on her right shoulder.

It was a typical outfit for a streetwalker. She wasn't half bad looking though. I guess it would give her an edge when picking up her *tricks*.

Then it hit me, Rosy resembled an actress I've seen a couple of times in the movies, Katharine . . . something or other; pretty and sexy.

I said, "A street walker. She shouldn't be too hard to find."

Clearing his throat, he said, "There's more."

"Sure. Why make it easy."

"What?"

"Never mind, go on."

Knowles was saying, "I've been so mad with Rosy for not calling in, that I threatened several times to forfeit on the bond, and throw her back in jail. But after leaving message after message on her answering machine, she still was not responding."

I nodded a couple of times, trying to act as if I was truly interested in his jumper. I wasn't really.

He paused and looked at me waiting for a reply or confirmation that I heard him. I just stared at him, but didn't say anything.

"You have to understand. It's her third go around, Mr. Alvarez. With not showing up for her court date, this could really get her a year or two in jail. I think she knows that too."

As he finished he closed the file folder.

Katharine Ross!

That was whom Rosy reminded me of, though somewhat younger. I remember a movie she was in — *Red Headed Stranger*, where she played Laurie something or other, which I enjoyed immensely.

I saw a look of what could have been impatience written all over his face. I didn't care one way or another.

I said, "So, who put up the bail money on her?"

"Her father did, in cash. He didn't want her in jail again. He's always been bailing her out of trouble and jail."

"Let me get this straight. He's not turning in the bond, but you are. Right?"

Now, all bondsmen have the legal right to surrender a bond and his client whenever certain written terms were not fulfilled by the client.

"Right, when I called her old man he still refused to throw her back in jail. I explained that he didn't have a say in it at all this time, since she failed to show up in court and skipped out."

I asked, "Has he heard from her at all?"

"The old man said if she did, he wasn't telling."

"Okay then, how about a husband or boyfriend? A girl like that would have one for her protection, if not for any other reason."

"Yeah, a boyfriend, but he dumped her a while back though. I have him listed in the case folder in case you want to talk to him."

"Okay. So, she's out on her own then, and her father's not cooperating."

"That's right, hence hiring you."

"How did you get a hold of my number?"

"I called Fred Luna at Triple 'A,' and he recommended you."

Good old Fred, I'll need to talk to him about passing out my number.

There was something about Knowles, hard to pinpoint exactly but more than just his smoking habit that just didn't sit right with me. But a job is a job, even if I didn't like the guy who was paying me.

Before I left Knowles, he'd given me the case file on Rosy which listed friends and relatives, and addresses — things I needed to know in order to do the job. But the most important piece of paper I had tucked in the folder was a signed statement showing that he had hired me to find and bring Rosy to jail. I made sure I listed my fee of three grand. I did this just in case he reneged on our contract. He looked the type that would. Just didn't trust him as far as I could throw him, which wouldn't be that far.

Chapter Forty-One

Lupita's Case

"So, what you got for me, Lupita?"

After leaving Jacob Knowles' office, I stopped off at a nearby gas station on Congress Street, and called home.

Dolores was so happy to hear from me, that after a few minutes of small talk, she wanted to let me know she was planning on a small vacation for us. It was exactly what we needed, and I told her so. She also thought that a trip to the San Diego Zoo would be a great place for the kids. Again, I thought so too. Then she mentioned Lupita had called several times wanting me to call her back ASAP.

I tanked off the LeBaron with some much-needed gas, and picked up a can of Pepsi and decided to take a ride on over to her office. Hell, I was only about a ten-minute ride from her place.

I arrived shortly thereafter to her office on North Stone Avenue. Traffic was sparse considering it was a late Saturday afternoon, and glancing at my watch I saw it was just past six o'clock. I also noticed it hadn't taken me the ten minutes I thought it would. Lupita was keeping late working hours, which wasn't all that unusual.

Lupita Shestko-Montiel, besides being a cagy, smart and powerful woman in Tucson, was also a force to be reckoned with. She always prides herself on the service she provided to her community. A service that far and above compensated her not just in her profit margin, but more so in the gratification she gets in helping her clients, big or small; no matter what she was asked to do. At only five-feet-three, she stood tall, proud and stoic. I took great pride in knowing and working with such a grand lady.

I pulled in, parked across the street from her offices and climbed out. There were four cars parked in front which necessitated my parking across the street.

Crossing the street, I slowly made it up to the front door. Once inside there were several clients waiting and she had another person sitting across from her desk.

Watching her from across the waiting area, I made eye contact with her and gave her a curt nod and sat down to wait.

Lupita momentarily turned her attention to me, and turning again to the person sitting across from her, said something to him. The man rose from the chair, turned and walked out of the office. He was murmuring and talking to himself all the way out. Guess he wasn't too happy to leave. But by then, Lupita had motioned me into her office.

Entering, I took the seat the man had just vacated, while she remained seated behind her desk.

I said, "Interesting guy that just walked out."

She went quiet for a moment, maybe thinking about her last client.

Wasn't like her not to quickly respond though. She must have had a lot on her mind. And she did.

Glancing over to me, she seemed to be thinking of something. I knew that look, and it didn't sit well for whoever was on her bad side. She then reached for a folder on her desk.

She said, "Victor, I don't have too much time. I have several clients waiting on me. I have this case I need you to take care of for me. Everything you need to know is in that folder."

I rose to get the folder she was passing over to me across her desk. Once I had the folder, I sat back down.

I said, "Okay."

She said, "And, I need him back in jail in two days' time."

I considered this a moment.

"Is this jumper going to present a problem?" I asked.

"It's nothing that you can't handle."

"Okay. I'll call if I need anything else."

"Thank you, Victor."

"No problem. I'll keep in touch."

I rose from the chair and walked toward the door. Lupita stepped from around her desk and started walking to the door as well. As she reached it, I was just about to step out, when she said my name. I turned to face her.

"Twenty-four hours, Victor. That's all I can give you."

Her words hung in the air for a brief moment. I just nodded, gave her a quick wink, and walked out.

Back in my car, I wondered why Lupita had mentioned the time limit twice. She had her reasons I guess. But she knew I usually pulled through in a pinch. I wondered too, what was so pressing about this case.

I was soon to learn why.

Chapter Forty-Two

Two Cases, Too Little Time

S o, I had two cases to work on. Not too unusual. Being a criminal investigator in the past, I've investigated several cases at one time, and managed to stay focused on them as well. It was a balancing act; sometimes you win and sometimes you lose.

I decided then to tackle Jacob Knowles' case first — the prostitute, before taking on Lupita Montiel's case. That one could wait for a few extra hours. And, it shouldn't take me too long to catch and return her back to jail.

The obvious place to start would be the streets she worked on. I reasoned, if anyone knew of her whereabouts it would certainly be another hooker.

According to the Tucson Police, Tucson's prostitute lane, as some have come to call it, extends from Miracle Mile west to Interstate-10 exit, and all the way to North Oracle Road, then from Miracle Mile south to West Drachma Street, extending through onto South Sixth Avenue, from Fourteen Street to Forty-Fourth Street. Then further onto South Craycroft Road through East Twenty-Second Street and ending at Golf Links Road.

It was a huge area. She could be anywhere along that route working on tricks. But when I'd gone through Jacob Knowles' notes in the case folder, I found a reference to a location or better yet, an area where she frequently liked to work.

I knew exactly where I needed to go which meant cutting across North Stone Avenue and Twenty-Second Street. Then it was a straight shot to Miracle Mile and El Burrito Ave. That's where I should find Rosy turning tricks.

It was almost seven as I pulled onto the curb at the corner of Miracle Mile and El Burrito Ave. It was a little early for the street walkers to start hanging around. So, I waited in the car keeping watch hoping to catch sight of Rosy as she made her way onto the streets.

About 8:30 things started picking up. A car packed with four girls stopped to let them out. Sure enough they were street walkers, getting ready to make some back breaking cash. Taking a close look at the women, I saw none that came close to Rosy's description.

Twenty minutes later another car pulled over by the intersection, and two more girls walked onto the street. But, I didn't see Rosy with them. Then almost as if they'd practiced their movements for days, the six girls took two to a corner, walking up and down the street waiting on their Johns.

I waited maybe twenty minutes before I made my move, and made sure that their pimps weren't around; I needed space and time to talk to the women alone.

Three of the girls got approached by three different cars and all climbed in and drove off. That left only three. That's when I made my move. Going through the case folder, I grabbed Rosy's photograph and tucked it in my back pants pocket, ready to show it to the women.

I climbed out of the LeBaron, shut the door and locking it started walking across the street to the nearest of the three. The cool crisp wind cut across my eyes, making me blink several times.

As I approached her, she looked calm, swaying a little, with a half smile on her lips. She was in complete control of her actions, smart and confident. She met my eyes and suddenly her smile disappeared as if she knew me, or of me.

I said, "Hi."

"Are you a cop?"

"No."

She was assessing me very carefully. I could just make her eyes giving me the once over, still not sure I wasn't a cop. She started to turn away from me, going over to a pickup truck that slowly passed us checking her out. But the pickup didn't stop.

She then stopped and slowly turned and noticing I was still there, she approached me very carefully and stopped again about two feet away from me, eyeing me suspiciously.

She said, "You look like a cop, man."

"Look, I just got a quick question and you can go back to work. Okay?"

"Ask the question. But the answer is going to cost you twenty bucks for taking up my time."

"Okay."

I quickly pulled out Rosy's photograph and showed it to her.

I said, "I'm a private investigator, looking for this girl named Rosy. I heard she works these streets. Have you seen her around?"

She laughed. "Damn, a private dick."

I just shook my head.

"What she done?"

"Nothing really, her father hired me to find her."

"Yeah, well. She works around here from time to time, but she hasn't been around in the last couple of days."

"Do you happen to know where I can find her?"

"No, her man drops her off and picks her up the next day."

I pulled out my wallet and gave her a twenty.

I said, "Thanks."

That was a waste of time and money. But it was worth a shot. Nothing ventured, nothing gained.

As she turned and walked away from me, I pocketed the photograph and thought about asking one of the other girls, but thought better of it. I'd probably get the same answers, and lose some more money in the bargain. So, I got back to my car, and drove off to the nearest gas station I could find.

I HAD MY MAP OPENED AND DRAPED OVER THE STEERING WHEEL, TRYING TO set a route to North Alvernon Way and Twenty-Ninth Street, out on the Alvernon Heights area in Tucson. It was to Rosalinda Garza's ex-boy friend's house where I needed to go, which Jacob Knowles was nice enough to provide for in his case file.

Earlier when I made the decision to start on this case, and before working on finding Lupita's jumper, I was hoping I'd catch Rosalinda within a fair amount of time and have sufficient time left over for the other jumper. And at the time it sounded like the right thing to do.

Once I had my route picked out I refolded the map and tossing it onto the passenger seat, got the LeBaron in gear and peeled away from the gas station. I was thinking that maybe once I get there, I'd get lucky on the first try; one could only hope. And in this line of business, I needed all the luck I could get.

It was taking me a little longer than I thought. I'd taken a wrong turn down Twenty-Second Street, but eventually found my way back a moment later.

After several minutes I was on Alvernon Way, just making my right turn off of Twenty-Second Street. I then passed "El Grande" Shopping Center on the left, and a moment later made a right turn at Twenty-Ninth Street.

I passed two unnamed streets but the one I needed was the third street on the right, which I made. Then up to Sylvane Street. I was looking for the fourth house on the left side of the street.

It was just starting to rain when I pulled up in front of Alex Arroyo, Rosy's 'ex's house. According to Knowles' notes, Arroyo lived with his parents. The one story house with a white picket fence had an '85 Buick four-door parked on the driveway.

Killing the engine, I sat there a moment, just letting the wipers do their work and waiting to see if the rain died down some. It didn't. Then I slipped out of the LeBaron. Closing the car door, I headed up the driveway to the front door, as the rain fell on my bald head.

Knocking twice, nothing happened. On the third knock an elderly man who seemed to be in his seventies, stood in front of the open door.

He stared at me for a second. His tone of voice was measured, belaying his age.

He asked, "Yes, can I help you?"

I pulled out my credentials, showing him my badge.

I said, "The name's Alvarez. I'd like to talk to you about Alex Arroyo. I understand he lives here. . ."

Suddenly, he looked at me, then my ID, turned around and started yelling inside. He said, "Alex run! Alex, run out the back, it's the police looking for you!"

"Sir, I'm not the pol. . ." I tried to explain, but it was no use, he slammed the door in my face, leaving me to wonder, what the hell just happened?

Chapter Forty-Three

Pimp's Hideout

Instinctively, I did the only thing I could do — I ran after him.

Damn. I thought. *This wasn't turning out the way I planned!*

I sprinted around toward the back then stopped, pausing long enough to just make out the end of the house that led onto an alleyway. And making matters worse, the rain was falling fast and hard now. And the darkness made it that much harder to see anything clearly.

I hoofed it to the alleyway, trying to catch a glimpse of him. At the entrance to the alley, I stopped again and scanned east and west along the alleyway. I couldn't see too well. I ran my hand over my bald head, wiping some of the rain off, when suddenly my eyes lit up as I caught sight of a figure running west.

I took off after him at top speed, and silently hoped it was Alex Arroyo.

Continuing at a dead run, I ran as fast as my two legs could carry me. I was getting closer to the fleeing figure by the second as the rain whipped through my eyes. Then I saw him trip and fall, and heard him yelling out in pain.

Ouch. I bet that had to hurt.

I was almost on him, maybe fifty yards away. Then, I saw him take a quick glance my way as he tried getting back on his feet. He didn't make it, falling back on his side.

But then, he finally got back on his feet.

Not knowing if he was too hurt to run, I put on a burst of speed. I jumped into the air, and tackled him just below his right knee. We both hit the wet hard-packed gravel alleyway, with me on top of him. I quickly struggled to my feet, drew my Colt and pointed it at his head.

Howling in pain, he twisted his body over on his back, bending at the waist trying to grab onto his right ankle.

He screamed at his touch. "Jesus, I'm hurt. I think I broke my ankle!"

He laid on his back, looking up at me and the gun pointed at his head. I needed to get his full attention and start asking the asshole some questions. So I fired a shot about a foot away from the side of his head. He saw the muzzle flash, heard the boom of the gun, and saw out of the corner of his eye where the round impacted.

"Don't shoot, don't shoot, I . . ." he cried out in terror!

I cut him off and said, "Do I have your attention now, asshole?"

"Don't . . . please don't shoot."

He cried out again as he struggled with his right knee, but he kept staring at the Colt leveled at his head, and crying out involuntarily.

I said, "Calm down, asshole. I'm not going to shoot you, unless you do something stupid again. Are you, Alex Arroyo?"

"Yeah. . . You're not a cop . . . . Right?"

This guy had shit for brains.

The guy was trying hard to concentrate, but his thoughts were swimming, considering the pain he was in.

"Uh-uh, I never said I was a cop. I'm a private investigator with a couple of questions for you about your ex-girl friend, Rosy."

"What . . . What the fuck . . . I . . .?"

"Pay attention, asshole. Rosy," I barked at him. "You know where I can find her?"

Arroyo went quiet, and I thought he may be going to pass out on me. I had to keep him talking before he lost consciousness.

"Hey asshole, wake the fuck up. Rosy, know where she is?"

As he cringed from the pain, he said. "No, man. . . I don't. Jeez, try her pimp over in South Tucson."

"What's his name and address?"

Once he figured out I wasn't going to shoot him, or take him to the police he regained some of his nerve. Still feeling groggy and not about to lose his consciousness, he quickly stared up at me.

He said, "Her pimp's name is Jose Molina. He keeps a couple of his girls up at his house in South Tucson."

He then recited the address, which I memorized.

I took a deep breath. "So, why did you run from me?"

Wiping the rain from his eyes, he said. "Cops had been looking for me for a while. My dad figured you for a cop, so I ran."

That's the second time tonight I'd been fingered for a cop.

Once I got what I came for, I holstered the Colt, turned away from him and started walking back to my car.

"Hey, wait a minute, you just gonna leave me here?"

"You're not my problem anymore," I yelled over my shoulder as I walked away. "You can crawl on back for all I give a shit."

Just then the rain slowed to a very light drizzle.

I PULLED ONTO THE CURB JUST AT THE CORNER OF SOUTH NINTH AVENUE and West Thirty-Six Street. I'd covered the fifteen minute drive in as little as ten.

It was almost a quarter to eleven and the desert sky was dark and starless. The only illumination was from a street corner light over on South Ninth Street. Otherwise it was pitch black. And so was the house with its two front windows covered over by black sheets.

I didn't see any signs of any recent activity. The house looked undisturbed. But, what I did notice was the attention of some gang activity as evidenced by some graffiti markings on the one side of the house.

I still couldn't see any lights coming from the front of it, which appeared to be an adobe structure. By the looks of it, it seemed to have no more than two bedrooms. It was an old whitewashed house slightly beyond repair, clearly ravaged by time. It was still habitable though at least by its current occupants.

Pulling away from the curb, I drove slowly on making my way up one corner of the house, then the other. On the east side corner I saw what could have been a bedroom window, boarded up tight. I could just make out a faint glow coming through the wooded slats.

Okay, maybe *someone* was home.

But I had to make sure. The only way to do that was to go inside and see for myself.

Coming back around toward the front of the house, I pulled in again onto the curb about a hundred yards away on the other side of the street. I parked and shut down the engine.

Dressed in my usual attire of blue jeans, black T-shirt, leather jacket, and cut-off combat boots, I sat quietly in the car, making sure no one had made me. Although the streets were deserted and devoid of traffic as well, one can't be too careful or overly cautious in this kind of neighborhood. I also had my Colt strapped on, locked and loaded, plus my ankle holster with the .38 down my right leg. I rifled through the glove compartment and retrieved a small pen light, which I pocketed.

I drew a deep breath, and slowly let it out.

I was moving into an unknown environment, with unknown dangers. And I was consciously placing myself in extreme peril. But it wasn't fear that I was feeling. No. It was just the excitement of it all. Taking another deep breath, and exhaling, I slowly opened the car door.

The drizzle came to a complete stop.

Climbing out of my car and closing the door I placed my Stetson on my head. I then stood there for a few seconds getting acclimated to the gloom and darkness. With my eyes now acutely used to the dark, I scanned the immediate area. Again, I checked for pedestrians or oncoming traffic. But there were none.

It was cold and quiet as a tomb.

Stepping forward, I made my way across the street. Keeping a steady even stride, I curled up the collar of my jacket and shoved my hands into my pockets. Continuing down the sidewalk, I slowly approached the house and ducked into the darkness just as I arrived at its corner. I kept an ear peeled for any sounds that could come from the house.

But I heard nothing.

I continued heading towards the back of the house. As I rounded its corner, I didn't see anyone about. I pulled out my penlight and turned it on casting its light onto the darkness and directing its beam onto the door. It was an old door that was virtually coming off its hinges, with a blackened window off to the right side. I also saw evidence of car tracks and foot prints by the back door. Evidently, they used the back door more so than the front.

Maybe the door was unlocked, I thought.

Just hope I didn't have to break it down to gain entrance.

Pressing myself up against the wall and staying low, I made my way to the door. I turned off the penlight. Grasping the door handle, I pulled out my Colt and cocked back the hammer, opened the door just enough, and slipped inside. I closed it behind me.

Keeping perfectly still for a short moment, I found myself in a darkened room. I turned the penlight on again and did a scan. It was a kitchen with stacks of dirty dishes on and around the sink, a trash can overflowing and trash thrown all around. As I played the light around, I saw couple of rats scurry away from the beam of the penlight.

Christ. The stench was overwhelming. The floor had been carpeted at one time or another, with just bits of pieces here and there, and bare concrete patches where the carpet had once been.

Then taking a few steps further inside, I stopped, when I heard shuffling and coughing of someone nearby. *So, there is someone in the house*, I thought.

With the penlight, I scanned further into the darkness. I saw a small entranceway and two doors; one opened and the other closed. I figured these for the bedrooms. I wasn't wrong.

Turning off the penlight, I again heard coughing this time closer and coming from the open door. Slowly pushing open the door halfway and keeping my Colt close to my chest, I took a step into what was a small bedroom. With a fast glance around the room I saw a small unmade bed, night table and lamp. It didn't feel well lived in. Beyond an open doorway a slice of light came through into the room — it was a bathroom. And someone was using it, as I heard water running. Seconds later the faucet turned off.

Quickly, I walked over and stood with my back up against the wall just to the right of the bathroom door, waiting for whomever to step out. Didn't have long to wait, as a woman coughing once, walked out, holding onto a towel.

Taking a quick step behind her, I roughly pushed her toward the bed, but she caught herself and turned completely around facing me. She was momentarily bewildered clearly shaken but unafraid, as she peered at the Colt leveled at her chest.

It was Rosy! Good looking Rosy.

"Maricon!," she exclaimed in Spanish. "What the fuck, *Cabron.* "What do you . . .?"

"I'm the one taking you back to jail," I said immediately cutting her off.

Throwing her towel on the floor, I saw she was wearing only a pair of pink panties. I couldn't fail to notice her firm naked breasts and pinkish nipples.

"The hell you say! Fuck you. You ain't taking me back!"

Without any warning and ignoring the weapon aimed at her chest, she threw herself at me. She tried grabbing for my gun at the same time. But in that instant, I transferred the Colt from my right to my left hand, keeping it away from her grasp.

And in the next instant she doubled over in pain, as I buried my right fist into her solar plexus. She just folded in half as both her knees gave up the attempt of staying upright. She then crumpled to the floor in a heap. I could've easily struck her across her head with my Colt. But, hell, where's the fun in that.

After that she was easy to handle. Guess I hit her pretty hard. She lay there, grasping but still very conscious.

Noticing her clothing on the bed, I quickly bent down, and grabbed her by her hair. She immediately grabbed my arm holding on with both hands. Then pulling her onto the bed, I told her to get dressed.

Once she was fully dressed, I pulled out my cuffs and had her securely handcuffed before she could do anything else.

Sitting her up on the edge of the bed, I saw she was coming around, maybe clearing her head and coming to grips with what just happened.

I said, "Listen, bitch, you try that again, and next time I won't be too gentle with you! Understand?"

She sat quite still, her eyes boring hard into mine, trying to make up her mind. She looked pissed. Then nodding, she glanced away and muttered something to herself.

I said, "You say something?"

Rosy drew in a short sharp breath, and then let it out.

"Yeah, fuck you, *Maricon!*"

She still had some fight in her.

I just smiled.

Suddenly I froze. . .

Just for a second I stood unmoving. Then, I slowly turned in the direction of the sound I'd just heard coming from the front of the house. It was unmistakable. I heard a car pulling into the driveway; then seconds later voices. It sounded like maybe there were three of them, and car doors closing.

Guess we had company!

Chapter Forty-Four

Escape with Rosy

Rosy heard it too.

She stiffened then tried getting up from the edge of the bed, but I pushed her back down. Rosy, took in a deep breath and glanced up at me with a smug look on her face.

She said, "Hey, asshole. That's my people coming back."

Right away I said with a straight face, "Shut your mouth, or I'll shut it for you!"

I watched her shake her head, but she didn't say another word.

I was on the edge here. I really needed to get the hell out of the house with my prisoner, before they knew what was happening. It was no time for a confrontation. Someone could get hurt or killed, and it wasn't going to be me. I was in a pickle and needed to think fast!

With Rosy on the edge of bed watching me, I pulled out my bandanna from my back pocket. Then I used it as a gag around Rosy's mouth.

I was feeling better now, really relieved that she was gagged.

Grabbing her by her left arm, I got her to her feet. Looking dead in her eyes I said, "If you make a sound, or do anything I don't like to warn your buddies, I'll make it very hard on you."

Her eyes glinted with anger then frustration.

Struggling somewhat in my grasp, I tightened my grip on her arm. She bowed her head slightly, and then stopped her struggles.

Then, I pushed her out in front of me. As we quickly walked out of the bedroom, I heard keys being inserted into the front door lock.

This was going to be damn close!

Just barely making the back door, the front door slowly opened. But by then Rosy and I were already outside. I reached the edge of the house, turned left and still holding tightly to Rosy prodded her along to the street. I stopped for a second on the sidewalk, making sure no one was lurking about and then we made for my car.

Still holding tightly onto Rosy, I got her to the passenger side, opened the door and told her to get in. Once I had her in the seat, I removed her cuffs, secured her hands to the iron post, and removed her gag.

At first, she just looked up at me, and then wordlessly she turned away from me.

Coming around toward the driver's side, I saw up at the house three figures. Two women and a man were at the sidewalk looking my way.

Getting in fast, I fired up the LeBaron, put it in gear, and turned the wheel over hard to the right. I made a fast U-turn and burned rubber getting out of Dodge.

As I picked up speed, I saw through my rearview mirror, the man run to the center of the street. He stopped and quickly raised his right arm. Then I saw two quick flashes come from his hand, followed immediately by the report of gunshots.

Then I heard low *pinging* sounds as if on metal. *Shit! Maybe those bullets found the back of my car,* I thought.

The pimp must've been really pissed seeing one of his girls being taken away from him so easily.

I finally made the intersection, then hung a quick left and pointed the LeBaron toward the Pima County jail.

Once at the jail house parking lot, I cuffed her hands behind her and helped her out of the car.

Just before we started walking her up to the jail's entrance, I stopped just long enough to check the trunk lid. Sure enough, I saw two bullet holes on the right side of the lit and said, "Christ! That's gonna cost me a pretty penny to repair."

"Yeah, right," Rosy said. "Too bad it wasn't your head."

I managed a grin, but didn't reply.

Two hours later, I had Rosy safely tucked in a cell. Afterward, I'd made contact with Jacob Knowles back in his office. I turned over the signed and sealed bond to his delight, as he handed over an envelope containing my three grand in cash.

I opened the envelope and counted out the cash, making sure I wasn't short-changed. I wasn't. Pocketing the envelope, I started turning and walking away from him, as I rubbed my tired bleary eyes.

"Hey, wait up," he said. "Stay a moment. Let's celebrate with a drink to the end of a successful and timely conclusion to our brief partnership."

Turning back stifling a yawn I said, "Don't think so, I have someone else I need to track down tonight."

Then once more turning toward the entrance, I took the last few steps then paused at the door. As I grasped the door handle to open it, my thoughts returned to the comments he'd made earlier about my phone number.

For a second longer, I didn't say anything. Then I turned my head slightly to the right, but not glancing over at him, and addressed him in a low voice sounding slightly menacingly.

I said, "Make sure you lose my number."

I didn't hear a reply, as opening the door I walked out into the night, quickly closing it behind me.

I felt a lot better now than when I took this case. Must've been the company I was in.

Anyway, that's one down, and one to go.

Chapter Forty-Five

Chavez and the Drug Cartel

I was kind of hoping the bar hadn't closed.

It would be perfect for what I had in mind.

So, I'd made a quick decision to stay out and not head for home. Knowing it would be virtually impossible to leave once I was there. The wife and kids would see to that.

It's been months since the last time I was at the bar and it was the type of place you frequently saw off duty police officers, but not what you might call a cop bar. On occasions, a poker game would be playing way in the back behind closed doors.

The joint wasn't packed, so I had my choice of seats. I'd decided on a booth in the back, far away from the other customers while I faced the main door.

Inside, I saw two off duty patrolmen that I knew, sitting at the bar nursing their drinks. As I walked by them, one of them turned in my direction and lifted his drink to me, in salute. Saw two detectives I'd met once or twice before, sitting with a small group off to one corner.

In a back corner, I saw a small Douglas fir tree with all types of trimmings nicely arranged, with its lights blinking on and off.

It was a very nice place to have a drink. But twenty years later, when I came for a visit, I noticed that most of my old hangouts were closed up and gone, and so was the bar.

Staring at the Christmas tree, I had a nagging feeling I was forgetting something my wife mentioned before leaving the house.

I'll remember soon enough, I thought.

So thinking about my wife, I walked over to the far wall and using the house pay phone, I called her.

I explained to her exactly where I was, and what I was planning on doing. She didn't like it. Not one bit. Sounding worried too. She had a right to be worried though. If she only knew half of the violence I'd had since becoming a bounty hunter, she'd be throwing a huge fit and maybe threatening me with divorce. But, her next words were a huge calming effect on my otherwise gloomy outlook.

In a soft measured tone she said, "Be careful and get home in one piece."

All I said was that I'd be careful. I couldn't promise anymore than that.

It was ten minutes later, while sitting at the bar and nursing on a Heineken — which I considered my old time favorite — that I was tempted to read through the case folder Lupita had given me. But I didn't. The beer had picked me up some. Then taking another quick pull, I felt it burn a little as it went down, and felt my eyes water a little too.

Boy, I was tired.

So, the bar was the best place I knew that was relatively quiet and safe. The waitresses weren't bad looking either. I kept peeking over at a cute little blonde number, maybe in her mid-twenties, with deep blue eyes, a slim waistline and legs that only Michelangelo could have sculpted. She was the one who'd been serving me. She would come to my table, even though I didn't need anything, and just strike up a conversation till she was needed somewhere else. But not before asking if I was married. Guess she liked what she saw. Oh, if I wasn't already married! Oh well, had to stay faithful.

Then music playing from the jukebox *White Christmas*, reminded me what time of the year it was. With all the excitement and fun that I was having, I nearly forgot. And I finally remembered too what my wife asked of me; I needed to buy a tree. How the hell can you forget something like that? Well I did. And I had to make this up to the family very soon.

First though my jumper, then going after the tree with the family came a close second.

And after watching the cute little waitress wiggle as she walked away in a very seductive manner, it was hard for me to get in the Christmas spirit, and the business at hand. Finally, with a little sigh, I managed to open the folder.

I read statement after statement of both the witness and of Jaime Moreno, the police report and the US Marshall's report as well. And of course, the statement made by Alfonso Luis Chavez. Then I pieced together what I thought was the back story behind Chavez, the jumper I was going after. It went something like this. . .

It was well over three years ago to the day that he'd teamed up with Jaime Moreno, his close business partner. And up to this point, business was on the upswing. Of course there were problems, but who doesn't have them in any business? His association with Moreno was tentative at best, but mostly they worked well together. Moreno did the driving, which of course was the most dangerous part, and he was the one who planned it all out. It was a team of three, with Chavez being the boss of the outfit.

The *smack* was being delivered on time, every time. They had never been stopped at the border crossing, or been pulled over by local police patrols, not once.

They'd been lucky in that respect, very lucky, or very smart.

His boss seemed very happy with the operation, and there were talks of increasing product distribution to his crew, which would raise the profit margin higher than he expected.

But then it all started coming down around him.

It was greed, pure and simple. And if he'd caved in, he would've seen those profits go down the toilet. It was obvious what he needed to do if he wanted to keep afloat — cut his losses.

It all started with his main man, Jose Luis Garcia, the third business partner in the outfit back in Nogales, Mexico. Garcia was his point of contact. Once the head boss approved the shipments, it was Chavez's job to put it all together. And Garcia was responsible to ensure the product was packaged and ready for shipment.

Once Garcia heard of the increase, the man wanted a bigger cut than what he'd signed up for. Jesus! The guy was already getting a sizable cut as it was.

Garcia wasn't supposed to die, but then one thing led to another and Garcia gave Chavez no choice. The guy was going to the Federales — the Mexican police, if he didn't get a better cut than what he was getting. Chavez didn't think Garcia would, but he wasn't going to take the chance.

It was stupid, just plain stupid of Garcia to think of it, let alone to say shit like that. It just wasn't acceptable and Chavez couldn't let that happen. The only way out he figured, was to put a bullet to his damn head. That would put an end to Garcia's threat.

So, one cold night, in Nogales, he did just that! Didn't think twice about it, just came up behind Garcia, pointed the gun to the back of his head, and pulled the trigger. That had been easy. Getting rid of the body was the hard part.

According to Chavez's confession, he disposed of the body and the weapon in a large grave somewhere out in the desert. A place even he wouldn't be able to find again. No one would miss Garcia. No wife. No children or family to speak of. With no body, the cops couldn't prove or disapprove his claim.

Then of course there was Jaime Moreno.

Moreno wanted out, completely out. He was worried the cops would eventually find out about the operation. And all he could think about was his family in Mexico. Not just wanting to get out, he also wanted all that was coming to him. And that amounted to well over a quarter of a million in easy cash.

But that wasn't the reason he'd shot Moreno. Oh no, Moreno had decided he needed cash right away. So, Moreno sold the last shipment on his own, all of it. Jamie had effectively sealed both their deaths warrants with the move. That was the argument he had with him at Moreno's apartment.

It was during the argument, when Moreno produced a gun and threatened Chavez with it if he didn't leave.

The argument had escalated into a fight, and in the subsequent struggle for the gun, Moreno was accidentally shot in the chest.

Chavez saw his chance and an opening. Still holding onto the gun, a Taurus .38 caliber revolver, he pulled the trigger and shot Jaime in the chest once more. Then with the gun pointed at Moreno's head, he pulled the trigger again, just to make sure. But the hammer fell on an empty chamber. He tried twice more, but the gun clicked on more empty chambers. He'd fired the last round. He flipped out the chamber and saw that it was empty and snapped it back in place. Then thinking him dead, he ran out of the apartment.

But little did he know Jaime Moreno had survived the shooting and fingered him as the shooter. He'd made the mistake of not putting a bullet in his head instead of his chest. And Moreno had been very lucky the gun had only those two rounds in it.

But according to Chavez, it hadn't always been like that. He'd never shot anyone in his life before, or stolen anything from anyone.

According to his statement, it had been a couple of years ago that he worked a normal eight to five job, as an assistant to an accountant.

He stated that in the beginning life wasn't all that good. He was shaken and had gotten in over his head in debt, and couldn't see any way out. What with a family of five, it just wasn't enough. One of his buddies recommended someone that could help him out with a loan. The trouble was that *someone* had been a loan shark. And when he couldn't pay it back in time, his troubles got worse.

One night as he came out of a bar, two ugly Mexican guys appeared out of nowhere. He was hit in the ear by one of them, and in the gut by the other, then held by his arms on either side and dragged to a dark alley behind the bar. There he was dealt crushing blows to his face. His mouth was filled with blood. Then they started on his gut, blow after blow. He almost blacked out, but somehow managed to stay conscious throughout the beating.

It was several days later after sustaining a broken arm the man behind the beating learned Chavez worked as an accountant, and offered him a temporary position as a bookie to help pay off his debt.

He couldn't believe his luck.

He had no alternative but to accept. His life would be forfeited and so would his family. But as luck would have it, that union brought greater rewards his way, till finally after establishing his trust, he was given an outfit all his own. But it didn't happen overnight. . .

Now it was all shot to hell, all that work gone and he saw no way out.

And it all changed when he had to shoot and kill Jose Luis Garcia, his Mexican contact and thought he'd killed Jaime as well. Those two deserved to die for screwing up the one good thing he had going.

Self-preservation and the safety of his family were the only things that mattered to him now. So, the first thing he did was to make sure his family was moved to an unknown place, where his boss couldn't possibly get to them. Once that was done, he stayed with some relatives on his wife's side, safe for the time being.

Or so he thought!

That's where the police tracked him down to and arrested him. After his bond hearing all he wanted to do was flee, and to hell with the courts.

SITTING IN MY CORNER OF THE BAR, IT FELT DAMP AND A LITTLE COLD. So, after spending the next several minutes reading a little more on the case, I looked around the bar. I noticed the joint was just about empty of customers. There were only three other customers besides myself left in the bar. And one of them was passed out with his head on the bar top.

Looking at my watch I noticed it was ten minutes after one, and the bar was getting ready to close-up. There wasn't anything else I was going to learn from the folder, so I gathered all the papers and stuffed them into the folder.

Stifling a yawn, I picked up the folder, stood and tucked it under my arm and headed off out of the bar and to my car.

Chapter Forty-Six

The Hideout

Unable to find refuge amongst his few family members, he was left with no alternative but to hideout at his warehouse.

Alfonso Chavez knew there were only three people who had knowledge of the warehouse and its location; his two partners, one that was dead, and the other in critical condition, and of course his only brother, Esteban-Luis.

It was the safest place he could come up with in such a short period of time. The warehouse and its two other buildings were old, built back in the 1960s. The area they were built on he'd purchased four years back for a song. They consisted of the large warehouse, and two smaller buildings. All three buildings had ragged holes in the sides, broken window panes, all needing a good paint job and proper maintenance and upkeep. Except for the inside of the warehouse proper where all the work was primarily focused, and of course including the office area, all new inside.

The tract of land and the three buildings were surrounded by large trees and high grass, and completely enclosed by high, six-foot, chain-linked fencing with a gate shack in the center that at one time was manned by an armed guard. But now it was just padlocked.

He didn't think anyone could get to him here. He felt somewhat safe.

Now thinking back, it just seemed like nothing had been going right for him. With a little luck, he could see himself out of this in a few days' time. He just needed a little more time, then nothing or no one would be able to stop him.

He thought about it several times, and several times he came to the same conclusion; he could never get to Jaime Moreno and finish up what he'd started.

He discarded plan after plan.

He just couldn't make it work. There was no viable plan that didn't amount to him being arrested, or worse, shot. So as easily as he thought of it, he discarded it. He knew Moreno would be guarded day and night by the police; it just wasn't worth the effort. Hell no, not his life, that's for sure.

So for now he waited in solitude, with Garcia's gun a constant reminder of the way it was, as he sat in his chair in the office shack of his warehouse. He knew full well the authorities were looking for him. But his worst fears were of his boss, and the men he'll be sending. They'll be gunning for him for sure, and would kill anyone who stood in their way.

If they got to him, his life wouldn't be worth a plugged nickel, and neither would his family's. He knew quite well how they operated. Once they got their victim talking nothing was kept from them — nothing at all. Not even the whereabouts of his family. They would be cold and ruthless. He couldn't let that happen.

He waited patiently for the right time till he could get back to his place, dig up the money he'd stashed in a safe place saved over the years, and make his way to Mexico and his family.

His brother Esteban was the only one who knew he was hiding out at the warehouse. And Esteban was due to meet up with him in the next two hours, bringing with him much needed food, a change of clothing and ammunition for the Taurus.

He stood up from the chair and started pacing back and forth in the small office, trying to come up with ideas to make this easy. But try as he could, there simply was no way around it. He'd even thought of letting Esteban go for the money. But damn, it was a question of trust. He just didn't feel that he could trust his own brother. Not with so much money. No. He needed to do it on his own.

So, Chavez waited, growing impatient. Time was slipping by and he could do nothing about it. He kept staring at the phone on top of the desk, waiting on Esteban to call. He put the gun on the table, stood up and turned the thermostat down low. The room was overly warm. *Or was it me?* he thought.

He went back to his chair, which had become very uncomfortable and sat down. Picking up the Taurus, he liked the feel and its compact design with a two-inch barrel that fit perfectly in the palm of his hand. Making sure the safety was off, even though it was empty, he felt a sense of security just holding on to it. Looking around the office, he'd also noticed something he had never even remotely felt before; there was very little sound coming into the warehouse from the outside. Strange, he'd never thought of that before.

Then yawning for a tenth time, he fell into a troubled sleep. Twenty minutes later the phone rang.

In his sleep, he thought he heard an insistent shrill ringing tone coming from far away.

Suddenly he was wide awake.

He jumped up from his chair, pointing the gun here and there. Then he realized it was only the phone. Christ, he was getting jumpy. He sat back down shaking the feeling away, and picked up the receiver.

Chavez said, "Esteban?"

"Expecting someone else, my brother?" Chavez heard his brother chuckle through the ear piece.

"No, of course not," he said.

"I didn't think so, brother."

"How much longer will you be?"

"Well, I haven't got everything together yet. It's taken me longer than I thought. So, I should be there in about three hours. Then we can sit and plan out whatever you have up your sleeve, my brother."

Chavez said, "Okay, try to see if you could possibly cut that down to two hours."

Then, after hanging up the receiver he started working on a plan. Overall, the plan's chances of succeeding were a lot better than going after Moreno, without the risk of getting caught.

ONE HUNDRED AND SIXTY-TWO MILES TO TUCSON, FROM THEIR HOME IN Santa Ana, Sonora, Mexico while driving their Ford pickup, would take them about two hours, more or less. That's if the weather held and traffic wasn't heavy.

This was the time of year when most of the rich Mexicans families took to the road, traveling into the US for holiday shopping looking for bargains. They did their shopping mostly in the closest bargain outlets in Tucson, and the surrounding areas. That's way they decided on leaving at night when traffic wouldn't be too congested.

It was just the two of them. And the boss said they should be able to take care of his problem and get back home in a fair amount of time. He had other pressing business the two men needed to work on that couldn't wait.

They took the back roads, or what went for roads that let across the border from Nogales, Mexico into Nogales, Arizona. They were armed, and for that reason alone, the back roads were the only way to travel.

They knew exactly what paths they had to take. Hell, they'd traveled this route several times before. But on their return trip, they would get rid of the weapons, thereby crossing back without trouble at the main border crossing. But for now, the back roads it was.

These were hard, capable men. Experienced men, both at killing and making people talk. They didn't foresee any problems with the mission their boss had set out for them. They knew what had to be done; first take care of two men, and then Chavez family came second. No loose ends.

They left Santa Ana and drove north on Highway-Two, passing the town of Magdalena. Later they stopped in Imunis, a small little sleepy town. They found a restaurant and had a bite to eat. A couple of beers later, they were back on the road.

Thirty minutes after that, they came to the end of Highway-Two, just to the spot where their path started up into the woods. The path cut almost straight for a couple of miles, then meandered through steep turns and bends. Then they passed two gullies and a wide river. They kept their headlights off, in case border agents were in or around the area. Slowly they made their way.

Chapter Forty-Seven

The Apartment

Back in my car, I started it up and just sat there awhile, thinking things over.

There were no two ways about it. I reasoned there were two things needed to be accomplished. First, checkout Chavez's residence, determine if his family still lived there, and if they did, pull surveillance and wait for him to come to me. Second, stakeout Chavez's brother's home. According to Chavez's bio-sheet, the brother was the only blood relative this side of the border. I had to arrest Chavez on this side of the US border. Couldn't go into Mexico and grab him there.

I'd always made it a strong point of not going across the border looking for bail jumpers. Too many things could go wrong. Considering I had no resources that I could turn to if I'd gotten myself in hot water, thrown in jail or worse shot — no one whatsoever.

Besides that, the *Federales* didn't abide with bounty hunters coming in grabbing someone and dragging them back across the border without their *cut*. Any self-respecting hunter knew better.

The practical point then was to not let Chavez get anywhere near the border. So, logically speaking, Chavez's residence was my first stop off.

I MADE A QUICK STUDY OF MY MAP. I WAS LOOKING FOR A FAST AND DIRECT route to Chavez's residence — an apartment dwelling.

Having found what I thought was exactly what I was looking for, and doing what I'd always done, I remembered all the right and left turns to get there. But there weren't that many.

Then, after placing the map on the passenger seat, I shifted the car into first gear, slowly eased out of the bar's parking lot, and made my way onto Speedway Boulevard. After making a right turn, I remembered I'd needed to make my second right turn about a mile up ahead.

Driving on Speedway Boulevard, I couldn't miss all the Christmas decorations being displayed from one business to another. Even though it was still a few weeks to go before the twenty-fifth, it seemed like the season's spirit was in full swing.

Making the second right turn onto South Kolb Road, I kept driving on till I made a quick left onto East Lakeside Road. As my heater kept me warm, fighting the coldness and the winds blowing just outside my car window, I hung another right. And there on the right side of the road was the apartment complex I was looking for — Springhill Apartments.

The complex was in shadows. There were barely any streets lights throughout the area, and most of the lighting came from the office building straight ahead. The complex was only two stories high of adobe style construction, like most in Tucson. The buildings were all cared for, all well maintained. The area seemed clean and properly policed. There were no overgrown trash bins that I could see from the buildings I'd passed. It was a nice place to live, if you liked the apartment scene.

I came around the apartment's offices looking for unit number 15. Passing two buildings, I finally found Chavez's apartment. It was on the ground floor, which would make my surveillance easier. I parked across the street from his apartment in the complex parking lot. The lot was full of cars, and a lot more were parked on the curb. Some were newer models but most were about five to six years old; one or two that could use a paint job. There were barely any free parking spaces, till I came across one just across from Chavez's apartment behind a late model, four-door Buick.

Killing the engine, I sat to watch.

But I wasn't going to stay there all night waiting and hoping Chavez shows.

No way.

I'll give it fifteen minutes and I'll go and check out the apartment for myself, I muttered.

MAN, WAS I DOGGED TIRED.

Blinking and rubbing my eyes trying to stay awake didn't help any, but I kept vigil just the same. I was anxiously hoping someone was in the house. But as yet, I'd been unable to see anything unusual or any of the house lights being turned on and off, to suggest anyone was home.

Nada.

Nothing.

So, I turned my attention on the rest of the apartments nearby. A few had shown house lights switching on then off like maybe going for a bathroom break, and back to bed. A few seconds later I saw someone coming out of a ground floor apartment, with a small dog in tow. The guy was in his pajamas with a jacket over it, constantly yawning which caused me to yawn as well. After the dog was finished, they went back inside and the lights were turned off.

So, I figured with the coast clear, time was at hand for me to do my thing.

After a few minutes had passed and making sure the dome light in the car was turned off, I swiveled on the leather seat, got my legs out of the car and climbed out. Standing next to the open door I drew my Colt, cocked the hammer back, released the safety and slowly returned it to its holster.

I closed the car door but left it unlocked — didn't know if I was going to make a fast getaway, or not. I always liked to be prepared nevertheless. I paused for a second or two and took a deep breath. Then I turned left and slowly traced my way in the darkness down the street.

In the distance, the sirens of a police car or fire truck wailed. Then with a quick turn to my right, I walked around toward the back of the building.

There I found a slightly open window with just enough clearance allowing me to insert my fingers through. I used one hand to soundlessly get it open sufficiently for me to climb in. Not hearing any noises coming from the inside, and getting one leg in at a time, I made it inside and left the window open.

Then I moved sideways pressing my back to the side wall, drew the Colt, and then got a hold of my penlight and switched it on.

God Almighty, just hope this plays out good, I muttered, as I slowly traced the penlight's beam into the darkened room. It was a small child's bedroom with a night table, dresser and a small bunkbed with no one on it.

The bedroom door was wide open.

I turned off the penlight, and waited for my eyes to adjust to the darkness. Then slowly I made for the open door. Halfway there, I tripped over and stepped on a small stuffed toy that emitted a low trumpet noise, much like an elephant would make. I immediately stopped, hoping no one heard it. I didn't hear anything unusual. If they weren't home, they sure left in a hurry leaving the child's toy behind.

Going through the bedroom door, I made it through the whole house without incident. All of the furniture, books, pictures on the wall, and beds were all still there, except the occupants. Shit. Guess I'd missed out.

Contemplating my next move and deciding on not going back out the window, I gambled on going out the front door.

Quickly arriving at the main entrance, I counted a slow ten. Then I released the deadbolt, and grasped the door knob. I slowly opened the door and slipped out.

Closing the door behind me, I stood there making sure no one was about. Then making it back to my car, I started it up and drove away.

Not a happy camper.

I could've called it a night if he was at home. But it's not rocket science. It's what happens when jumpers go on the lamb. So, I had to put the next part of my plan into action — the brother was next.

Chapter Forty-Eight

Cartel Enforcers

It was 2:25 a.m.

I stopped at a 7-11 convenience store where I filled up on a much needed pick me up — black coffee, strong and a couple of donuts for the road. I paid my four dollars and fifty cents for it, got back in my car and headed out toward Esteban's home thirty minutes away.

As I munched on the donuts and drank the strong black coffee, I found myself rolling though some very secluded dark side streets which eventually led me onto South Craycroft Road. After two miles, I passed the Triple "T" truck stop just off of I-10 on the right side. I hung a left onto East Elvira Road, then a block more I made another left toward South Van Buren Avenue. Esteban's house was the third one on the left.

I made a slow drive-by of the area.

The house wasn't anything really fancy. A two-story long place which had brown bricks built all through the front facade. It had a gravel walkway and a one car garage that was open. And parked inside was a brown Chevy pickup. The garage lights were on, but no one was in or around the pickup.

As I slowly made my way around the block and five houses further on, I saw a parked Ford pickup. The engine was running and white plume smoke was coming from its exhaust. The funny thing about the pickup was the two men. They looked to be Latinos maybe Mexicans. They both just stared over at me as I drove past them.

In that brief glance, I started to feel a little apprehension and a tickling sensation that crept up my spine. *These two were up to no good,* I thought.

Just hope it was nothing to worry about. But the more I thought of them as I drove on, the more I felt something was wrong here.

There was no mistaking the two guys in the Ford. They looked like they were there for something nefarious. They both appeared like they knew what they were doing. I also couldn't help noticing the Mexican license plates.

And that's what gave me pause.

What were their intentions? Were they there for something other than surveillance of the house, the same one I was there for? I thought.

"I'm not going to worry about them now," I murmured. Just hope their attention wasn't on Esteban Chavez's house.

The night was dark, quiet and lonely, a typical suburban atmosphere. I came back around the block and parked at the left side of South Van Buren, killed the lights and the engine. I reached over into my equipment bag and pulled out my powerful night binoculars and scanned over to the house.

There were lights on and the garage door was still open. Something didn't seem right though. It was a little past three in the morning, and Esteban's house was the only one with their lights on.

Something was up. And I didn't know what.

I scanned past the house to the Ford pickup. All I could make out was the back of the guys' heads, and the lights of cigarettes burning from inside the cab.

God, I hope those two guys are not mixed up in my case, I thought.

Nevertheless, the way my night was going, I just hope this turns out for the best, with me going home in one piece, and my jumper in jail.

So, I sat watching the watchers and watching for the brother as well.

It was later, when I learned the Mexican's were actually cartel enforcers. They were working for the same boss who once employed Serrano. And now, they were after Serrano's head and of those of his family. If anyone else dared to come between them and what they were paid to do, they faced the same consequences.

I just had to stay alert.

So, I waited. Feeling confident, seemingly relaxed and patient, like all surveillance's I've conducted. And not jump to conclusions.

It was getting on to 3:45. The LeBaron was still warm, comfortable. Outside was cold and the wind seemed to gust now and then. I drank all of my coffee and had eaten the last of my donuts, and felt rather refreshed.

I was hoping for the best on this early morning surveillance.

Yeah, hope for the best!

Forty minutes later, things began to happen at the house. Through my binoculars, I noticed that the Ford pickup made a U-turn and parked on the other side of the street, facing Esteban's house.

So, the Ford it seemed was in on the action too. Oh hell. I just hoped it wasn't anything I couldn't handle.

Chapter Forty-Nine

Follow the Leader

As I scanned back to the house, things were starting to look up.

For not long after observing the Ford pickup with the two guy's relocate itself across the street from its previous location, the house lights were turned off. A moment later a man in a brown winter jacket and Boston Red Sox baseball cap, carrying a small tan suitcase and a small wooden box walked out of the house and into the garage.

Storing the suitcase and box in the Chevy's bed, the guy walked around to the driver's side and climbed in. He cranked the engine but it failed to start. It caught on the second try and then slowly backed out. After clearing the garage door, he came to a stop. Climbing out again, he grabbed the garage door at the top and pulled it all the way down closing it. Then getting back in the cab he backed up onto the main road.

I quickly scanned over to the Ford, and heard it crank up as well.

As the Chevy pickup eased onto the road the driver, whom I took to be Esteban-Luis Chavez turned the wheel to the left, and rolled forward slowly. The headlights came on as it gained speed coming toward the intersection, just across from my location. As the Chevy's headlights came closer to my car, I ducked down trying to avoid being seen. Once his headlights beamed across my car, I came back up and watched as he completed a right turn.

Then headlights came on up by Esteban's house — the Ford. I saw it roll forward slowly then increasing its forward momentum it started picking up speed. It was nearing my spot and my car would soon be totally visible to them. So I ducked down once again as its headlights flashed across my windshield. Coming back up I saw the Ford make a tight right turn on squealing tires, quickly picking up speed trailing a plume of white smoke in its wake, trying to catch up with the Chevy pickup.

A few seconds later after firing up the LeBaron, I eased out of the curb, rolled through the intersection, hung a left turn then floored the gas pedal as my engine's power smoothly kicked in.

I played follow the leader.

TRAILING FAR BEHIND THE FORD, I SAW ITS TAIL-LIGHTS UP AHEAD AS IT turned onto Craycroft Road. A mile further, I followed as it made the I-10 Frontage Road access. After a right on Valencia Road, I continued to stay far behind hoping they wouldn't suspect anyone was on their tail. I was gambling they stayed focused and trained their sole attention onto Esteban's Chevy and not suspect anyone was following *them*. I needed to catch them off guard in whatever they had planned for the night.

We came to South Palo Verde Road, then a quick left to East Universal and the intersection of Brosius Ave. The Ford slowed and so did I, staying back about nine car lengths, and turned off my head-lights. I slowly inched my way forward, and saw the Ford had also turned off its headlights and came to a dead stop.

I was still moving slowly forward, when I saw the two men climb out of the Ford. I pulled over about two hundred yards and came to a complete stop alongside the curb, killed the engine and waited.

The streets ahead and behind were completely empty and the area was silent. I was overly apprehensive of those two guys. From what I saw of them, they screamed out dangerous. I knew then that I would have to face them down soon enough. Not looking forward to it though.

Not at all.

Looking around and getting a feel for the area, I found myself in a densely wooded and secluded area. Over to the left side of the road was a high fenced in area, which appeared to be a warehouse of some sort. One large building to the right with two smaller ones completed the overall structures of the compound.

The area was in total darkness, only light came out of the gate shack. It was lit from the inside and illuminated just a few feet around the shack. The buildings were built in a horse shoe configuration, with the gate shack just center of the two outer buildings with an iron-post drop down gate, left wide open.

A large wooden sign just off to the right of the gate read: Chavez Transport. And from my vantage point, the buildings looked deserted.

After a few seconds had passed, I watched as the two guys walked toward the open gate then onto the grounds and disappeared around one of the two side buildings. They both had drawn weapons in their hands.

All of a sudden, I knew this was going to get ugly, if not downright dangerous.

Slipping out of my car, I just let the cold wind blow against my face, cooling me down some after the warmth of the car. For a few seconds I just stood there shaking off any apprehensions I was feeling. Then, removing my Stetson, I threw it in the car and closed and locked the door. I pulled my Colt and made sure a round was in the tube, and clicked off the safety. Again, I cocked the hammer, and returned it back to its holster. Then slowly I made my way to the warehouse.

I was determined to meet any menace waiting in the warehouse, just like I've always done, cold, hard and fast.

"Damn, now the fun is about to begin," I murmured, as a blast of heavy, chilled air blew itself on me like a slap to the face.

With dark clouds rolling in out of the west and no visible stars nor moon to guide my path, the darkness was complete as I slowly inched my way forward toward the gate.

I'd heard somewhere, that nothing is more horrific or uncomprehending to the human mind than total darkness. The mind can and will always play tricks on one's imagination. But I didn't let that sensation get to me, and as far as I could see, the path was the only visible means of getting onto the warehouse compound.

Crossing over the main road, I pulled out my Colt, holding it in both hands, trigger finger along the side, barrel pointing toward the ground, I crept up to the gate. I kept low, and passed through without hearing any sounds from the compound.

I continued on slowly still not knowing what to expect, as the cold wind picked up, blowing my leather jacket flaps behind me. The wind made my eyes water, and I used my right-hand sleeve to wipe the wetness away.

About a hundred yards ahead and to my left was the west side of the large building, which I assumed was the main warehouse. A little further on was Esteban's Chevy pickup parked parallel to its entrance. I crept up to it, as my boots crushed the gravel under my feet.

Making my way to the side of the building, I stayed in the darkness and inched my way a little faster and stopped just by the Chevy pickup. To my right was a partially opened door. I moved toward it. And after a slow count of ten, I opened it just wide enough for me to go through, and stopped again.

Chapter Fifty

Deadly Shootout

In front of me and through the dim lighting of the warehouse, I saw four aisles of twelve-foot high metal shelving stacked with palettes of boxes. Two more aisles were on the right side of the wall. The other two on the left side had an eighteen-foot wide gap in the center. Off to the left side was a parked yellow forklift.

Toward the far end of the building I saw more dim lighting coming through an open doorway, probably an office of some sort.

From my place of concealment behind the right-side aisles, I made a quick examination of the warehouse. It was an old building. Trash littered the aisles as dust covered the concrete floor, and windows had broken glass panes. There seemed to be no signs of recent activity. The warehouse may have been used as a front for criminal activities.

I wandered slowly toward the left side of the warehouse wall, glancing around the dusty aisles and found a small gap in between the racks and the metal wall.

Slowly making my way up the aisle, I made it to the end without mishap and stopped. Leaning against the metal racks, I saw a closed window on a small office and lighting coming from the inside. There were the faintest sounds of movement and moans and groans from within. Over that I heard someone speaking in Spanish, but couldn't detect what was being said.

Moving again, I slowly made it to the far end of the office structure. On the other side of the closed window I stopped again, and leaned my back on the wall. Taking a quick glance through the window I made out four men; the two Chavez brothers tied up in chairs, and the enforcers I'd seen before in the Ford hovering close to them. Both brothers had blood seeping from several cuts on their faces. One of the enforcers held a gun loosely with his left hand at his side.

Ducking down low under the window sill, I crawled over to the other side, stood back up and made my way to the end of the office wall. There I glanced to my left and saw the open door.

It was do-or-die time. I kept telling myself I had the upper hand in what could happen next. I had the element of surprise in my favor, and their backs to the door helped out too.

With the Colt by my chest, I caressed the trigger and stepped close to the open door, stopping once again. That's when I overheard someone ask in Spanish, "Where is your family hiding out?"

Then from the other one, "Yeah, you'll tell us soon enough."

I didn't hear any response from the brothers. Apparently they couldn't speak from the battering their faces had received or they were keeping the information to themselves. They knew full well what would happen to their family if they gave them what they asked for. They probably also knew the longer they held out, the safer their family would be. No, they weren't going to part with that information, even if they killed them which more than likely they were going to do in the end.

"Well, time to make a house call," I muttered under my breath.

Then, taking a deep breath I slowly let out a short sigh. I paused just long enough to slow down my breathing and my heart rate. Then quickly and quietly I took a step into the office.

I had my Colt pointed directly at the guy with the gun, who was still holding it at his side. He was my focal point. Danger would come from him first. I would turn on the other guy next as soon as I'd dispatched his partner.

That was my plan!

The moment I walked in I was assailed with the pungent smells of blood and other unmentionable fluids. Things I'd smelled only in the killing fields of war.

Casting a quick glance inside of the office, I saw it had the usual "L" shape desk, grey metal filing cabinets, several shelving units and chairs. Stacks of paperwork littered the desk, with three rows of in-out bin boxes also stacked with papers. The lighting came from two over-head fluorescent light fixtures. And sitting on chairs with their hands tied behind them were the two Chavez brothers.

Still looking in, a slow smile crept across my face. *Here I come ready or not.*

I said, "Knock, knock. Hey . . . am I late for the party?"

I stood directly behind them, just inside the threshold of the office.

As I figured, the low-life thug with the gun acted first. And as he turned toward his left side, I saw his gun hand start to come up trying to track me with it. I didn't let him get off the first shot. Pulling the trig-ger, I shot him once as he turned in my direction on his left hip, just below his waist line. I missed, because I was aiming for his leg.

"Ahhhh, cabron!" he screamed.

I saw his face then. He didn't say anything else, but his face said volumes. Maybe like; *what the fuck?* or *who the hell are you?* or *Oh shit, I'm shot.*

One bullet was enough to put him down. I didn't need to go into over kill, since I still had the other thug to contend with.

The gunshot was overly loud and explosive in the confines of the small office. The guy continued on in his turn as the bullet's impact propelled his momentum and he was thrown back about a foot. Then he went straight down to the floor as if gravity itself was heavy, and as he did, the gun went flying out of his hand landing on the other side of the office well away from him and the other guy. Not a killing shot, but a disabling shot nevertheless. It was what I was hoping to achieve.

The other guy turned on his right side, coming out of his shock of seeing his partner down and out. Then in a blur, he flipped over the flap of his jacket, reached into his right side and pulled out a gun and fired almost point blank at me.

He was faster than his buddy, I give him that. I was just getting ready to raise my Colt to track him, when he drew and fired his weapon, then I pulled the trigger on my Colt twice.

His bullet had just grazed my left shoulder as I heard and felt it ripping my jacket.

But he only had time for one shot, as my first bullet struck him on his right shoulder. My second bullet struck the ground between his feet.

"You son of a fucking bitch, you shot . . ." he muttered in a low hoarse voice in Spanish. Then his face went blank, and before he could complete his sentence, he fell back dropping down on his knees holding onto his wounded shoulder with his left hand, as if to stem the flow of blood. Then, he slowly rolled onto the floor losing consciousness.

Keeping my Colt pointed at him, I walked over and kicked his gun far away from him. I then searched him for any further weapons and found a six shot .357 Colt Python. Taking it away from him, I checked the cylinder. It was fully loaded, so tucking it in my belt I kept it as a souvenir.

I also searched his partner, who was still out cold, but came up empty for guns. But instead, I found an old Italian-made, switch-blade with a bone-handle and in pretty good condition. So, I kept that too.

I took stock of where the guy's bullet just grazed my left shoulder, and knew I was just a centimeter away from being shot.

Only then did I look over to the two Chavez brothers who had been staring up at me from the moment I entered the office.

I read shock, disbelieve and a sense of relief written on their faces.

Ignoring the two guys I'd shot, I approached Alfonso Luis Chavez, my jumper.

Holstering my Colt, I stopped in front of him. Staring down at him, I saw he hadn't fully recovered from his beating. Slowly shaking his head side to side, he looked around then stopped. He finally took notice of what had happened around him as he kept opening and closing his one good eye.

Christ, his face had been worked over pretty good. His lips were puffed up and bleeding from several cuts and his right eye puffy and bleeding, was swollen shut. He was also bleeding from his right ear and blood was seeping out from a cut on his right arm. Glancing over at his brother, Esteban, I noticed he'd been worked over too, but not as badly as his brother.

Pulling out my handcuffs, I walked behind him and cuffed his hands together. Taking out the switchblade, I cut the rope binding his hands and his feet. I wasn't taking any chances with him, in case he still had some fight left in him.

Coming back around, I saw he was still somewhat in shock, but stared straight up at me.

Alfonso Chavez said, "Why are my hands cuffed?"

"Because you're the one I've come after."

"Come after? Who are you, do I know you?"

I shrugged, pausing a moment and smiled.

"Me? I'm no body. You don't know me, but I know you. I was sent to bring you back to jail."

"Let me guess, Montiel. Right?"

"Yeah, no one else but."

"You know, you could've been killed coming in here. Those two guys were professionals."

"If you say so," I said. "It was a gamble I had to take, before they killed you both. And I've survived far worse from better men than these two."

Alfonso Chavez was silent for a moment, but kept staring at me shaking his head.

"So what happens now?" he asked.

"Now, I take you back to jail."

Again, he went quiet for a moment, and then I saw his brother, Esteban Chavez, turn to face me giving me a serious quizzical look.

He said, "Hey, how about me? Are you going to cut me loose too, or leave me here like this?"

Turning to face him I said, "That all depends."

"Oh. Depends on what?"
"If you're going to do something stupid once I cut your bonds."
No answer for a beat.
I said, "Well?"
"OK, man. I won't do nothing stupid, promise."
But, he didn't live up to his promise.

Chapter Fifty-One

Blind Attack

Coming around to the two shot-up cartel enforcers, I stopped at the one I'd shot in the hip. Kneeling next to him, I placed my finger on his neck feeling for a pulse. It was weak, but still there. He was breathing rather shallow, but would live.

Removing his pants belt I used it to bind his hands behind him. Then using the switchblade again, I cut off his two pant legs and used them to stem the flow of blood. Once I'd finished with him, I turned to his partner.

The guy had managed to prop himself against the wall. He was wide awake looking at me holding on to his wounded shoulder. Again, I knelt beside him and removing his belt, tied his hands behind him. Cutting off one of his pant legs, I used it on his wounded shoulder. I noticed my bullet had gone clear through. After I finished with him, I stood straight back up and started walking away.

"Hey." I heard the guy behind me say. Turning around facing him, he stared up at me for a moment.

I took a step toward him.

I said, "What?"

The guy stared up at me. "Hey. Who are you, what do you want with them?"

I said, "Not your concern on either count. You're in no position to be asking questions."

"But, what are you going to do with us?"

"Shit, I haven't decided on it yet."

"You're not going to kill us, or you wouldn't have bothered to treat us."

"Aren't you the smart one," I said. "I clearly haven't decided yet. But yeah, the question is what to do with you and your partner. I'll think of something."

Turning back around, I walked over to Esteban Chavez who was still seated in the chair, hands tied behind him and his legs also tied to the chair legs.

Stopping next to him, I bent down and cut the bonds to his legs, then walked behind him and cut the bonds to his hands. Coming back around to face him I slowly back pedaled a couple of steps and watched as he massaged his hands and legs before standing on shaky legs.

My gun hand was nowhere near the butt of my Colt when he suddenly charged straight at me like a bull . . .!

He came at me fast, with his head down and bent at the waist, arms outstretched in front of him, with a loud yell.

What happened next took all of a few seconds. I wasn't given time to think, but acted out of pure instinct, driven by years of martial arts training.

A nano second more and he would be on me. Then, the moment he was inches from making contact, I quickly stepped forward to his right side with my left leg, thus removing myself from his direct line of attack. With my left forearm I forced him off balance in his forward movement. Moving fast, I pivoted withdrawing my right leg to my right-rear side. Then, grabbing his right arm, I spun him around me, while with my right hand I was guiding his head down into a circle to his rear in a windmill motion of my arms. He went flying and landed onto his back hard, hitting his head on the concrete floor, and was completely motionless for a few minutes.

"Oh, that's gonna hurt!" I muttered.

Suddenly, I heard someone coming up behind me. . .

Immediately I turned, drawing my Colt, cocked the hammer in one fluid motion and leveled it onto the chest of Alfonso Luis Chavez, who stopped dead in his tracks.

He yelled out, "Don't shoot! Please don't shoot me."

"Get on your knees, asshole."

"Ok, ok, just don't shoot."

He dropped down to his knees and stayed where he was, while I lowered my weapon and walked up behind him. Holstering my Colt, I made sure he still had the cuffs on and made sure I double-locked them.

He said, "My brother . . .?"

"He'll be okay. Just got the wind knocked out of him is all. He'll come out of it soon."

Coming up behind him, I grabbed his cuffed hands, and with a slight sudden grimace and moan, I had him standing back up. Then eliciting a short outburst of indignation he cursed me out in Spanish.

I ignored him.

He kept on yelling saying I was hurting his arms.

"You weren't cooperating with me, asshole. You try anything else, and I won't be as kind as I was with your brother. Understand?"

"Yeah, I understand."

He fell quiet after that.

Our walk to my car was uneventful. Once there, I led him to the back seat where I cuffed him to the iron post. After that, I headed back to the warehouse office where I still had some unfinished business to attend to.

Walking through the office front door I noticed that the two hitmen were still where I had left them, but Esteban Chavez was slowly trying to stand. Apparently, none the weaker after having the wind knocked out of him. This was good. It meant he could walk, and I needed him mobile for what I had in mind. I was making an assumption that he could help me. Not sure he would. Didn't cost none to ask nicely though.

I said, "I see you're up and about."

"Christ, my back hurts like shit and I got a terrible headache."

I said with a slight grin, "Yeah, guess you did land hard there, friend. It could've been worse, maybe taken a bullet."

He looked at me for a second while wiping away blood from behind his head.

He said, "Yeah, guess so."

A brief silence.

"So, what now, are you going to let me go?" he asked.

"Let me take a look at your wound."

Pulling out my scarf from my back pocket, I approached him and tied it around his head, stemming the flow of blood.

I said, "There you go. That should help some."

Then I addressed his question of letting him go.

"Not just yet. I have something for you to do first."

"Oh, like what? And do I have a choice?"

"Hey, you already made your choice when you helped out with your brother. So, what I'm asking isn't anything difficult."

Esteban looked at me, quizzically.

"So, what do you want me to do?"

"To begin with, I need for you to rest up a bit. Then you're going to help me put these two in their truck. After that, you're going to drive them across the border following me throughout. We'll drop them off in the desert somewhere and I'll bring you back to your apartment. Sound fair enough?"

"Okay."

Then taking up my offer to rest, he turned away from me and pulled up a chair and sat down massaging his legs and arms, trying to get more feeling into them.

"How soon before we start?" he queried.

I shrugged. "Just as soon as you're able."

"Give me a minute or two."

"Take your time, no rush."

Looking up at me he asked, "Are you still taking my brother to jail?"

Not bothering to make eye contact, I nodded, "That's the plan."

Once we secured the two cartel enforcers onto the bed of their Ford pickup and with Esteban Chavez in the driver's seat, I had him drive me to my car.

Once there and walking around to the driver's side, I unlocked the door and climbed behind the wheel. I fired it right up, put it in gear and slowly pulled away from the curb.

The moment we were moving, I heard Alfonso Chavez muttering from the back.

"You say something?" I asked.

"Yeah, it's about my brother?"

"What about him?"

"What have you done with him?"

"Nothing, he's okay."

"Where is he?"

"He's driving that Ford pickup."

"Where is he going?"

I adjusted the rearview mirror, saw his face and said, "That doesn't concern you. Just sit back, shut yourself up and enjoy the ride."

He muttered something I couldn't understand, but nevertheless he went quiet after that as he dropped his eyes from me and looked out his window as if resigning himself to his fate.

And then as I led the way, we pulled away heading toward Interstate 10.

Getting my bearings as best I could in the darkness, I went over in my mind a best route to the border crossing I'd used before, which suited my plans for disposing of the two Mexicans.

We traveled through a part of South Tucson I hadn't driven through before. Although it was in total darkness, my headlights beamed through into the area. I noticed that the structures and homes in this part of town were in a remarkable state of decrepitude. Garbage was strewn about on the sidewalks and the streets, and trash cans overflowed. The streets were completely deserted. After two or three miles, the surrounding landscape changed to empty lots, then to open grassy areas, devoid of buildings or homes. Then, approaching the I-10 onramp we got on the highway and made good time to Nogales, Arizona.

At last, after driving for about two hours we made the outskirts of

Nogales and got off I-10 then onto Highway 19. Turning off our headlights and driving slowly, I found the path I was looking for and ten minutes later drove through an almost invisible dirt patch of road, not readily seen from the highway. We stopped to make sure Border Patrol vehicles weren't hiding in the bushes. Not seeing any, we continued on in darkness moving slowly and crossed over into Mexico. Turning on our headlights we drove on for about two hours through a lonely stretch of deserted dirt road.

Finally, I found what I was looking for. It was so far away from civilization that it made for the ideal spot to release our two Mexicans. It was atop a small wooded bluff overlooking a small lake, surrounded by large rocks, Palo Verde trees, prickly pear plants, and a wide range of Cacti and Succulents plants. Tall grass grew throughout the area. It was a perfect spot to dispose of some bodies, dead or alive. But in my case, live ones.

Coming to a dead stop, I climbed out of my car, and waited for Esteban Chavez to pull up behind me.

Alfonso Chavez poked his head out of his window.

He said, "Hey, bounty hunter, I know what you're planning to do here, you thinking of killing those two. Don't blame you one bit, they deserve it for what they did to me and my brother. Go for it. I won't tell anyone."

As Esteban climbed out of his truck, I turned to Alfonso Chavez, looked him in the eyes, smiled, but didn't say a word. I let it hang in the air.

Meeting Esteban half way, we walked back to his truck and unloaded the two Mexicans. It took us about fifteen minutes, but once finished we had them lying on the ground by some rocks, still tied, still alive.

One of them looked around to where we were going to leave them, and turned to look at me. He was if anything, glad to still be alive.

He said, "You just going to leave us tied up like this?"

"Well, would it be better if I just put a bullet in both of you? Solve everyone's problems."

He didn't say anything after that.

I said, "With a little time you and your partner can get yourselves untied. Don't hear any wild animals nearby, so you'll be okay till you get loose in a day or two."

He glanced about him, saw his partner was still out and raised his head to look at me.

"You say wild animals?"

"You're not scared, are you?"

He didn't say a word, but I saw the concern and the fear edged in his eyes, before he dropped them from mine. It was true. The Sonora desert was rich in animal life and some were known to roam this part of the desert. Wild animals like the fierce pot-bellied lizard known as the chuckwalla, javelin, mountain lions, cougars and coyotes, made their home in the area.

After obtaining the truck keys from Esteban Chavez, I threw them far into the tall grass, but not too far where they couldn't eventually find them.

Starting to walk away from them, I noticed the other partner had regained consciousness and started to look around and then he glanced once at his partner, then at me.

For a moment, they were shocked into silence.

The closer of the two turned and stared up at me. He struggled with his restraints, but I'd made sure they were tight. He slowly started to plead and beg for his life.

He said, "Jesus, please don't leave us like this."

I didn't say a word.

Considering it for just a moment and against my better judgment, I reached into my jacket pocket and pulled out the switchblade. I then threw it into a tall grassy area far from them, but not too far they couldn't get to it. That is if they could find it, and if the animals didn't get to them first.

Seeing where I tossed the blade, they both started struggling with their bonds. They wriggled, twisted and turned their bodies in a vain effort to reach the blade.

I wished them luck.

With Esteban in the passenger seat and me behind the wheel, I quickly made a U-turn on the tight dirt road, and slowly drove out the way we came in and headed back to Tucson.

Arriving back at the warehouse to pick up Esteban's truck, I parked and shut down the LeBaron. Once he had exited the car, he leaned up against the passenger door, bent down and looked though the open window at me.

"Eh, I like to thank you for not shooting me back there."

I glanced at him.

"Yeah, it could've been worse."

"Now's that?"

"I could've killed you."

"Guess you could've at that."

I nodded.

"Listen," I said. "You can take this with a grain of salt, but I would leave here for someplace far away. I mean far from Tucson or Arizona. Those two, if they live out the night, will probably return for you and your family. And if not them some others would be sent. Mark my word, they will come for you."

"On the drive over here, I was thinking the same thing. Thanks."

And that was my last good deed of the day.

Driving away through the warehouse gate I decided on taking a shortcut to the Feds' lockup. And with Alfonso Chavez in the back all cuffed and secured, he wasn't going to give me any trouble — except with his mouth. He ran it a mile a minute, just couldn't keep it shut. And like most of my jumpers, he offered me a large sum of money to turn him loose.

It doesn't work with me though.

After listening to him run at the mouth, I pulled off to the side of the road and turned around to face him.

"Listen closely," I said. "If you don't shut the hell up, I'm going back there and ram my fist into your face and make you uglier. Do I make myself clear?"

Not a word, just a brisk nod.

THE TURN-OVER OF MY PRISONER TO THE FEDS' TOOK ALL OF THIRTY minutes. Sitting down at the patrolman's desk area, I started writing the arrest report. I included; who, what, where, when and why of police report writing into my report leaving out the shooting and the two enforcers from the report. The courts just needed to know why the prisoner was being remanded back into custody, which I did.

Finishing up my report and turning it in to the booking sergeant, I requested permission to speak with one of their prisoners, Angel Serrano.

Twenty minutes later, I was led to an interview room by one of the guards. And there he was cuffed to the desk, waiting. The moment I walked in his eyes lit up and his mouth opened to let out a yell for the guard to let him out of the room.

The guard came but I waved him off. Taking a seat across from him, I stared him in the eyes and smiled.

I said, "Didn't think you'd see me again, did you?"

He didn't say anything as he turned his head away from me, avoiding any chance of eye contact.

"You know I have a few people in here that would take you down with just a word from me. You try sending anymore of your goons after me, and so help me you won't live long."

Then I just got up and left before he could say anything.

Out of the room I thanked the guard and walked back to the front desk.

After getting my copy of the bond signed and sealed, I headed home to a hot bath, a hot meal and the waiting arms of my wife and kids.

This was going to be my last case of the year. I'd promised the family a vacation to the San Diego Zoo and Christmas to celebrate together, and I wasn't going to let them down. My social life had been rather anemic lately, and I was going to change that. And of course, it hadn't been too shabby for several hours of work and a good paycheck added in.

Now that my business with Serrano was over, I felt rather pleased with myself.

Book Five

James Jennings

Chapter Fifty-Two

Home Front

Mid January 1988, Tucson, Arizona

THE ONE STORY SINGLE FAMILY HOME LOCATED IN THE GROVES LINCOLN Park, in Pima County, Tucson, Arizona, was built back in 1977, and was well maintained and immaculately preserved with its desert landscape; it still maintained the Old West charm and had a lone eight-foot tall Saguaro Cactus just to the right of the front door.

The home boasted four large bedrooms, a large kitchen and an open carport. The cooling system consisted of the typical evaporative coolers predominately used in the Southwest, and used forced air for heating. I also had a large back yard that the kids loved.

And it was home!

Not too many knew of the address, or that a licensed bounty hunter lived in the neighborhood real close to them. But appearances can be deceiving, and I liked that sense of anonymity.

I was in the living room catching up on my reading of a book entitled, *The Icarus Agenda* by Robert Ludlum, one of my favorite authors. It was mid-January, and the weather forecast was slated to be in the low forties this evening as the night wind brought a chill to the air.

But, it was warm and cozy inside.

It was quiet and very peaceful in the house. With the boys fast asleep in their rooms, Carmen-Melissa, my six-year-old had dropped into a sound sleep on her mother's lap. Dolores barely kept her eyes open though, dozing on and off. She was wearing a pair of my gym workout pants she'd worn all day with a white blouse. Her hair flowed freely down over her shoulders. She was looking quite beautiful as always and so peaceful sitting there with Carmen that I hated to wake them.

Nothing disturbed my reading, which was a God sent. It was a breather of sorts from my private investigation and bounty hunting cases. But, as I sipped on a cup of hot coffee, Dolores woke with a start as the kitchen phone started ringing.

She sighed and rose from her chair.

She said, "The phone, Victor."

"I hear it too, honey."

I reached for my coffee cup, left my easy chair and walked the few steps to the kitchen. Reaching the phone, I saw Dolores picking Carmen up in her arms and walking down the hallway to the bedrooms. Taking a sip of my coffee, I reached for the receiver just as it ended its fourth ring.

"Hey Victor," came a heavy voice I'd recognize anywhere on the other end of the line. "How's my friend, the Huntsman?"

"Well, if it isn't my buddy, Mike. Hello, Mike, it's always a pleasure hearing from you."

Mike Hernandez was a member of FIST, the Fugitive Apprehension Division of the Pima County Sheriff's office, and my friend.

A little dry chuckle.

"Hey, I'm joining a few of the guys tomorrow for a little shooting, thought you'd like to tag along."

I paused, thinking of the last time we went shooting together. It didn't fare well for him, but it did for me.

"I'd love to go, thanks Mike."

"Good. I knew you couldn't turn down my offer to beat you in shooting."

"Hey, if I remember correctly, I beat you in the combat twenty-five-yard range and the fast draw shooting as well. You remember that. Right? Or are you getting too old that you could forget something like that?"

"You're an asshole, Victor. But that's the reason I'm inviting you along. I'm going to beat you this time."

"Sure you are. Whatever gets you through the night."

"Anyway, we'll meet at the Pima pistol club say about ten in the morning. You know the place?"

"Think so. Is that the one off Lago Del Oro Parkway?"

"That's the one. Hey, smartass Puerto Rican bring some dollars with you. I want to win back my losses I had from the last time."

"See you there. But you're sure asking to lose some more dough. Your wife's gonna get pissed at you again, Mike."

"I don't see it that way."

"We'll see."

As I replaced the receiver, I recalled the first and only time we'd gone shooting. I'd barely beaten him. If his last two shots had come just a little closer to the bullseye, I would have lost. But as it was, I won four hundred bucks on that bet. We'll see what tomorrow brings.

Before retiring for the night, I left a note on the bedroom dresser for Dolores, with the phone number to the range, just in case she needed to contact me.

It was eight in the morning when I woke up from a very sound sleep. What woke me was the racket the kids were making as they thundered through the house, and it dawned on me that this was Saturday. No school.

Christ!

Slowly getting out of bed, I walked toward the shower in the nude, just as my wife entered our bedroom. She was dressed in a loose fitting white robe.

I said, "I see you're up and about too."

She glanced down at me.

"I, ah, see you're up as well."

I saw a slight mischievous smile play across her face as she slowly undid the robe's belt. It opened just enough for me to see she wore only panties underneath.

She closed the door behind her and slowly approached me.

She said, "Just came in to let you know I've made breakfast."

"Is that all?"

Stopping right in front of me, Dolores stared at me with those big brown eyes as she wound her arms around my waist. I held her tight as we melted into each other with a burning hunger I knew was mutual. Then gently, I held her head in my hands as I inclined my head and meeting her warm soft lips, we kissed softly and passionately. She began caressing my chest, then her hand slowly crept down between my legs and she tenderly stoked there too. I was fully aroused, letting myself be completely taken by her caress, wanting her. Then gently she pushed away from me, turned around and walked toward the bedroom door and opening it she started walking out of the bedroom, closing up her robe.

"Ah, oh honey," I said in a soft breathless voice. "You're just going to leave me this way?"

She stopped at the door and turned to face me with a smile on her face.

"Oh. What way is that?"

"You're a big teaser, honey."

She didn't say a word as she walked out of the room.

I took a deep breath, slowly exhaled and with a sigh and a little cough, I prepared to take a very cold shower.

I LEFT THE CITY OF TUCSON AND AFTER ANOTHER FIFTEEN MINUTES OF driving, I finally turned onto State Route 77, which would eventually take me to the Bowman Road access. Then a dirt road and a few minutes later, a sign came into focus along with the main entrance to the PPC, Pima Pistol Club.

The PPC is one of the oldest outdoor shooting ranges in Tucson, dating back to 1920, when it first opened its doors to the public.

Entering, I made for the parking lot up ahead. The lot was almost packed and I saw scores of people walking around involved in some quiet conversations and enjoying themselves. Finding a space way in the back of the lot, I shutdown the engine, and as I climbed out, I grabbed my gun belt, equipment bag and my black baseball cap, and locking the car, walked over to the main office.

Once inside I saw Mike and three other cops I'd met before looking over at me. Walking up to them, I saw they had already picked up their targets.

I was wearing a black sweatshirt army camouflaged pants, and noticed the rest of the guys were similarly clad.

I said, "Hey, Mike, guys."

"Hi Al," Mike said. "You know the rest of these guys, don't you?"

"Yeah, I've seen them around," I said, extending my hand out to them. "Glad to see you all."

After a round of handshakes and exchanging pleasantries, I picked up some targets of my own and started walking behind the pack over to the range proper.

One of the guys, a short man, not more than five-foot-eight and starting to show a pot belly, with brown thinning hair named Andy Morales, took a glance my way and smiled.

"So, Al," he said. "You ready to lose some money today?"

"And who said I was going to lose?"

"Mike did," he said.

"Well, Mike's full of crap. He doesn't know he's already lost."

"We haven't started shooting yet," Mike said. "And he's already shooting off his mouth."

We all laughed.

I nodded, then winked at Andy Morales and kept on walking.

I said, "We'll see who's shooting off his mouths soon enough."

I tried sounding confident and self-assured in as much as I could.

But also knowing how good Mike was, I'd have to be able to best him once again. Unless of course he'd been training, and if he had been, well that could spell trouble for me.

Chapter Fifty-Three

Guns and Bullets

With clear skies and no wind to speak of, the weather was cooperating today making this a great day for shooting. The temperatures held steady at sixty-five degrees and it was expected to climb towards the high seventies just about noon. So, we didn't expect to be shivering in the cold.

We'd just entered blue-range number-one, which was primarily used for pistols. The maximum target range was set at seven yards, enough to get a good tight shot-group.

There wasn't anyone else firing on our range, which for us was a blessing of sorts. It was just us, and that suited us just fine.

After getting our paper targets setup down range, I settled in to my firing bay, as Mike and the other guys set up to my left, with Mike next to me. I then laid out three empty magazines and three boxes of .45 caliber ball ammunition on the shelf before me along with my Colt. The rest of the guys followed suit with their Department issued Smith and Wesson model-66, 6-round capacity revolvers and boxes of ammunition. That is, except for Mike. Like myself he had a Colt M1911 .45 caliber. I opened a box of ammo and began loading my magazines.

Then I grabbed a pair of hearing protectors from my equipment bag and placed them over my ears. Picking up one of my full magazines, I loaded it into the Colt and racked the first round into the chamber, primed for firing.

Seconds later, the report of gunfire from the other guys was partially muffled by my ear protectors. Mike Hernandez's weapon roared to life on my left as I carefully took aim and fired off two quick shots. Looking down range I'd noticed my rounds had just nicked the outer circle left of the bullseye. I adjusted my shooting by gripping my Colt a little tighter, which should stop the barrel from moving up and down and off the left side, and let loose the rest of the rounds. As the Colt locked after the last round I'd fired, I laid down my weapon. I saw that all my rounds hit within or about the bulls' eye marker.

It's been my experience that a tight shot group really doesn't matter as such. But rather it's hitting the right target and in the right place that truly counts. Muscle memory is the secret. If you consistently and constantly worked those muscles, you should acquire a good tight shot group all the time, regardless of the distance from which you're firing.

Then I inserted a fresh magazine and fired off the last of my full magazines, in quick load and fire fashion taught in all police departments.

After my last round was fired, I noticed that the other guys had stopped firing as well. We then took the opportunity to check out the targets, and proceeded down range.

No one said a word till we reached our targets.

As we approached them, I immediately noticed that only three of us came within or on the bullseye, Mike, James Franklin, the older of the three cops, maybe forty-three, six foot and ramrod straight, and myself. But only Mike and I had a fairly tight shot group.

Mike had five rounds on the mark, and three that were too close to call, with all the rest on or about the head area. James, with his six shot revolver, had four rounds on and two out. While I had five rounds on, with one round out and another way off to the left. And like Mike's, the rest of my rounds hit on the head portion of the target. So, Mike was the winner, with me coming in second and James third.

We were all milling about, taking turns looking over the targets, admiring the tight shot group of Mike and myself.

James had been looking at Mike's target.

He said, "Now that is some good shooting, Lieutenant."

Mike said, "I'll be lucky to repeat that again, for my yearly qualification."

"Hey, Al," Dan Warren said. "The LT beat you."

I said, "Yeah, yeah. He got a lucky break, is all. For now, that is."

"What's next?" Andy Morales asked.

Mike said, "How about we do the quick draw competition with three rounds into the target's bullseye with the best time wins. Winner takes the purse."

We decided that a hundred dollars apiece would go into the purse for the quick draw competition.

I said, "Okay by me. I brought along my pro-competition stopwatch just for this."

James asked, "Who's up first?"

"Well," I said. "How about the three of you guys go first, and Mike and I will go last?"

James said, "Sounds fair enough."

"What was your best time, Al?" Dan asked.

"Let's see," I said. "When I beat Mike before, I believe it was about one-sixteenth seconds. Not my tops, but it was good enough then."

Andy said, "That's pretty good, Al."

The rest of them, even Mike, nodded their agreement and gazed over at me with what I thought was a hint of admiration.

As we walked back to our bay, I didn't say anything, but gave them a little smile.

Ten minutes later, we were all setup for the quick draw competition. But in this case, only one target was used.

After all three of the guys had taken their turns, with Mike at the stopwatch, only one of the guys, Andy had come close enough to beat my best time. He had one-nineteenth seconds, so we had to beat that time, and that left Mike and me.

It was at this juncture when they all placed separate bets on a winner, and Mike was the favorite to win. I didn't blame them for betting that way, cops looked after cops, it was their nature, and although I was a friend, I was still considered an outsider.

With a new paper target set-up, we decided that I would shoot last. James asked to be on the stopwatch. We all agreed.

Mike started getting ready by loading a magazine with just three rounds, all that was required to shoot. Then picking up his Colt, he walked around and in front of the shooting bay and holstered the weapon.

Wearing our ear protectors, James called out to Mike, "Are you ready, Lieutenant?"

After a brief pause, Mike nodded.

"On the count of three," James said. "Draw, shoot and recover."

James had his finger on the stopwatch button.

"One," he said.

Everyone looked over at Mike, who had his back to us.

"Two."

I held my breath, and watched as Mike let his shoulders slacken. I saw him slowly bringing his left arm up close to his chest, ready to receive the Colt, as his right hand slowly creep up to his holster, in anticipation of the next count.

"Three."

I relaxed, and breathed out, knowing that's exactly what I'll be doing next.

As if in slow motion, I watched Mike draw. Then fire three quick shots down range. His Colt locked out after the last round, and he holstered it in one smooth motion. He had good posture and good control.

Then after a short pause, James shouted, "Time! One-sixteenth seconds!"

Mike walked back around the bay, and was greeted with handshakes and big, warm smiles.

I said, "Damn, Mike. You have the same time I had when I beat you last, but you certainty beat out Andy's time."

Mike shrugged. "It felt good, too."

Andy nodded rapidly. "Shit! I was hoping on taking home the five hundred bucks."

"Ah come on seriously?" I said. "I guess you weren't counting on me?"

Then turning away from us, Andy went down range and pulled Mike's target and set-up another, which was for me. On his return, we saw that all three rounds were grouped around each other in the bullseye.

"Yes sir," I commented again. "That's some real good shooting."

Mike kept staring at me.

He made a happy face. "Thank you, Al. So it's your turn. Do better if you can smartass."

There was something in that stare.

"Sure," I said.

A ghost of a smile played across my lips as I dropped my eyes from his, understanding the challenge. And it definitely was a challenge. Two things came to mind, as I thought, *should I beat him in front of his close buddies? Or should I just let him win?* Yeah, I understood it quite perfectly.

At least we weren't in competition for a woman! I thought.

I said, "Well, let's get this show on the road."

Stepping up to the bay's shelf, I loaded a magazine with three rounds. I then locked the magazine into the Colt, racked a live one down the tube, clicked off the safety, and holstered the weapon.

Coming around the bay, I felt all eyes on me. I took a deep breath and breathed out. Seven yards, that wasn't the problem. I'd made easier shots in the past. No big deal really. When Lieutenant Mike Hernandez called me to participate in the shootout, I wanted the purse that went along with the invite. But I didn't want to lose the friendship I'd made with him.

It was a decision not to be taken lightly.

Shit, a little voice in me said.

Then smiling, I gently nodded.

With shooting still going on through the ranges, I closed my eyes and tried to isolate the sounds, and just thought of what I had in front of me. Opening my eyes, I grabbed my ear protectors from the shelf; I then placed them over my ears. No one had said anything as I walked around toward the front of the bay, stopped and faced my target downrange.

Then as if from far away I heard James, call out to me.

"Are you ready, Al?" he asked.

After a brief silence, I nodded.

"On the count of three, draw fire and recover your weapon," James said. "Once your weapon is back in its holster the time will stop."

I waited, not saying anything. Back straight, knees slightly bent, I let myself stand relaxed with both hands down my sides — breathing in breathing out. In good position, as called for in police training. It was a typical tactical pose for reflexive control shooting.

"One," James called out.

Still and calm.

"Two."

I slowly raised my left hand and placed it on my chest ready to receive my weapon, as my right hand crept up to the butt of the Colt.

"Three!"

I took a quick breath and exhaled hesitating slightly. Then as I drew my Colt, my left hand moved to receive it as I grasped the weapon in both hands, trigger finger resting along the side of the Colt, close to my chest, elbows bent in. Extending the hands, I locked into my target as I subconsciously felt my finger slide onto the trigger. Squeezing the trigger, I kept on squeezing till I heard and felt the slide locked in place after the last round had fired, and then in one smooth motion, holstered the weapon.

"Time!" James yelled out. "One-fourteenth seconds!"

The second I holstered my Colt, I kept my gaze on the target. I saw that the rounds had scored within the bullseye. But that didn't matter one bit now. I knew my time wasn't good enough to have beat Mike's. And consciously, I knew it from the moment I hesitated prior to drawing my weapon.

I let him beat me.

It was only five hundred dollars, but our friendship meant more to me than that.

With a contented smile, I walked around the bay and approached the guys. Andy blew a little whistle my way, showing his appreciation for my shooting.

As Mike and I met up, Andy walked the down to the target, removed it and came back to meet up. We gathered around the target, as Andy placed it on the bay's shelf.

James said, "Would you look at that?"

I said, "Read it and weep, guys."

Mike said, "Damn, that's the tightest grouping I've seen yet from you, Al."

I didn't say anything, just smiled.

Dan piped in, "Looks like they're grouped tighter than a half a dollar piece."

"Yeah," Andy remarked. "But not good enough to beat Mike's time though."

A while later when we walked back to our cars, with Mike walking at my side, he looked over at me with a wry little smile. Then he placed his hand on my left arm slowing me down a bit.

He said, "You hesitated back there, just before you drew. You mind telling me why?"

"Don't rightly know, Mike. Something in my eye I guess."

"Eye my ass! And I think I know why."

"Sure?"

"Yeah," and in a low whisper he said, "Thanks for not showing me off in front of my guys."

"I don't know what you're talking about, Mike. You beat me fair and square."

"Yeah . . . right."

Chapter Fifty-Four

Holdup and Arrest

Late February 1988, Tucson, Arizona

THE BLACK '79 CHEVY EL CAMINO, WITH ITS TWO ORANGE STRIPES running sideways down the hood was parked in the shadows up by a lamp post.

With this part of town almost deserted, hardly anyone took notice neither of it nor of the only occupant sitting behind the wheel.

The guy was smoking, listening to some hard rock station on his car's radio, not loud, just barely high enough so only he could hear it. He didn't want to draw attention to himself. The inside of his car was filled with cigarette smoke, and after three back-to-back Marlboros, he had to crack his window down to let some of the smoke out.

He also had a small bottle of whiskey in a brown, paper bag from which he'd been taking long pulls. Slowly but surely he was gaining courage for what he had planned on doing tonight.

It was a little after two in the morning, cold and windy for a February night. The driver, a pale looking guy, with long dirty blond hair down to his shoulders, wore a sad miserable look. Miserable because he needed cash right away, cash to support his meth habit. No one knew he was here, not even his girl friend, Julie. And if she knew he would be a dead man. So, he kept a steady vigil on the Circle K convenience store across the street. After nearly thirty minutes of constant watch as several people came and went, and hoping for the right time, he finally saw his chance.

With only one person that he could see inside the store, the cashier, he donned a blue sailor's cap and picked up his father's old .38 caliber Smith & Wesson two-inch detective special from the glove compartment and tucked it into his waistband. He then pulled his coat over it, finished the rest of the whiskey, and slipped out of the Chevy into the cold windy night.

Closing the driver's door, James E. Jennings stood there a moment and cupping his hands, blew into them. As he looked up and down the street and before taking a step toward the Circle K across the street, he saw two young punks walking down Twenty-Second Street approaching the store.

He held his breath, hoping against hope they would just walk right on by. Reaching the convenience store they passed without entering, and he quickly exhaled, giving little thanks that they didn't enter. Then, seeing no one else coming around, Jennings ran across the street, slowed then stepped onto the sidewalk not three feet from the store's entrance. Taking out his gun, he palmed it in his right hand and pulling open the door, he walked inside.

Jennings walked up and down the aisles acting — he hoped, as if he was shopping for goodies. He then came back around to the front of the store, reached the front desk and pointed the gun at the cashier ordering him to empty the cash register.

With the register full of cash and another nine thousand in the safe behind him, the cashier, and a sandy-haired, twenty-one-year-old guy named Jimmy Hicks did as he was told. Hicks, a local high school dropout, had been robbed at gunpoint twice before. So, without a word Hicks opened the register, pulled out all the bills and laid the cash on the counter.

"Put it in a bag, asshole!" Jennings snapped at him, shoving the gun in Hicks' face.

Hicks, again without saying a single word, grabbed a paper bag from under the counter, stuffed it with the money and handed it over to Jennings.

Grabbing the bag, Jennings turned and ran out of the store, only to have the Hicks seconds later, run after him.

Hicks saw the thief running across the street to a black Chevy El Camino. Saw him get in and speed off down Twenty-Second Street. Running back into the store, Hicks called the police, gave a description of the robber and of the vehicle with the direction it had taken.

It didn't take long before an APB, all-points-bulletin, was out on the El Camino and broadcasted on the police band.

A patrol officer in a black and white happened to be nearby on Twenty-Second Street, and called in that he was within two blocks of the scene.

With blue lights cutting through the night and sirens whining its warning to traffic, the police officer rushed to the scene, just as the El Camino sped past him in the opposite direction.

Immediately recognizing the vehicle, the officer executed a quick U-turn and gave chase to the fleeing Chevy. Jennings, watching the black and white prowl car bang the U-turn, knew it was just a matter of time before it caught up to him.

With three other patrol officers joining in on the chase, within a few minutes Jennings stopped and was arrested without incident.

***

APPEARING AT THE PIMA COUNTY COURT HOUSE THAT NEXT AFTERNOON, Jennings was arraigned and charged with armed robbery. A day later, during his bail hearing he was granted bail. Having no prior convictions and not considered a flight risk, bail was set at sixty-five thousand dollars.

In the packed court house that day sat Julie Ann Moss, Jennings' girlfriend and Frank Marshall from Triple 'A' Bail Bonds. They sat in the back, waiting their turn.

Julie, sitting across from Marshall saw Jennings being led into the courtroom handcuffed. Jennings saw her and his face lit up with a smile as she waved over at him. A half hour later once the bond was satisfied and posting the necessary ten percent in cash, Jennings was a free man.

Besides the cash, Julie Ann Moss also signed over a quick deed to her home to Triple 'A' Bail Bonds, making her responsible for Jennings. If Jennings didn't show for his court appearance, or if he failed to live up to the conditions of his bond, Julie stood to lose the cash and her home. But Jennings had assured her that wasn't going to happen.

Earlier that day, Frank Marshall was in his office at Triple 'A' Bail Bonds, when Julie Ann Moss came in. She needed to bail her boyfriend out of jail and asked what was required to make that happen.

Looking up from his desk, Marshall saw a woman of medium height, with jet black hair growing long down her back. Slightly pale faced with small round eyes, a pretty good looking young lady of about twenty-three. Once he briefed her on the procedure, and getting all the necessary information from her, John Marshall made the arrangements to be in the court house with her.

He'd been awake for some time now.

But, he lay in bed under the covers debating on whether he should get up at all. But, he knew he was going to be late if he didn't.

Shaking his head, trying to wake up after a night of partying and drinking, James Jennings turned over and gazed at the beautiful blonde who was starting to wake, and kissed her forehead. Then rising out of the bed, he picked up his clothing off the floor a piece at a time, slowly because of his huge headache.

It was still slightly dark in the bedroom as beams of sunlight filtered through the half open slats of the venetian blinds from the two side windows. He stared at the alarm clock on the night stand. And as his eyes focused on it, he saw it was just half past seven in the morning.

Christ, I'm going to be late, he thought.

The blonde, Tiffany Barnes, was in her late twenties, just barely pushing thirty, a pretty good-looking woman with a lot going for her; beauty, blue eyes and a body any man would love to devour in bed. She worked at The Desert Diamond Casino out by the airport, dealing blackjack. Between tips and wages, she made a very good living. Jennings knew that, since he was always able to get her to loan him a few dollars here and there, whenever he wasn't working.

Tiffany stirred on the bed and sat up blinking rapidly, trying to shake the hangover she was feeling as the sheets fell on her lap, exposing her small firm breasts and pinkish hard nipples.

Placing the clothes at the foot of the bed, Jennings slowly turned and watched her for a second, looking at her breasts, and thinking if he only had some more time, he could get in one last screw to hold him till tonight. But he was already late.

She saw him looking at her half naked body and smiled.

She said, "Hey. Are you leaving already?"

It gave him pause.

He knew she was having her fun with him, exposing herself to him like that.

Then he smiled a little crooked smile.

"Yeah, guess so, got to go to work."

"Are you going to be coming back tonight?"

As he sat on the edge of the bed getting ready to put his clothes on, he looked into her eyes, cupped a breast in his hand, and caressed her firm nipple. They kissed as her hand slid over his face. He gently laid her down onto her back.

As his hand moved down her leg to the mound at the apex, she shuddered a little and stiffened, waiting for what was to come. But with a little sigh he got up quickly, and started putting on his shorts and pants.

She was trying very hard to keep her composure after he let go of her breast without entering her.

She said, "Well, are you?"

"Am I what?"

"Coming back tonight?"

"Don't know. I'll call you later."

She bristled, a pout on her lips. "You're going to *her*, aren't you?"

He stood there frozen like a statue for what was just a second, and turned around to face her.

"Like I said, I'll call you later."

"You're still seeing her, aren't you?"

Jennings was pulling on his pants, and sat back on the bed, not looking at her. She looked at him waiting for him to say something. She loved him, and couldn't bear having another woman share his bed. It was tearing her apart.

"She bailed me out of jail. What am I supposed to do?"

"Leave her. That's what you need to do. That's what you said you were going to do."

He turned his face to look directly at her, and said, "I'm leaving." He pushed himself up from the bed, grabbed his shirt, put in on and then his shoes.

"James, you're going to blow a good thing with me."

"Cut the crap, okay? I'll be leaving her, so don't push it."

"Don't make this harder than it is, okay?"

"I'll call you tonight."

He turned and walked out of the room, past the kitchen and then to his car.

Chapter Fifty-Five

Bond Surrender

At the Triple 'A' Bail Bonds office, she came in wearing a solemn face.

It was a most unhappy face, with sorrow lines narrowing her eyes, but I detected anger behind them as well.

She walked into the office and came to a stop just at the threshold. A gorgeous brunette with a large brown handbag hanging from her shoulder, she was wearing a light coat open, showing a blue blouse and short dark blue skirt. No nylons. Her hair was neatly brushed back into a ponytail.

She was candy to my eyes.

I was sitting across from Fred Luna, one of my bondsmen and friend as we both looked up and saw her framed against the door. She stood there for a second, not saying a word, and as her eyes fell and lingered on us, she walked over. She stopped right in front of us. For some unknown reason, her eyes locked on and stayed on Fred.

I kept glancing at her.

She was slim from what I gleaned under her coat, with pale skin, light eyeliner, golden earrings, light red lipstick, and a very sweet tender voice.

She said, "Hi. Is Mister Marshall in today?"

Fred stood up extending his hand.

"No. He's off today. How can I help you?" he asked.

After gently shaking the proffered hand, she nodded but went quiet for a few seconds like maybe trying to think of what to say.

"Mister Marshall," she said, "Helped bail my boy friend . . . ex-boyfriend, and I need to speak to him or someone else about it."

I immediately stood and offered my chair to her. Taking the seat, she reached into her handbag and pulled out a copy of a bond and handed it over to Fred.

Reaching for the form and opening it, he read through it briefly. Fred sat back down.

He said, "Ah, yes I remember John talking to me about this case. Again, how can I be of help to you?"

She slowly bowed her head and placed her hands on her lap. Seconds later, she raised her head and looked at Fred, then started telling her story.

Pulling up another chair I sat in the front of the office listening to their conversation and the story she told.

The gist of the story went like this; her name was Julie Ann Moss, and her boyfriend was James E. Jennings. According to her, she'd broken up with Jennings over a week ago, because he was romantically involved with another woman. She didn't want to be responsible anymore for him or the bond. She didn't know the name of the other woman, nor did she care. It was through a close girlfriend of hers that she'd found out about the other woman. When Julie confronted him with it, he denied it. She had immediately seen though his lie though. But the damage was done, and she immediately parted ways.

Fred and I didn't say anything.

Then, she broke the brief silence.

She asked, "How can we go about getting me off this bond?"

"Let me take a look at the file first," Fred said. "I'll see what can be done. I'm not making any promises though."

She shrugged.

"I understand," she said.

Fred Luna stood back up, went into the back of the office and came back with a manila folder and sat back down behind his desk.

As he read through the folder, I sat up straighter in my chair, already sensing the possibilities of a job here. I was thinking that maybe this could be another Snatch and Grab affair, if she agreed to the terms.

A slow smile touched my lips. But my eyes came to rest on her and they opened a little wider, as if in sympathy to her plight.

Once Fred was finished, he said that the only way would be to surrender the bond and Jennings to the courts. But that would mean tracking him down first and that cost money. Then, after introducing me to her, Fred mentioned that I could be persuaded to help, for a fee. Fred said, "Mr. Alvarez is a private investigator and a bounty hunter we use from time to time."

I came up front again, dragging my chair with me. I placed it beside her, sat and saw her glanced my way, as I extended out my hand.

"You can call me Al," I said. "I handle Fred's difficult cases for him."

She gently shook my hand. "And would you consider my case difficult, Mr. Alvarez?"

"Al, please."

"Al, then, would it?"

I shook my head. "As a matter of fact, I don't. This wouldn't be difficult at all. I'd say a day or so, at most. No more than that."

She looked over at Fred then slowly back to me.

"You can get him in a day?"

"Yes ma'am, I believe I can."

She kept looking at me, trying to make up her mind. She started to say something, and then she stopped. Then she just shrugged and closed her eyes for a second or two.

She nodded. "Okay, I'll pay the fee."

IIT WAS LATE THAT AFTERNOON.

After kissing my wife and kids, I'd started out on the case. I was hoping to catch and return Jennings back to jail by nightfall. My family had made plans for the day, and naturally they weren't too happy about my going out. But that couldn't be helped; I had a job to do.

Seems the address Julie Ann Moss had given me turned out to belong to Jennings' parents. They were two seventy-year-olds which was unexpected. Their house turned out to be a Rambler out by Green Valley off Highway-19. It was a good thirty-minute drive just south of Tucson.

It was an old ranch by the looks of it, and not well kept either. I parked my LeBaron in a thicket under some trees setting myself up for a little surveillance.

It was a cool, crisp February afternoon, cloudy and somewhat over-cast as I kept watch on the house. It was a half hour later, just as I finished the last of my cold coffee that I heard out in the distance the approaching sounds of a car.

A few minutes later I caught the front end of it as it approached the intersection. By the looks of it, it was a black car. As it entered the inter-section it made its turn toward the house. I knew what it was and who was driving. It was an El Camino, James Jennings' car!

I was getting myself ready to take him down once he parked in the front of the house. But Jennings didn't help my course; he just drove straight through to the back.

Damn, there goes that idea, I thought.

I made a strong effort to control myself, thinking of how to effec-tively proceed. If it had been the cops, they would have surrounded the house, used a bullhorn to persuade Jennings to turn himself in, and then waited it out. I didn't have the luxury of a police department at my call.

It was just me.

So, I couldn't just go busting into the house, not with an elderly couple inside who may or may not get involved or injured in crossfire. Just didn't know for sure if he was still armed. I didn't want to take the chance.

So, I did what the cops would do in my situation — wait him out.

Then, follow him when he departed to wherever that would lead me. And hope for a better scenario in some other place to effectively make my arrest, without any collateral damage.

Four hours into the surveillance and as the darkness enshrouded the area and my hiding place, my patience was finally rewarded. I heard the El Camino start up and saw it pulling away from the house. With its headlights on, it slowly approached the intersection, and then made a right onto Highway-19.

I caught the shadow of only one person in the Chevy. As it accelerated fast away from my location, I turned the key in the ignition. Slowly pulling out of my hiding place, I got onto the highway as I caught sight of the El Camino's taillights.

With very thin traffic out so late at night, following him was a rather simple task. And staying back five or six car lengths would keep Jennings off guard.

Moreover, he didn't know anything was up. No warrants had been issued for his arrest, and since he'd been keeping up with his court appearances he was assured of a safe bail.

But, what he didn't know was that his ex-girlfriend Julie had turned in his bond. If he had known of it, he would've been more cautious, looking over his shoulder as it were.

It was twenty minutes later when we made the I-10 turn-off. Here traffic was heavy, and it became somewhat harder to keep the Chevy in sight what with drivers cutting me off twice. I had to drive faster just to keep up with the Chevy.

I remembered when I was a military detective we would use the old method of following a suspect — the leap frog method. Although there were other very effective methods, this one only required the presence of two vehicles to be effective, with one vehicle in front of the suspect and the other in back, keeping tabs on the suspect. It was used in either vehicle or foot surveillance. This method prevented being 'made' by the suspect. But once again, I didn't have the luxury of a partner or another chase vehicle.

Making the outskirts of Tucson a short time later, I followed the Chevy El Camino to the Alvernon exit, then to Valencia Road. Jennings for some reason or other blew through a small traffic jam, but we caught all green lights after that.

Finally, he made a left onto Country Club Road, then to East Elvira Road. After a quarter of a mile, he arrived at a housing complex on the right.

I slowly followed right behind as I saw Jennings parked in the driveway of the second one story house on the left. Jennings slipped out of his car and walked toward the house. The front door opened. Walking in it was closed behind him.

I parallel parked a block away, grabbed my binoculars and again sat to wait it out.

My first question was, who did the house belong to? My answer was, probably the new girlfriend. But I needed to make sure.

Not yet though.

Who was in the house with Jennings was my second burning question. There was just one other car, a white Toyota, parked in the driveway. Did it belong to *her*, whoever *she* was?

Only time would tell.

So, for the time being surveillance was the key factor here as well. A few minutes later, the front house lights came on making my watch that much easier to see who came in or who came out.

Chapter Fifty-Six

Bushwhacked

It was getting late and my patience was wearing thin, so I decided to do the unthinkable.

Not knowing the occupants or how many there could be in the house, I threw caution to the wind as it was, and went with my gut feelings. I took a wild-ass chance and went for the house, deciding on breaking my way in.

I left my Stetson on the passenger seat, opened the driver's door, and climbed out of my car. I slowly made my way to the house and the front door.

Once there, I twisted the knob, and gently pushed it open and entered — didn't have to break in. I quickly stepped into a living room; lights were on, no one in sight. I decided to keep my gun holstered once I entered the house. My thinking was there could be children present. I didn't want to take the chance there could be several innocent lives also involved.

"Jennings, I know you're in the house, I'm here to take you to jail!"

I was hoping by my yelling I would try to avoid any sudden

confrontation with whoever was in the house. Didn't see anyone, but I heard talking come from a room with an open door.

I slowly turned and walked toward the open door on my left, when suddenly, I heard a muffled bang coming from my right side. Spinning toward the sound, I caught Jennings running out of the room to a back door. He opened it and bolted out.

Instinctively, I ran after him. Dashing through the open door, I came to a stop as I saw him trying to climb the wooden six-foot fence surrounding the back yard.

He was too far away from me to rush him. Not knowing if he was armed, I took the most prudent method of just slowly approaching him. So, walking forward a few paces, I stopped about three feet in front of him.

"Jennings," I said. "Stop, you're not going to make it out of here."

He stopped his attempt to climb the fence and slowly turned in my direction.

Jennings tensed. "Who are you?

I just smiled, not saying anything yet.

I took in a breath walking forward again, and stopped within two feet of the guy. He was breathing hard, and I could just make out the strong smell of alcohol on his breath. So, he was under the influence, which could embolden him in his actions. He was wearing a T-shirt and jeans.

I smiled again.

"I'm the guy taking you back to jail."

He still kept staring at me, his mind probably processing the meaning.

"And why is that?"

That's when I saw he had a gun in his right hand, as he held it down by his leg.

Seeing the weapon, I tucked the front end of my jacket behind the butt of my Colt, and waited to see what he would do. I knew he wasn't a killer, or he would've fired it by now. So, I waited for him to raise it or drop it. I was hoping for the latter.

"Your old girl friend turned in your bond."

"No shit!"

I smiled. "Yeah crazy. Right?"

He saw me as I cleared my jacket, exposing my gun.

He said, "You're crazy you know if you can draw before I shoot you first."

"You bring it up an inch and I won't be responsible for what happens next."

"You ain't that good, mister."

"You want to gamble on it?"

"You haven't seen me shoot."

I then said, "I ran into a situation like this once before."

"Yeah, what happen?"

"The guy held a piece down by his side, just like you. He made up his mind and raised it, I drew and shot him before he could let go a shot."

I saw him shaking his head.

"You make up your mind, make the right decision and you'll live. If not, well. . ."

He just stood there, his face not telling me a thing.

"What's it going to be, the morgue or jail?"

Seconds ticked by, then.

"Shit, the hell with it."

He dropped the weapon on the ground and raised his hands over his head.

"That was a smart move, Jennings."

"Yeah, go fuck yourself."

I'd just starting walking up to him, and saw his eyes had diverted to a point behind me.

Then it happened.

One second I'm staring down on Jennings, the next getting bush-whacked from the back. I felt someone walking up behind me, and before I could turn, felt myself getting hit just below my shoulder blades.

It wasn't a hard blow, just hard enough to move me a step or two forward. Spinning around, I saw the shock on the woman's face, as she realized I hadn't gone down yet, and with a yell, she swung the bat she was holding a second time.

Stepping in before she started the swing, I balled my right fist and struck her on the jaw. She went down on her side fast, unconscious, blood immediately dripping down her jaw.

Then I turned quickly back to Jennings and saw the gun still lying on the ground as he rushed over to his girlfriend.

He said, "You didn't need to hit her so fucking hard, asshole."

"She shouldn't have hit me then. Grab her and take her into the house."

Once he had his girlfriend cleaned up and making sure she was all right, I got Jennings handcuffed and into my car for the ride to the Pima County jail house. Then it was a simple matter of writing out the arrest report, turning in my certified copy of the bond, and driving over to Julie Ann Moss and picking up my fee.

It didn't take me long to drive over to Julie Ann Moss. I'd just pulled up in front of her place, when I saw her standing just inside the open front door. As I walked up to her she said, "You're a man of your word, Mr. Alvarez."

"I try, ma'am." She was wearing a blue bathrobe and had her hair curled up into a towel. I couldn't keep my eyes off her. And she knew it, as a small smile swept across her face.

"Please come in," she said. "I'll get your money for you." Then she slowly walked away and into another part of the house.

As I softly closed the front door behind me, I just stood there at the threshold, not wanting to tempt fate.

Oh my God, I thought as I watched her walk back to me. She had this come-along-look to her, that wasn't completely lost to me.

Handing me an envelope and opening it, I saw my fee in cash. I didn't bother to count it though.

"Would you like to stay for a while and talk about it over a drink?" she asked rather sweetly like.

If I didn't know any better, I thought she was trying to seduce me. I was flattered, but my wife's face crept up suddenly in my subconscious.

"Sorry, can't stay. I need to get back home to the wife and kids."

"Oh," was all she managed to say smiling.

Book Six

Billy Bob Landon

Chapter Fifty-Seven

Hail of Bullets

October 1989, Somewhere in Nogales, Arizona

I SLOWLY GUIDED MY LEBARON OFF OLD TUCSON ROAD, AND HIGHWAY 19, just north of the Mexico and Arizona borderline in the small town of Nogales. I'd been following a Ford pickup for the better part of an hour, at a good safe comfortable distance, so as not to get myself burned.

I'd been in these parts on numerous occasions, and knew that the temperatures in the open desert can range between 60 degrees in the day, to a downright cold 30 degrees at night this time of the year. And with the cold comes the monsoon soaked weather as well.

The patch of Highway 19 I was currently on, and up until one gets to the outskirts of Nogales, is devoid of any highway lights. I only had the pickup's taillights and my own headlights guiding my way. And with a half-moon overhead, it gave me a cold eerie sensation driving in the cold desert night.

The name Nogales is derived from the Spanish word for "walnut" which refers to the large stands of walnut trees that once upon a time stood in the mountain pass, where the city is currently located.

The city of Nogales borders Sonora, Mexico. It has roughly sixteen thousand inhabitants and is a major port of entry, not just to vehicles and pedestrians, but also drugs. Highway 19 ends at the border in Arizona, and Highway 15 picks up in Mexico, which from the Arizona side, is only a skip-and-a-hop into a different world.

Traffic on Old Tucson Road was light, but once on Highway 19, it was just the two of us. The driver was a bail skip I'd been tracking. After a few moments, the Ford rounded a curve and was briefly lost to me. I took the time to turn-off my headlights, just in case they were close by.

Coming around the curve, I saw his taillights as they dimly shone about a quarter mile up ahead and then again disappeared into darkened woods. I drove on slowly onto a gravel road, which eventually took me to a dead end, and a yellow painted, iron bar gate that effectively blocked any further progress.

As I approached with darkened headlights, I came to a stop a few feet from the gate post. Then grabbing my binoculars from my equipment bag laying on the passenger seat, I slowly raised it to my eyes, adjusted the focus and surveyed the area out to my far right as a slow steady stream of rain started to fall pitter-patter against my windshield.

Not letting the rain darken my spirits, I scanned further toward my right. Then, a Klick down the road and dimly visible through the light rain, I saw a large well kept ranch.

It had two small size structures, one a barn, and the other resembling a bunk house of sorts. It was devoid of outside lights, just some diffused lighting coming from two small windows.

Then I came to a stop, and as I focused my attention on the scene, I saw the Ford pickup I'd been following. There were three other pickup trucks present as well — parked at the further end of one of the smaller buildings.

As I panned over toward the larger of the structures, which I took to be a ranch house, I spied a bevy of activities on the veranda as I counted seven men and two women in a party atmosphere; and one of them was the guy I'd come after, my jumper, Billy Bob Landon, his big bulky form unmistakable even in the distance.

"Ah hell," I grunted. Then shaking my head and taking in a deep breath, I slowly exhaled between my teeth.

Silence all around me.

"This sucks, this sucks big time," I murmured.

I kept staring at all those men. And it started to look grim for me.

My first reaction was to get out of Dodge and return with people to help, preferably the cops!

But after a few seconds, I went with my second reaction.

Damn, I knew this day would come. The day I would have to fight it out with a large group of men on my own. Just wish it hadn't been today.

I shook my head again, and cursed my damn luck.

And I started to think I may have gotten myself into a nice pickle.

Oh, yeah, I didn't see any way around it. It was no use, risking life and limb over one man. There were too many of them for me to go breaking in all gung-ho like and affect an arrest.

Uh-uh!

So, my second reaction was to wait it out, and see if a better opportunity presented itself. I wasn't going anywhere. I didn't want to go tracking after my jumper all over Arizona again.

No way!

Dropping the binoculars on the passenger seat, I put the gear in reverse, and backed away several feet from the gate post. I parked in among some high grass and some tall leafy trees just off the gravel road, enough so that it completely concealed the LeBaron. I kept low in the car seat, hugging myself, trying to stay warm as I hunkered down for the wait.

As I rolled down my window some, trying not to get the inside fogged up, a cold breeze and the smell of wood smoke drafted up from the ranch and with it the sounds of loud laughter.

It reminded me of my youth, when at the age of thirteen, I worked on a horse ranch in Huntington Beach, Long Island, New York, owned by one of my high school teachers. It was a lot of fun, and I got to get out of the city for once, a welcome change for a city kid, who had recently gotten out of the Barrio gang life.

So, settling in for what could very well lead me into a long night of surveillance, I thought back to the events that brought me here in the first place. . .

It began just a little past three o'clock on that cool rainy October afternoon. I was keeping watch on my children as they played in the backyard. Bundled up nice and warm in their boots and rain coats, they jumped in puddles or tried to catch the rain with their tongues, hands and even their feet, all three of them enjoying the rain.

They wanted to be out of the house for a while, so I let them have their fun. With their mother out grocery shopping, it was my turn to watch over them.

I was sitting at the dining table and sipping a cup of hot coffee and munching on a chocolate chip cookie I had stolen out of the cookie jar. My eyes taking in my children, but inevitably my thoughts revolving around my business, and of not having had a job in quite some time.

I sighed and shook my head.

I was running out of funds, so I needed another sizable bail skip or get called from some law firm. But, the outlook for that wasn't looking too promising. In this business, we all have our ups and downs, and it seemed mine was on the downswing.

I inclined my head and munched on my cookie. Downing the last of my coffee, I returned my attention to my kids, trying to forget my troubled thoughts.

After a while, it seemed nothing could disturb my thoughts or concentration. The only faint sounds I heard were those of the kids, yelling from beyond the closed porch kitchen doors. Apparently they were having a great time.

As I kept my vigil, my concentration was completely broken. I watched as the porch doors were thrown open and all three of them flew though running into their rooms down the hall, without so much as a glance my way. Not even a wave.

"Hey, stop running before you guys hurt yourselves," I yelled as they flew past me. "Don't want your mother yelling at me for that." It dampened my spirits just for a second or two.

Mind you, I did feel a little hurt. But I'll get over it.

Then out of the corner of her bedroom door, Carmen-Melissa, my six-year-old and first born, peeked out.

She said, "Hi, Daddy."

Aha! See, I got over it quick enough.

A half hour later the front door opened quietly and my lovely wife, Dolores entered. Closing the door behind her, she started walking through the hallway and into our bedroom, but not before she said, "Groceries need to be brought in from the car, Victor," as she continued down the hallway into our bedroom.

I paused for a few seconds, my mouth halfway open. Not even a by-your-leave, or honey or sweetheart. I stood up and just shook my head.

"Yes ma'am. I'm on it."

Then I began making my way to the garage.

But before I could, the living room phone rang. From out of our bedroom, I heard my dear wife calling out to me.

"Victor, answer that."

"Yes dear, I'm getting it now."

Such was my lot in life. Women!

Walking into the living room, I grabbed the phone on its third ring and lifted it to my ear.

"Yeah, it's your dime."

And from the other end, I heard a familiar voice.

"Al, its Frank Marshall. Can I ask you to come right over to the office?"

I quickly took a seat on the sofa, crossed one leg over the other and thought of only Dolores; what was going to happen after I hangup and told her of my impending plans. My expression turned to worry then regret. Worry, because she'd made her own plans for the rest of the afternoon. Regret, because I was about to break them once again.

I sighed. Not because I didn't want the job, but because Dolores was going to be mad as hell once again, knowing I'd be off on another case.

I shrugged and swallowed slightly uncomfortably. Closing my

eyes, I thought; *there just isn't anything I can do about that now. I need the job and money.*

Seconds later, my reverie was broken as I remembered Frank was on the line.

Frank Marshall, although not the head-guy at Triple 'A' Bail Bonds, that title belonged to Fred Luna, had worked hand-in-hand with Luna since the late 70s. When Marshall came to work with Luna, their business surged and eventually they had written more bonds than most of the other bail agents combined. And with me in the fray, I'd recovered quite a few of their jumpers, saving them a considerable amount of money in the process.

I leaned back on the sofa. "Hey, Frank, let me guess. You got a job for me?"

"Yeah, and I can sure use your help with it."

"Yeah, okay. Give me about two hours or so."

But, first things first — the groceries, that was the most important item of the day, next to having to watch our children. I had to keep the little lady happy, one way or another.

After bringing in the groceries and from our bedroom, I heard my wife asking me to help her undress. Walking into our bedroom, I saw she was patiently waiting for me sitting on the edge of the bed.

She stood up and turned her back to me.

"Undo my zipper."

Naturally, I approached her, and started getting aroused by her closeness. It was her perfume that set my senses on fire. I wanted to rip off her dress and take her then and there. She turned around facing me, and her next words gave me pause.

"That was another job, right?" she asked.

I winced and fell silent for a moment before I replied, "Now, don't freak out or nothing, honey, but yeah. Frank wants me over there now."

"Damn, Al! When are you going to stop and listen to me? You need to get out of this business and leave Arizona."

"I'm sorry, Dolores, but this is who I am. This is what I do. And anyway, we need the money. You know that."

She took a step back and closed her eyes.

"Get out and close the door behind you."

I looked at her as she opened her eyes, and saw compassion replaced with anger.

There wasn't anything I could say then. I walked out and closed the door behind me.

Afterward at the front door, as I was leaving, I left Dolores shaking her head.

I didn't look back as I headed toward my car feeling slightly guilty and hurt both at the same time.

IT WAS JUST A FEW MINUTES AFTER FIVE WHEN I MADE IT TO FRANK Marshall's office.

The moment I walked in, Marshall, who was sitting behind his desk, looked up from the book he was reading or leafing through. He gave me a curt nod, and stared straight at me with what I thought might be a frown.

Walking up to his desk, I planted myself on the empty chair across from him, took off my Stetson, crossed my legs, placed my hat on my lap and stared straight back at him.

"Well, if it ain't Victor freak'en Alvarez," he said jokingly.

I shook my head almost unnoticeably and smiled.

"Hi, Frank, well I'll be damned."

"What?" he asked as he swiveled in his seat almost turning his back to me, putting away his book.

"You're actually reading a book without pictures."

Swiveling back around, he stared at me with half closed eyes and smiled.

"You're an asshole, you know that?"

I snuffed a laugh. "That's okay Frank. I always knew you could read."

Frank sighed wearily.

"I didn't expect you so soon."

And that was my cue to get this meeting going.

I nodded. "Well, I'm here now."

His silence was a little too long.

He nodded, staring away to the side. Something was eating at him. And obviously it wasn't the case, because he never took this long in laying it out for me. It wasn't lost on me. He may be having problems on the home front.

I said, "Hey, Frank, so what have you got for me?"

Finally, he nodded again, and with a slight frown, he cleared his throat. "A damn red neck asshole it's what I got, and a pain in the ass if you ask me."

"Oh, do tell. It's starting to sound interesting already."

"I wouldn't use interesting as much as dangerous. His name is Billy Bob Landon. But he answers to Billy-Bob. The guy went FTA, for his court dates. I've spent days trying to make some type of contact with him, with no luck."

"What was he in for?"

"Burglary and unlawful possession of a firearm, and he has a rap sheet that reads like a damn phone book."

The office was hot and stuffy as I sat patiently across the desk from Marshall. I watched him as he opened and rifled though a manila folder on his desk. I bid my time. I was in no hurry. He was ambivalent, relaxed, but also concerned. A lot of money must be involved with this guy, I thought, or he wouldn't be asking for my help. Or could it be something else?

I saw Frank looking at a photograph he'd taken from the file folder which he passed over to me. As I took the photo he said, "That's Landon."

The guy staring back at me from the photograph had slicked back blond hair, with a cleft chin, blue puffy eyes, and a broken nose that may have seen too many fistfights in his time. And according to his file, he stood six-foot-one.

I said, "A real unsavory looking character and an ugly son-of-a bitch, I see here."

Frank shook his head and shrugged.

A slight pause.

"It's like this, Al. Last month, about two in the morning, Landon broke into an affluent upscale house out at the foothills. Fortunately, there was no one in the house at the time. Before he broke into the house, he was seen on several occasions walking up and down the neighborhood. According to the cops, he was probably casing the joint."

I nodded thinking the same thing.

I said, "Yeah. How was he identified?"

There was a very slight hesitation on his part.

I kept staring at Frank as he looked away, and then slowly he returned his gaze on me. His voice was pleasant enough, but tight. I sensed his mind was elsewhere. It was much later that I found out from Fred Luna, that Frank was having marital problems.

Seems he wasn't the only one.

Marshall, in response just leaned back in his chair, scooped up the file folder and glanced back at me.

"Ah, a couple of witnesses who placed him at the scene identified him from mugs shots. Also, seems he got a little careless, leaving a finger print behind. A few days later, he was arrested up at his apartment without incident."

"For a guy who makes a living out of breaking into houses, he got very sloppy, or not very smart."

"No kidding. You got that right. But whoever said crooks were smart. Anyway, with no family to speak off, it was his high school buddy, a guy named Jacob Brayden, who bailed him out. Bond was set at one hundred thousand. I settled with cash and property, a ranch belonging to Brayden, in affecting his bail."

"That was a pretty high bail."

"Yeah, like I said, Landon had some priors like assault and battery, a B&E rap and another weapons charge. But it was the second weapon's charge that caused the high bond."

"So, where did Brayden come up with the cash in such a short period of time?"

"I asked that same question myself. Brayden said it was his inheritance from his uncle."

"And you believed that?"

"Hell no, I'm not that naive. Shit, I know for a fact that they're into all sorts of criminal activities, but cash is cash and the home he put up is paid in full too."

"Such a sweet caring guy this Brayden character is."

"I wouldn't go that far, Al. Friends that they are, they're also business partners. I did a little checking on Brayden. Seems he has an extensive rap sheet all his own, and besides that his friends call him Big Jake; a big tall son-of-a-bitch. You get the picture?"

I took a deep breath and knew these two guys were going to be trouble with a capital T. I looked over at Frank.

I shrugged. "It doesn't bother me."

After a brief silence, Frank looked at me again kind of expectantly.

"So," Frank said. "What do you think?"

"About?"

"Are you going to take the job or not, Al?"

"Yeah sure, no problem, I'll take it. Got a deadline that I should know of?"

"Yeah, warrant for Billy-Bob's arrest is going to be issued within three days, unless we bring him in before then."

"What's this . . . *we* crap?"

He looked at me grinning.

"Well, I meant of course you."

I looked Frank over a bit.

"Of course you did. Anyway, it should be enough time."

"Landon is not going to be easy, Al, and if he's with his buddy Brayden, they could very well make it difficult for you."

Yeah, they usually can be, I thought.

I asked, "And when were two guys a challenge for me, Frank?"

Frank shrugged with a faint knowing little smile.

"Yeah, you never disappoint, Al."

In answer, I just smiled.

Any thoughts I had of not having another bounty and a substantial payday soon, went flying out the window.

With dark rain clouds looming overhead and the chance of a heavy rain fall, it was six hours later that I finally made contact with the redneck and his buddy Brayden.

The rain was coming down so hard, it made visibility poor. I got back to my car completely soaked. Turning on the ignition switch, the LeBaron started up quickly enough. I turned on the wipers at full blast, and with light traffic on the road, I left Frank's office. I swung the LeBaron toward the last known address Landon had given Frank — an apartment complex out on Swan and Golf Links Roads.

I drove on as my view outside the windshield grew quite grim. It was slow going. The rain made my drive difficult to see four feet in any direction. Twenty minutes later, pulling into the open gates of the apartment complex, I found his apartment building. And, parked up against the front of it, was the Ford pickup belonging to Billy Bob Landon.

"Well, well, what do you know?" I muttered.

I paused just long enough to register my surprise on this bit of luck that came my way.

I grinned and said to myself, "OK then, and let's see what happens next."

Parking my car a half a block away, I waited to see if he came out and who he was with, if anyone. I really preferred my jumpers to be alone, it made my job that much easier. Then, I remembered what Frank Marshall had said about Landon's buddy. I was soon to learn that it was wishful thinking on my part.

The rain continued unabated making it very difficult to see up to the apartment building, so with the engine idling and the wipers doing their job, I sat to wait.

Several hours later, as the rain slackened some and visibility got slightly better, I caught sight of a door opening on the second floor just above the parked Ford pickup. As the door swung completely open, I saw two white guys slowly walk out of the apartment. One of whom I immediately recognized as my jumper, Billy Bob Landon. He was dressed in blue jeans, cowboy boots, untucked red long sleeve-shirt and a grey jacket vest with a John Deere baseball cap.

The other guy was a heavy-built younger looking thirty-something, I took to be Jacob Brayden. He was dressed in blue jeans, cowboy boots, tucked in multi-colored long sleeve shirt, brown jacket vest and a wide, straw style cowboy hat. I didn't see any weapons. Of course, that didn't mean they weren't packing.

But as was my custom, I took it for granted they were.

They were laughing, joking and mocking each other as two close friends would as they came down the stairs. Nonetheless, I caught Landon furtively checking out the area for possible police presence or for anyone else who could be on the lookout for him.

These two guys were huge!

Billy-Bob was a little taller than Brayden, who looked like a football full-back, hence the moniker — Big Jake.

I watched as they ran through the rain to the Ford. Once they were in the pickup's cab with Brayden behind the wheel, they drove off away from the complex headed down Golf Links Road.

It was a cold afternoon about six o'clock, and as the rain picked up in intensity and not telling when it would stop, I got in behind the Ford following at a discreet distance.

After a little over an hour of following, as I kept far behind them, we arrived at a ranch house in the middle of nowhere. There weren't any other ranches or homes visible for miles.

According to my case file on Landon and Brayden, this was Brayden's property — the one he used as collateral to effect bail for his buddy, Landon.

TWENTY MINUTES LATER, MY REVERIE WAS BROKEN AS STILL INTO MY surveillance of the ranch, the rain suddenly stopped. The night was dark and starless. The only illumination now came from the main house porch lights, turned on earlier, and the dim lights from the windows. The night air was cold outside my driver's side open window.

Training my binoculars again on the ranch house, I kept my lonely vigil. And as my thoughts took me to all the fist fights, car chases and gunfights I'd been involved since becoming a bounty hunter, I hoped a good opportunity would present itself where I didn't have to use deadly force to effect an arrest this go-around.

I shrugged. "We'll see," I said to myself.

Into my fifth hour or so of surveillance, I felt dazed and a little groggy. Lack of sleep does that to a person. I fought myself to remain awake and vigilant. I wasn't going to let them get away me anytime soon.

But, it then appeared my long wait had paid off.

Glancing at my watch it read half-past four. Grabbing my binoculars once again, I scanned back to the house. This time there wasn't anyone outside.

The party had been taken inside.

Then twenty minutes later, I finally caught sight of Landon and Brayden along with two other men emerging from the house. They stood talking at the door, in what I thought was a small heated argument, with Landon doing most of the talking and finger pointing. Then the two unknown men walked back into the house, as Landon and Brayden headed toward Landon's pickup.

Excellent, it started to look most promising. Hopefully, my luck was changing for the better.

With Landon doing the driving, the Ford was fired up a few seconds later. Backing out he straightened out the Ford, and crawled slowly away down the gravel road.

They pulled up at the gate and stopped.

As Brayden exited the Ford and swung open the iron post, Landon slowly drove through as Brayden closed the gate behind the Ford. A few seconds later they drove past my hiding place. I cranked up the LeBaron, rolled up my window, turned on the much needed heater, and backed up from the grassy area. I swung a quick U-turn, and leisurely paced down the gravel road as I turned on my headlights.

I don't recollect exactly what may have spooked them. Maybe my headlights gave me away. Or maybe just at that same precise moment, the Ford's driver had glanced at his rearview mirror. He must've caught sight of my headlights. Whatever it was, I guess I'd spooked them real good. For at that very moment as the driver spied my car as I was quickly as gaining on them, the Ford accelerated, pulling away from me with each passing second!

I whistled softly. "*Madre De Dios!*"

The wind had started blowing through the tree tops, and the rain had picked-up again. It started falling in sheets all around me. There was no warning. One second it was dry, the next it was soaking wet outside my car. Definitely felt as if the monsoon season was upon us. Arizona historically experiences more severe weather than most states.

Giving chase through the wet dark night, I knew then that I'd had been made. They knew someone was after them now. No use hiding the fact. I gave the LeBaron a burst of speed as I stomped on the gas pedal. And with the tires digging in deep, and the patter of rain falling heavy around me, I heard the gravel spurt up from behind my car.

Slowly closing the gap between us, I saw their taillights wavering in the rain. Then I saw the Ford was fast approaching an intersection where two cars were stopped at a red light.

Suddenly, the Ford veered around the two cars, in a fishtailing turn, slipping and sliding, almost losing control but showing no signs of slowing. Then in a burst of speed, the Ford accelerated through the intersection.

A four-car interval separated the Ford and my LeBaron, as I sped through the red traffic light. I veered around the two stopped cars just as the light turned green. Then slowly I started catching up to the Ford again.

Just about gaining a two-car advantage, I saw an arm appear out the passenger's window. Then a series of bright flashes and the stutter of gunfire filled the night as a hail of bullets pinged on the hood of my car. I saw dirt kick up gravel from the impact of some bullets in front and to the right side of the LeBaron!

I took a deep sharp breath, my eyes widened as I tightened my grip around the steering wheel.

Holy shit, so they are armed! I thought.

That answered that.

Chapter Fifty-Eight

Ambushed

Trying to keep my wits about me, a few seconds or more may have passed. I then did the only thing I could do, under the circumstances — I slowed and hung back some. I was trying to avoid the fusillade of bullets, as I heard the ping pinging sounds as more bullets hit on or around the hood.

The chase accelerated, as we both surged dangerously toward the 90mph speed mark.

The Ford pickup swayed side to side down the wet gravel road. A couple of minutes later, the Ford's driver drove onto the hardtop of Old Tucson Road and I watched it accelerating, leaving me in the dust.

Straightening the LeBaron as I approached the hardtop, I quickly down shifted to first gear, stomped on the gas pedal and in an instant of burning tires and shifting gears, I continued the chase with only my headlights guiding me in the darkness. Far out in the distance all I saw were the diminishing taillights of the Ford pickup.

It was just a few seconds later, after completely losing sight of the Ford's taillights around a curve, that I started to realize that I may have lost them for sure.

But, I hadn't given up quite yet.

Not by a long shot!

Cautiously slowing to about 75mph, I approached the start of a pronounced sharp curve in the road. Seconds later, just out of the curve, and through the pouring rain, I finally caught sight of the Ford once again.

But this time it was stopped on the side of the road, parked ass end, with the front just jutting out over the shoulder and the beams of its headlights shining out over the hardtop.

I started to get a bad feeling about this, "Oh, son of a bitch!"

Suddenly, slowing down as I drove past them, and out of my peripheral vision, I caught several bright flashes coming from the drivers and passenger side windows. Then over the loud engine roar, I heard the unmistakable crackle of gunfire once again.

Mere seconds later, my car was assaulted as bullet after bullet slammed into the right side. A bullet or two must've hit one of my tires, as I then heard the blowout.

As my car swerved side to side, I fought desperately to regain control fighting with the steering wheel, before I ran out of hardtop and could've headed into some sort of a ditch alongside the road.

Several miles further on, after gaining control of my car and creeping slowly along, I pulled onto the shoulder, stopped, and killed the engine. I cursed myself for being easily drawn into an ambush. I wasn't feeling totally happy about it, but at least I hadn't taken a bullet or worse been killed.

Shrugging off my second brush with death, I struggled somewhat to collect my wits once again, and waited till my hands stopped shaking and to quickly get back into the chase, if that was even possible.

So, not knowing if they had made a U-turn and taken another route to wherever they were originally headed too, I got out of the LeBaron into the sweeping rain.

The front left tire was almost off its rim. Knowing I had a good spare in the trunk, it was a simple matter of replacing it and getting back on the road, and maybe somewhere, somehow catch sight of the Ford once again.

As I stood there contemplating my next move, and as the wind whipped through my wet soaking clothes, I heard the approach of a vehicle. A minute later, I saw through the rain, a set of headlights coming around the curve. It sped up fast as I heard tires squealing and rubber burning as they dug into the wet roadway. And just before it came parallel to my car, I saw it was the Ford pickup!

"Awe, *shit*," I said out loud. Then I thought, *they are trying to finish me!*

I hesitated as my body began to tense, but quickly recovered.

But my heart almost stopped.

For at that same moment, as it came abreast of my car, I saw several flashes and the crack-crack of gunfire coming from the passenger's side window as they sped away.

Immediately recovering from my sense of shock, I heard more gunshots ring out. Then round after round striking the side of my car. And as my rear right passenger side window blew up into pieces, I quickly ran toward the front of my car, threw myself to the ground and kneeling behind it, drew my Colt and returned fire as best I could. But by then the Ford was almost out of range.

With my head still spinning from the gunfire, I quickly got up from the behind the car. I was totally pissed. I kept firing at the Ford and yelling at the top of my lungs, *fuckers* again and again. I walked onto the hardtop, continuing firing my Colt, until it finally locked back on an empty magazine!

Taking a slow breath, I let it out. Then ejecting the spent magazine, I replaced it with a fresh one. Jacking in a live round, it was ready again in case they returned. Then holding the Colt by my side, I stared into the darkness and the rain.

After a few minutes of waiting, and watching for their return, I gave it up. I holstered the Colt, and got back to my car. Popping the hood, I didn't see any major damage to the engine, and even though I'd counted quite a few bullet holes on the hood and besides the shattered passenger window, it was still fit to drive.

In the predawn darkness of that cold October night, sitting behind the wheel of my car, I'd contemplated my next move. I knew I had just one or two options left open to me.

Once I'd replaced the flat tire, I was speeding down Highway 19 toward Interstate 10, hoping to at least catch sight of the Ford somewhere along the way.

Fat chance, I thought. But stranger things have happened.

They had too much of a head start on me, I'd give them that. My only option at this point was to get on back to Landon's apartment and maybe just maybe, I'd find them there waiting for me. Or, if that fails pull a little surveillance on Brayden's house again. Christ, all I needed was a little bit of good luck to get me through this safely with no further bullets flying my way and with my jumper in jail.

But first, I had to take care of my car.

At the parking lot of a low rent sleazy motel by the Triple 'A' Truck Stop, just off I-10, in Tucson, they sat in silence for a minute, not saying a word.

After getting two magazines loaded and tucked away, they inserted fresh magazines into their weapons. Then, they just stared over at each other and smiled.

They'd known each other from way back in their youth. So, they knew better than to just talk, just for the sake of hearing themselves. It stood to reason that this time, it was no exception.

They had their own take on what just transpired.

He didn't know who had come after him or how many were in *that* car, but one thing was for sure — *someone* had. And it had been his idea to put whoever it was away before they could get at them. That third attempt at stopping whomever was after them should've put the fear of God into them, and make them think twice about coming for him again.

Or so he hoped.

Jacob Brayden asked, "Think they were cops?"

Landon watched Brayden rolling a good sized joint, working his fingers around it. Once he had it lit, and after taking his hit, he handed Landon the joint.

Landon took a long pull. He paused, and then exhaled slowly. He said, "Don't think so. If they were, we would be followed by patrol cars, and not just by one unmarked car."

Brayden frowned looking at his buddy.

"Yeah, you could be right. But the car didn't look like an unmarked police car."

Landon looked at his buddy thoughtfully. He said, "So who could it be then?"

"It could be your bondsman, or maybe a hired bounty hunter."

Landon's jaw dropped. "Shit—"

Brayden idly glanced outside his window and said, "My thoughts exactly."

A terrible feeling suddenly crept over Landon. "Christ, bounty hunters!" Landon exclaimed, shaking his head and passing over the joint.

Reaching for the joint, Brayden took his last hit.

He said, "Bounty hunters are badass dudes, worse than cops."

Landon looked over to his buddy. He shrugged and managed to ask what he was already starting to feel. "Scared?"

"Fuck no."

After some silence, Brayden just shook his head. But out of the corner of his eye, he saw a flicker of fear etched in his buddy's eyes.

"Think we scared them away?" Landon murmured.

Brayden shook his head again.

"I don't know. What I do know is we may have pissed off someone, and I think they're going to try again."

Billy Bob Landon sighed, hard thinking what to do next. But after a few seconds of silence, he just shook his head. He knew the bondsman would be coming for him, just didn't think it would be so soon. As he turned his head to look out the window a plan slowly started to take shape. But he realized he may only have one option left — Mexico.

"What time is it?" Landon asked.

After a brief pause and glancing at his watch, Brayden said, "Five o'clock give or take."

Billy Bob glanced around outside the truck's windows, and drew in a sharp breath.

"Well, first things first, we need to get a bunch of money together, some clothing and I need to get my passport."

Before they became sleepy from the weed, they drove away. Landon knew he had a lot to do and a short time to do it in. It was a short while later when he detailed his plan to his buddy, Brayden.

I was home, sitting patiently on the living room sofa, watching the sun peek through the windows. I felt relaxed sitting there in my T-shirt and pants resting, after what I'd been through the last couple of hours. So, it felt nice taking a breather and not have anyone looking over at me, or over my shoulder, if I'd been anywhere else but home.

I didn't nap or fall asleep. I was too wired up as it was. I just sat hoping against hope on catching up with my jumper today. The clock was ticking down till the courts issued a bench warrant for my jumper.

I couldn't let that happen.

I kind of enjoyed the quiet time though. But I knew it wouldn't last.

I waited just long enough for the sun to come peeking through in the night sky, before I moved from the sofa. Then grabbing my shirt, I tucked in my pants, strapped on my gun belt, swung my rain jacket over me and prepared to hit the road.

The day promised to be a dry one.

I left home at six in the morning without so much as breakfast, not even a cup of coffee, or kissing my wife and children goodbye.

I was in a hurry.

Under the circumstances, I never should've gone home. But I needed to wait till dawn for what I needed to do, And what better place — than home. The house was as quiet as a tomb. I didn't have the heart to wake them.

I decided first to make an appearance to the one person that could get my car fixed; the same one who transformed it from the wreck it had been when I purchased it from the junk yard.

"WELL, HOW LONG DO YOU THINK?" I FINALLY ASKED HIM.

I leaned back on my car's fender and crossed my arms across my chest, and regarded my friend Luis Garza, with a hopeful collected gaze. He didn't say a word. Just kept wiping his hands on a shop rag, as he walked away from a car he'd been working on.

I kept staring at him, thinking about the length of time needed to get it fixed. And silently hoped it would only take less than two hours – tops, if that. But as he slowly walked toward me, he kept looking away from me in a contemplated manner.

Then he stopped in front of me.

I was at Luis Garza's auto body and paint shop in South Tucson, trying to get the LeBaron fixed. I knew he kept unusual hours, and for that reason alone, I was there early. Garza, a dark skinned, short pot-bellied Mexican walked around my car, shaking his head.

Then he stopped again just by my side. Grinning, he seemed to consider my question for a moment. Then he gestured me to follow him.

Garza asked, "Man, what the hell you did to your poor car?"

"I didn't do it . . ." I started to say, as I was led to the back of his shop and his office.

We both went quiet as I followed him into his darkened office. Once inside, he flipped a wall switch and two overhead fluorescent lights snapped on with an audible hiss.

"Two red neck assholes did it," I went on, undeterred before we were halfway through into the office. I was a little hurt that he would think I would do such a thing to my LeBaron.

He just smiled. Coming around his desk he flopped his bulk onto an old beat-up office chair behind his desk, and pointed at an empty chair.

He kept smiling at me.

"Go on, Al, have a seat and tell me all about it."

"What's so funny?"

"Just all the shit you get into."

I came around to the indicated chair.

"Yeah, well about that."

The chair, another old decrepit thing with a cracked leather cushion, cut in several places, should have seen the landfill years ago. Just hope it was safe enough to sit on. But despite its popping creeks and groans I sat down; it didn't break under me. Then I watched as Garza lit a cigarette.

I began by telling him everything that transpired up to this point, leaving nothing out and watched as he gave me a sidelong glance, maybe not believing my story. But the evidence is in the pudding — my car.

After a pause of several seconds, he gave a loud hmmm, and shook his head.

"You get involved in stuff like that often, Al?"

I found myself a little amused by his question.

"Well ah, more or less."

Garza frowned as he took a drag of his cigarette, blew it out, looked at me and took his time answering. "Give me maybe three, four hours, depending when I get the parts in. Besides the auto glass, you have two hoses need replacing."

Then he asked about the bullet holes, as he flipped his ashes on the floor.

"So, you want me to take care of that too?"

"Can you cut that down to an hour and a half? I really need to get back on the road and catch those two redneck son's of a-bitches. You can take care of the bullet holes next time I bring her in."

"Okay then. No promises. I'll see what I can do."

A little while later, I used Garza's office phone to call on Dolores. The conversation was short.

After I told her of my plans, there was a silence on the line.

Then, I heard a slow almost quiet exhalation of breath, and all she said were three little words; *come home soon,* almost in a whisper. But I could almost feel and sense the worry and dread in her tone.

I slowly hung up the phone.

Slowly I shook my head, because nothing haunts us like the things we don't say. And what she didn't say spoke volumes. She knew my job was dangerous. That's why I would never tell her of my constant brushes with death. On several occasions when the situation got too tense, she brought out the idea of moving to Seattle, Washington. It was something to think about.

An hour and thirty-five minutes later, Garza was a man of his word.

Once in my car, I was back on the road again, with Garza's parting words, *"Stay safe, Al."* As I prayed for lady luck to once again watch out for my ass.

Chapter Fifty-Nine

Javier

I was hungry and needed to get some coffee in me as well, but knew if I did, it would give my jumper that much more time to go to ground, making my job harder or impossible. So, after leaving Garza's shop, I headed out to Landon's apartment complex.

About half a mile or so to the complex, I passed a JESUS SAVES sign, up on a billboard, jeez, how the hell could I've not seen that before? The things you missed when you're the one driving.

I stayed on the Interstate till I came to the Golf Links exit. Then I hung a right on Swan Road. Up ahead was a 7-Eleven. I pulled in, filled the tank and got me a quick cup of coffee for the road. I also placed a call to my old buddy Javier Martinez to see if he could help me out once again.

Martinez, or Javi as he liked to be called, was a medically discharged army captain and ex-Green Beret who lost the use of his left leg in his second tour in Vietnam. But worse, Javi was an ex-convict having served a few years for assault and battery. He never told me the details of it, but if I had to guess, it was over a woman. But one thing for sure, he's never failed me in a pinch, and I hoped he could do so again. And as friends go, I don't have many. I distrust people in general. I have acquaintances, but very few people I'd call friends. Javi was a man I'd call a very good friend.

All in all, I hadn't taken more than ten minutes. I just hope I didn't pay for that missing time later on.

Fifteen minutes later, I parked across the street from the complex. I didn't need to me *made* anywhere near there by my jumper. But I did do a drive through.

During my recon, I didn't see any vehicles parked in front of the apartment, which was a good thing, or bad depending on the outlook. Also, there were no lights coming out of the apartment. Now that was a good indication no one was home.

It was two hours later when Javi met up with me at Landon's apartment complex. He was driving an old Chevy pickup, leaving behind his much-loved candy apple Chevy Corvette, which wouldn't do for what I had planned. When I called him earlier I'd instructed him to leave the Vette at home and come in some old beat up vehicle. His words still echoed in my ear.

"Al, what the fuck have you gotten yourself into this time?"

"Nothing I can't get out off without your help."

"So, Al, why couldn't I bring my 'Vette?"

"You don't want any bullet holes in it, do you?"

"Did I hear you right, bullet holes?"

"Yeah, ah, plus the jerks I'm after know my car."

"Christ, Al, how the hell do you get into so much shit? The last time I went out with you, I got a bullet in the chest for my troubles. Remember that?"

"How can I forget?"

It if hadn't been for his Kevlar body armor vest I loaned him, Javi would have suffered dearly with his life. As it was, it only threw him back a step or two before he fired his weapon wounding his attacker.

"You want me to bring along my vest just in case?"

"Oh, yeah, buddy. It may come in handy."

Now with me behind the wheel, and Javi on the passenger seat of the pickup and our gear stowed away, I made my way onto the complex. Then, finding a free parking space just two spaces from Landon's apartment, I parked ass-end and sat to wait.

It was then, that I took the time to get Javi up to speed on my jumper and his buddy.

He was taking it all in without saying a word. Although he hadn't moved throughout, I couldn't sense any desperation or misgivings about joining me, which was a good omen.

Once I finished, I glanced his way. He was looking forward with a slight frown.

It was becoming obvious to me, from his silence, that he thought there was more to the story.

"Is there anything else?" he finally asked.

Still looking over at him, I gave a brusque shake of my head.

"Nope, don't think so."

He didn't move, just sat there ramrod straight, arms on his lap.

"I'm curious, Al."

"Yeah, what about?"

"How much is my cut this go-around?"

I didn't reply right away, just sat back taking in his words. I hadn't thought about it till he brought it up. But it was a good sensible question. If I offered too little, he wouldn't help out in the future. He was the only one I could trust enough to watch my six.

"How does three grand sounds?"

He slowly nodded, and turned toward me with a childish grin.

"It sounds more than fair."

I gave him a thumbs-up by way of saying I agree and thanking him too for being there with me.

After that, we both lapsed into silence for a while.

Then the conversation started again, but changed somewhat to the personal side.

He said, "So, you thinking of maybe doing this job for another few years?"

"Don't think so."

"How come?"

"The wife's getting serious about moving away to another state, maybe Washington."

"So, are you having problems?"

"No, but she is."

"You're a good friend, Al, sure hate to see you go."

"Yeah well, ain't left yet."

"Right."

I leaned slightly forward, and clutched the steering wheel with both hands.

I said, in a conciliatory tone, "Have you found work yet?"

I glanced over to him waiting for a response, but didn't get one right away.

Then he casually turned his head my way. His eyes boring right though me. He lowered his brows some, maybe thinking of something or maybe searching for something he'd forgotten from long ago — or maybe someone. Then apparently not overly surprised at my question he answered slow and easy, "Off and on, nothing steady. It's really hard finding anything good being a convict and all."

"I imagine."

"Yeah, it's the way things are."

We both went quiet after that.

Chapter Sixty

The Cops

After spending two hours of steady surveillance, I decided to give it up and take our chances at the ranch. It was a challenge of sorts. I'd hoped it would've panned out here at the apartment, but it just wasn't looking that good.

The ranch was altogether a challenge all its own. It presented too many variables to contend with; for instance, there were entirely too many innocent people who could needlessly get shot or killed in a crossfire. It was too much of a risk for the two of us, let alone one. I wasn't looking forward to it. But worse, Javi and I could get killed for our trouble.

I could've asked for police backup. But not knowing anyone in the local jurisdiction, I couldn't assume they would come out and help. And if they did, they would try to control the situation to their advantage, leaving me and Javi in the dark. No way was I going to let this payday slip through my fingers.

It was at that moment, as I started turning the ignition switch on, that I caught sight of an approaching truck, or pickup to be exact, coming from the left side of the road.

Javi was fast asleep.

I said, "Heads up, we've got company."

All at once, he was wide awake and turning his head looking out his window.

"Where from?"

"My left, I think it's them."

Javi turned on his seat and glanced over me to the approaching truck.

"Is it them?"

"Will know in a moment."

The street leading onto the apartment complex was a double tree lined street facing east and west. It was a quiet enough place, and it was sandwiched in a nice residential area. The truck was slowly approaching from the west, from my left side of our truck's window.

It made its way up the street, and slowly past Landon's apartment, where it came to a stop.

It was then that I made a positive ID on the pickup.

Turning toward Javi, I gave him a slow smile. "It's them, Javi."

Javi leaned back in his seat.

"You want to take them out here?"

Damn right I wanted to take them out. And this was clearly the place for it.

"Of course, once they get into the apartment, we make our move."

"Sounds like a plan."

Glancing over at the pickup, I saw only one person getting out of the truck — Landon.

For a moment I'd figured that would throw a wrench into my plan, if Jacob Brayden didn't get to join him too.

A few seconds later, Landon made it up to his apartment, unlocked it, walked in and closed the door behind him.

Jacob Brayden hadn't moved out of the pickup.

Shit, of course it wouldn't be easy, I thought, just when I thought I had them. Something was up. Just didn't know what.

I said, "Javi, change of plans. I need you to move on over to Landon's apartment, and keep him from getting back to the pickup."

Listening to my plan, I watched him light a cigarette. "Roger that. What about you?"

"Me? I'm going over to Brayden and put him in handcuffs."

Javi turned to face me.

"Ah, naturally you'd given me the bigger of the two."

"You want to change it up?"

"Nah. Think I can handle it."

"Fine, why complain then?"

He stared at me and smiled.

"I'm just pulling your chains, Al. Pulling your chains."

I simple nodded, smiled and went to open the driver's side door, when suddenly Javi grasped my right arm keeping me from getting out.

He said, "Whoa, whoa."

"What's up?"

"It would appear there's going to be another change of plans."

"What are you talking about?"

"There's a patrol car with two cops in it, coming in from the east side."

"Christ, now what?"

"You should be able to see it in a second of two."

Then I saw it.

This was unbelievable. Just when I figured to have this case wrapped up here and now, this happens!

The cruiser drove slowly as if they were looking for something. Then it pulled up and parked at Landon's apartment building, just four doors away from his unit.

Clearly, this was an unexpected turn of events.

The officers, one male and the other female, stepped out of their cruiser. They both walked toward the ground floor section and knocked on a door. They were let in by a white female as the door closed in after them.

"What do we do now, Al?" Javi asked.

This most assuredly put the wrench in our plans.

"We wait, see what happens."

"Roger that."

Chapter Sixty-One

The Ranch

Several minutes later, I saw Landon stepping out of his apartment. He closed the door behind him and started walking to the stairs, when suddenly he came to an abrupt stop.

"Javi, I got Landon stopped at the upper stairs landing."

"What do you want to do?

"Let's play it by ear, see what he's going to do."

Landon had fear and shock written all over his face on seeing the police cruiser. As he turned over toward the landing and the stairs, I saw him quicken his steps and start down. He didn't notice any cops around as he stepped off the last few steps.

My eyes just lingered on Landon as he made his way to his pickup. Not walking. Not running. And still no cops out yet.

So, I was in a dilemma. What to do? We could jump Landon before he made the pickup, and hope the cops didn't come out. Or wait it out and see what Landon does next.

I decided to wait it out a little longer.

It would just be my luck to have the cops come out just when Javi and I jumped Landon. No way was I going to let that happen. Too much explanation and the cops could very well take us three in for questioning or wait for their supervisor to make an appearance. Also knowing they were armed, bullets would fly and someone could get hurt, then the cops would have a field day with us.

Yeah, it wasn't much of an alternative. And I didn't feel like making front news headlines in the local papers, especially with Javi who could get arrested for packing a weapon, being an ex-con and all.

A few minutes later the two cops left the apartment and casually walked to their cruiser; just at the same time Landon made it to his pickup.

"What now?" Javi asked, looking somewhat amused at the turn of events.

Looking over at Javi, with a noncommittal look as he asked the question I began to smile.

I said, "Guess we play follow the leader."

WE FOLLOWED THEM HEADING SOUTH ON INTERSTATE 10.

As we drove on, I was betting I knew where they were taking us. Forty-five minutes later, I was proven right as we saw signs pointing toward Nogales — the ranch.

It took another fifteen minutes till we hit Highway 19. There I drove past the ranch exit and pulled over to the side of the road, engine idling.

Javi said, "You know they pulled into that gravel road back there, right?"

"Yeah, I know exactly where they are heading. I've been here before."

"You got a plan then?"

"We'll stay here for about ten minutes, then head on over to the ranch, see what needs to be done and take it from there."

"Yes sir sounds easy enough."

After my imposed ten minutes were up, I pulled away from the shoulder of the road with a screech of rubber. I made sure no oncoming traffic blocked my path and swung a quick U-turn, heading for the entrance to the gravel road and the ranch.

We arrived under clear skies and a half moon lighting our way.

A quarter of a mile from the gate leading to the ranch we came to a forest line which was set back a few feet from the road. I pulled into the tall trees hiding our pickup and came to a complete stop. I killed the lights and shutoff the engine.

"What's the plan, Al?" Javi asked.

"Get suited up, grab our weapons, and do a little reconnaissance. Then take it from there."

But I also laid out my full plan of action in taking down Landon and his partner Brayden.

Without another word, Javi and I got out of the pickup at the same time, like two hardened seasoned cops would do. As we came around toward the back of the truck, I opened the tailgate, and pulled out my equipment bag. Opening it, I let Javi take a look at what I had. He pulled out a Mossberg shotgun, and a Smith & Wesson model 5906 handgun, chambered for the 9mm round with several fully loaded magazines as well.

"Well Javi, which one?"

Javi said nothing.

With the Mossberg in hand, I noticed he kept eyeing the handgun. He stared at me for a second, then back to the handgun. He dropped the Mossberg back into the bag and hefted the pistol. Picking up a full magazine for the handgun, he inserted it into the weapon, pulled back the slide and jacked in a round. He set the safety and tucked the weapon in his belt. As three additional magazines that went into his pocket.

He said, "I'll take this one."

I cocked my head and smiled.

"Are you sure?"

"Absolutely, it feels good in my hand. And who knows if I'll need the use of my other hand."

That made perfect sense to me.

"OK then."

I waited a few seconds and just stood there staring at him. He kept his hand on the butt of the weapon as he took furtive glances around him. There was something strange about his face that I couldn't put my finger on. He noticed me staring at him and asked with a little irritation in his voice, "What?"

I nodded. "You okay?"

He was frowning and slowly shaking his head.

"Just want to get this show on the road. You know?

"Right on, buddy. Get out your Kevlar vest and suit up."

After we both suited up with our vest, I again explained my plan of action to him and all he did was nod in agreement.

With our guns in hand, we started toward the ranch.

THE MOON STOOD HIGH IN THE SKY LIGHTING OUR WAY DOWN THE GRAVEL road. The night was quiet, except for the howl of some distant animal. Maybe mating calls of the wild.

With the wind blowing around us in the empty expanse of the woods, we walked side by side till we came to the iron-bar gate.

We stopped in front of the gate, and I swung my gaze down toward the ranch in the distance. All seemed peaceful and calm. Only lighting came by way of two porch lights from the main house, its beams lighting up two parked pickups out in front. One of them our jumpers truck.

"Looks good so far," Javi said.

"I agree. But looks can be deceiving."

Javi didn't say anything, just a murmur of understanding and a nod.

With a full audible sigh, I started off down the road. Javi on my left flank, gun in hand, taking up our positions, just as I discussed in my plan.

With my senses now on full alert, and taking full advantage of the trees for cover, we made it to our first target, the left side of the main house and the bunk house. Everything was utterly still, the element of surprise still working in our favor.

Now the hard part begins!

Chapter Sixty-Two

Shit Hits the Fan

Kneeling down in the shadows in a thicket of tall grass, with the bunk house and the main house between us, we didn't move for a minute or two, just in case someone came out or went in.

"Let's do this, Al," Javi said.

He was cool and blessedly confident from what I could see of him, even though I kinda sensed he just wasn't.

For my part, I wasn't as confident. Knowing how things can go wrong at any given time.

I knelt there just a little longer, hoping we come out of this in one piece.

Then calming myself down, I turned toward Javi.

"Go for it."

Javi stood straight up and ran toward the back of the bunk house. Watching him as he disappeared around a corner, I stood up and keeping in a low stance made by way slowly to the front door.

Just before reaching the front porch, I noticed that both sides of the bunk house were being used as a dumping ground for trash and unneeded appliances. An old yellow colored refrigerator, a washing machine and dryer, plus three large metal trash cans littered the place. I hated to think what was inside of them.

With my Colt at my side, hammer cocked back on a live round, I stepped onto the porch with a resounding loud creaking of loose floor boards under my foot.

Quickly reacting, I moved swiftly up to the right side of the door and hugged the wall, hoping against hope that no one had been alerted to the sounds. Holding my breath, I waited for a slow count of ten. When no one came to investigate, I slowly started opening the door just enough to get my body through.

Raising my gun hand up to my chest and pointing the barrel straight out in front of me, I stepped into the bunk house, and into a large room. It was dark inside and I had to wait for my eyes to adjust to the darkness. Seconds later, I stepped within three feet into the room and then it happened. . .

Suddenly, from out of the darkness, I heard someone yell. Quickly I turned around toward the sound, and was tackled about the waist from behind before I was able to see my attacker. And through an open door in a room close by, I heard more yelling, but by then I was only paying attention to my attacker.

Down to the hard wood floor we went rolling around. Back and forth we changed positions, he on top of me punching me about my head and face. And with blood streaming from my lips, it was my turn on top of him. I used my elbows striking him about the side of his head and face.

Back we rolled again; I tried to wrap my legs around him, when I heard two shots coming from behind me. But I didn't have time to think about that now. All my energies and expertise was on Landon — my attacker.

Finally getting my legs locked around his waist, I lifted him up off the floor and slammed him back onto his back, knocking the wind and the fight right out of him.

As I stood there, I started looking for my Colt, and remembered my Smith & Wesson .38 caliber detective special in my holster down on my right leg. But before I could reach for it, Landon, attacked again.

This time I saw the glint of a blade as he charged me straight on aiming for my stomach. I didn't have time to reach and draw my .38; instead, I met his charge. Just before the point of his knife met my vitals, I side-stepped to his left, grabbed his knife hand and swung him around once. Then bringing his knife arm up, I bent his elbow and redirected the point of his blade to his body aiming for his stomach. As the blade entered his body, Landon went limp and dropped to the ground without a sound.

I pulled out the knife from his body waiting to see if he attacked again. But he fell onto his knees then rolled onto his side trying to stop the flow of blood that seeped out of his wound with his two hands. Landon wasn't going anywhere after that, except to jail.

Taking stock of my situation, I noticed my right eye wasn't working as it should and it hurt like hell. My vision was becoming blurry from that eye. And, I could taste blood in my mouth that was leaking from a cut to my upper lip. I pulled my bandanna from my hip pocket and wiped at the blood.

Then I remembered the two gunshots and Javi. I yelled out his name.

Javi called back, "I'm okay, Al, just a little shaken. But I can't say the same for the other guy though."

"What happened? I heard gunshots."

"Yeah well, that. As soon as I heard the ruckus, I blew through the back. If I hadn't dropped to the floor the moment I blew through the door, his bullet would've found my head. As it was, it flew over me as I returned fire aiming at his muzzle flash."

"Did you kill him?"

A slight pause.

"No. He's nursing a shoulder and a leg wound. I'm over here with him now attending to his wounds. And from what I see of it, four inches more or less to his right shoulder and it would have been his heart."

"Good. His death would've caused trouble with the local cops."

"Yeah well, don't have to worry about it now."

"Find out who he is. Get a name."

"No need. He's the same guy we saw with your jumper."

"Ok, I know who it is. That's Jacob Brayden, Landon's buddy. Leave him and come over and help me with Landon."

"Be there in a second."

We got Landon cuffed and bandaged ready for his ride to jail. His knife wound wasn't that deep. No vital organs had been punctured.

I gave Javi the keys to our pickup and asked him to bring it around. A few minutes later Javi showed. Then we saw lights turning on over at the main house.

I said, "We need to get out of here before someone comes out to investigate."

"Roger that."

Getting Landon into the pickup took all but a few minutes, and then with Javi doing the driving, we drove out of there. I watched through the outside mirror and saw someone at the front door of the main house pointing at us. And that was the last I ever saw of the ranch.

I didn't know it then, but October, 1989 would be the last bounty case I would be involved in.

Epilogue

Reflections

September 2016, San Antonio, Texas

My writing room was quiet and peaceful as I finished working on the last of my stories.

My children from my second wife Dolores have grown up and are living their own lives doing one thing or another. Now as I sit back in my easy chair, I reflect on my life since leaving Tucson, and what the future may have in store for me.

So, between October 1989 and November 1990, I did some boring work for a couple of law firms, nothing really interesting. But it was in December 1990 that the U.S. Army recalled me for active military duty from retirement to participate in Operation Desert Storm. After serving a short period of eight months, they retired me once again in August of 1991. I had fun and enjoyed my brief time back in uniform.

After parting ways in September 1991, with my bail bondsman friends at Triple A and Montiel, my wife and I decided to say goodbye to Arizona, and headed for Tacoma, Washington. So, with our bags packed and children in tow we moved to Lacey, Washington, a sleepy suburb of Olympia, the state capital.

But finding employment was hard; jobs were scarce.

Few opportunities presented themselves. Then in 1994, I opened and operated the Lacey Shotokan Karate Dojo or school. It grew to be a highly successful and very profitable endeavor. With well over 320 students at any given time, it was a business I would have loved to have passed on to my children. In that time frame, we had another birth, a daughter we named Marisol.

Then, the moving itch hit my wife once again.

In 2002, we once again packed our bags and moved to San Antonio, Texas. But in 2009 our lives took a bad turn, and my wife Dolores and I parted ways in a divorce, which left some bitter taste in my mouth. Prior to the divorce, my firstborn Carmen-Melissa had given birth to our beautiful grandson, Carlito.

Now along with my present wife, Jill Shively, we live on my military pension and retirement. What else life may have in store for me is anyone's guess, but I hope and pray it will be better than what I had in the past.

Acknowledgments

It has taken me over thirty years of writing and editing my stories, and along the way I'm quite indebted and grateful to so many for their valuable support.

To Lupita Shestko-Montiel, who first approached me to write about my life as her bounty hunter, I owe her a tremendous debt of gratitude and special thanks.

I'm also grateful to Dan Russell, Ira Harrison, and Jesse Murrah, for taking the time to read through my first draft and offering their indispensable advice.

Additional thanks to Mike Valentino for his professional editing services.

The Law Of The Bounty Hunter

In 1872, the US Supreme Court issued this finding regarding the rights to apprehend a fugitive for failure to appear (FTA).

In Taylor vs. Taintor—83 US 366 (1872)

"When bail is given, the principal is regarded as delivered to the custody of his sureties. Their dominion is a continuance of the original imprisonment. Whenever they choose to do so, they may seize him and deliver him up in their discharge; and if that cannot be done at once, they may imprison him until it can be done. They may exercise their rights in person or by agent. They may pursue him into another State; may arrest him on the Sabbath; and if necessary, may break and enter his house for that purpose. The seizure is not made by virtue of new process. None is needed. It is likened to the rearrest by the sheriff of an escaping prisoner."

This US Supreme Court case is what most refer to regarding the rights to apprehend a fugitive for failure to appear (FTA) in court. The single paragraph above explains the "principal" who "is regarded as delivered to the custody" of the courts.

Afterword

1989, NEWSPAPER EXTRACT

The following news extract appeared in *The Arizona Daily Star Metro/State News*, Tucson, Arizona in July 1989 and written by staff writer Susan G. Price:

"Prepared for danger"
"Private bounty hunter follows few rules"
"Tracker for bonding firms shuns police procedure."

Victor Alvarez has a wide, pearly-white smile and eyes that look like he has something to hide.

The only thing Alvarez wants to hide is his identity. It could ruin business. Alvarez said he used to get into trouble with gang fights when he was growing up in New York City's Spanish Harlem.

Now, he goes after the bad guys — he is one of several independent bounty hunters in Tucson.

He searches for suspected criminals who have either fled while on bond or broken the conditions of their probation. If he catches them, he pockets 10 percent of the bond.

Bounty hunting can be lucrative. Alvarez once made $17,500 in 18 1/2 hours, which he split with his friend who helped him. He took home $11,000. He would not say how much he made in a year.

"I don't need a warrant or anything else to break and enter. I can break in and use any force necessary next to death. It's just like when a prisoner escapes from jail," Alvarez said.

"The suspect has already been arrested and his constitutional rights are forfeited — I don't have to worry about reading their Miranda rights.

"Cops can't do that," Alvarez said. "Their hands are tied."

Bounty hunters, according to a federal statue on the books since 1873, can do anything within "reason" to catch an alleged criminal who has fled on bond.

"Cops have to walk a thin line. I don't," Alvarez said. Unlike police, Alvarez does not have to wait for a search warrant — he can rush past police to break down a door.

Under Arizona law, anyone can call himself a bounty hunter, but he must be authorized from a bonding agent to go after a particular suspect. Most tend to be licensed investigators.

Once Alvarez catches the suspect, he takes him to jail. An arrest never takes place, he said.

Alvarez, who is a licensed private investigator, said he keeps a set of leg irons in his car and carries handcuffs and a 9mm pistol — loaded with high-impact bullets.

"If criminal fires, I intend to get him down with the first bullet," Alvarez said.

But he never shot at anyone, Alvarez said. Mostly, he uses karate — he said he has a fifth degree black belt — and choke holds if the bond jumper becomes violent.

"I use a lot of choke holds and a nerve control technique to cause them to faint. It's much easier to put handcuffs on that way," Alvarez said. "But I won't do anything where the person can come back and sue me."

He said a lot of it is instinct. "I think I cover my bases much more than the police," he said. He described how he usually surveys the area where he thinks the suspect is during the day, noting possible escapes routes. Then he returns at night for the catch.

One time, Alvarez sat in his car for 13 hours during surveillance. Out of the 21 bounty hunts since he started 3 1/2 years ago, only one was easy. He did not even need handcuffs — he just picked the person up at his house, said Alvarez, who works primarily with Montiel's Bail Bonds and AAA Bonds in Tucson.

Alvarez fits the part. He said he was considered a "jungle expert" when he served 2 1/2 years in Vietnam. He was in the Army for 22 1/2 years before retiring and worked with the Canal Zone police in Panama, he said.

But Alvarez said he has had problems with the Tucson police. "They are more of a hindrance than anyone else," he said.

In June, Tucson police arrested Alvarez after he chased and lost a suspect. The suspect's wife called the police saying that someone was shooting at her husband.

It took awhile to convince the officers that he was legitimate, he said. He was never charged.

Alvarez carries a certified copy of the suspect's bond to prove he is the bonding company's agent.

According to the Tucson Police Department regulations bulletin still in effect from March 1985, the police must let an authorized bounty hunter do what it takes to catch a suspect, breaking down doors and sneaking up on the suspect at 3 a.m.

But they all don't know the rules, he said. "The police usually want to control the situation — it's a great disadvantage to me," Alvarez said.

But according to Sgt. Robbie Mayer of the Pima County Sheriff's Department, bounty hunters are useless. Mayer heads the Tucson's fugitive task force, called FIST. Last year, the team handled more than 2,000 warrants and made 600 arrests, Mayer said.

"I don't trust them — that's the bottom line," Mayer said. "The problem is they aren't cops. They can break into houses and all kinds of stuff," he said.

"We don't get involved without a warrant," Mayer said. Suspects that flee on bond do not necessarily have a warrant.

"But with a warrant, we call the shots," Mayer said.

"If the bounty hunter contacts us and gives us information, we say thank you. They don't come with us, and they don't participate in the

arrest. Mayer said it has been the department's policy which began in March 1988.

Alvarez said even with a warrant, he just has to get the right papers signed to collect his money.

Mayer said his department decided to do something after a Phoenix incident in May 1987 when two bounty hunters, a father and son team, from Banning, Calif., shot a fugitive in the back as he was fleeing.

The son, 18 at the time of the shooting, was sentenced to six months in jail and five years probation in Maricopa County.

Alvarez said he starts a search using information the bonding agent complied before granting the bond, which includes everything from the person's best friends, relative's addresses, and phone numbers and their Social Security number and bank accounts.

If the suspect gives the wrong information, the bond is forfeited, Alvarez said.

Extract From <u>The Arizona Daily Star</u>
Sunday July 23, 1989

About the Author

Victor Manuel Alvarez was born in Puerto Rico, and moved with his older brother and his mother to New York City when he was nine years old. In 1963, while living in the Big Apple, he was ultimately drafted into the US Army.

His military awards range from Jump Wings, Vietnam Cross of Gallantry, awards of the Purple Heart, Air Medal, and Army Commendation Medal, among numerous other awards.

Alvarez attended the University of Maryland while on active duty and studied criminal justice. He served as a CID agent, an army criminal investigator.

Retiring from the US Army after twenty-one years of service, he applied for and received his private investigator's credentials in the state of Arizona and became a licensed Arizona bounty hunter.

He currently makes his home in San Antonio, Texas.

CPSIA information can be obtained
at www.ICGtesting.com
Printed in the USA
LVHW080052111122
732898LV00003B/20